THE YEAR OF THE FROG

A Tattletale Fairytale

THE YEAR OF THE FROG

A Tattletale Fairytale

Juls Amor

iii

To my son, G, who understands—who understands this book without ever reading it, who understands life because he knows his soul and understands we are all good covered in muck just trying to learn our way back to love.

Contents

Introduction

I worked as a Therapist doing various forms of individual and couples therapy for patients of all ages dealing with stress, anxiety, depression, autism and countless other afflictions. Despite my ability to be good to others and help them follow dreams, I had difficulty following my own because I was always conforming. I have been writing since I was a little girl and went to graduate school in the hopes of writing but the scientific approach numbed my creative voice. My goal is to write creatively from my spiritual source within rather than someone else's scientific path before me. I want to inspire others to move in their own direction of happy.

Oh to be happy. Isn't that what life is about—to be happy? It is what motivates our every decision, forever seeking a happy ending. But ask someone what happiness looks like and watch them pause, blankly staring into space. It is at least the response I got from clients. What does happiness look like? What is it to you? One thing I know for sure is unless we can answer that question, we will never find it or, even worse, we will not recognize it until it is gone. It is our human journey to seek it out, yet so many are lost not knowing which way to turn. Even though it seemed I had the answers at my fingertips, I was no better off than the rest.

I used many forms of energy medicine while being a biofeedback practitioner. The idea was to teach focused relaxation. I saw clients make amazing changes requiring immense strength because change disrupts our life, our insides, and overwhelms our minds. We naturally like things to stay the same no matter how unhealthy it may be. As I watched clients conquer unhealthy patterns to move in the direction of happiness, I sought my happiness, often using the new-age equipment on myself.

In my travels I was introduced to similar ideas of old, sparking my interest in nature, eastern philosophy, and ancient skills teaching how to change frequencies without the use of costly fancy equipment or a prescription numbing guidance. If we drug feelings, it is my belief we will never find happiness, because feelings are sensory indications of which way to turn. Numbing those senses mutes the inner compass whispering directions. We will stay lost and we will never have the guts to change. Because my dear friends, those uncomfortable feelings are the guts it takes to move mountains.

For me, I thought happiness was the happily ever after presented in the stories I read—all things outside of my being; love of a man, a house, and kids is all I thought I wanted. But I learned the hard way the script I was following was not mine and therefore I would never find my peace on someone else's path. I began to feel I had been programmed to believe in phony fairytales of who I should be, while something erased my dream. As a child, I would write getting lovingly lost in my words. Days later when I went back to read it, I often got chills at words seeming to have come from a place so foreign to me, yet oddly feeling like home. That passion got lost over the years. This book is an endeavor to get it back.

I sat with clients offering them love and nonjudgmental acceptance as they told me the hard truths but I could not give myself the same gift. Many times I wanted to tell my clients who looked up to me how my struggle too overcame me. This is my way of honoring those who confided in me, finding the strength to tell me the hard truths that always broke society's rules. I tried to follow the rules in search of my fairytale too, only to miserably fail twice. By some unseen force, I began a path unwritten and thus I write it now in an attempt to identify my own unhealthy patterns.

This is an open examination of my life, my self-help history and journey to heal so others can hopefully relate to my difficulty. I do not want anyone to believe my beliefs. This is merely my point of view letting you see the process I went through. It is my walking the walk, I preached—to live my truth and accept reality. The greatest gift I can give past clients is a look into what life really looks like for someone they looked up to as "having it all and having it all together."

I started this unscripted journey with advice from a child I was seeing in my practice. He and I were working on ways to overcome his anxiety about beginning public school. He had been home-schooled his whole life due to Asperger's Syndrome. I knew full well how this precious baby had battled fear. It was a brave, huge step for him to decide to try public school. In an effort to help him prepare, I had simply asked him how he was planning to walk through that public school door the first day. His incredible answer was "1, 2, 3 GO!" This is the blog I wrote inspired by that brilliant boy.

1, 2, 3, Go! That's what I was told by a child on how to get started on a difficult task. For me that task is writing. When I began meditating almost 10 years ago, a recurring image would pop in my head of a piece of paper with words written on it. At the time my gut said "you should write." But about what, I had no clue. I cannot bear to think of the number of books I have started and left hanging helplessly out there in digital land. Where do some of them reside now? Your guess is as good as mine.

I chalked this urge to write up to meaning maybe I should go back to school and so I did. Be careful what you wish for? OMG, I got my feel of writing in Grad school, but nothing that soothed my soul. What I got was life sucking hours and hours of writing scientific, technical, theory themed essays and research papers I am almost positive drowned my creativity reference by reference. *Where is the proof? Whose theory is this? Add more references. What about the Mexicans? Ugh! (That last bit is in no way racist but an inside joke between a fellow student and me concerning a Professor's constant reprimands on ethical inclusion of all cultures.)*

I work in a field where I blurt out scientific facts left and right. On occasion, I hear my own muffled voice as my imagination looks over my shoulder and says "Who the Hell said that? That's brilliant. AHA!" I have always had deep thoughts. Even as a child, I recall sitting by a campfire for hours on end or watching the rain and doing nothing but thinking. My girlfriends and I used to drive out on a dirt road and watch the stars above, (drinking a $1 bottle of Strawberry Hill no doubt) and simply think.

Sometimes I discover someone brilliant already said or thought it, but sometimes not. I am tired of following rules, quoting science, filtering every thought while making sure I give credit where credit is due. It scares the bejeezus out of me to put it out there exposing my mind to be ridiculed. However, at 40 years young, I refuse to be wrangled by fear of anything one second more.

I have a goal list a mile long. This year has been one of my best at getting started on some of those goals—scuba diving, competing in races, learning Spanish, teaching myself to play my pink guitar, and now writing. Someone once said (and I'll be damned if I am going to look up who, in fact I am not even going to put it in quotes!)… to be an artist all you need to do is paint, and to be a writer all you need to do is write. I really yearn to finish one of my books so this blog is an attempt to get me moving in that direction. No rules, no set schedule, just writing what I think when I think it. I am certain some of my thoughts will be someone else's and I am in no way above quoting, but for once in my life I would like to just speak candidly about what ruminates in my head, rustles in my gut and resonates in my soul. This is the unedited version….. 1, 2, 3, Go! ~ Juls ♥

Genesis

In the beginning, God created the heavens and earth.[1] He made woman from the rib of a man. Rules were set. Man did not obey. Sin was born, dooming us with judgment and we all fell from power because man broke an apple rule. Lightning strike me now. Or better yet, strike you since you are still reading this. I commend your open mind for making it past the chapter title. I know how scary it is to step out on a lofty ledge of something so blasphemous. To question years of mass beliefs passed on from generation to generation is to choose an unknown frightening path of isolation. To anyone who is already offended, you are free to stop now and go write your own book. Or maybe you can set your beliefs down in faith you can pick them back up again punishment free.[2]

Please understand my first attempt at writing left me apologizing to my readers in an effort to say I was not condemning the Bible. But that is not true. I am condemning it. This is my tale about wanting to question it, the rules it established, the society it created, and the thoughts it engraved upon my female mind. It programmed me well by thwarting my idea of happiness with stories written by men and only men. (Even though there is speculation a woman wrote parts of it. Nobody was brave enough to tell me this.) I am no Bible expert,

---

[1] All scripture from this point forward is taken from my engraved brain. But for the sake of sanity let it be noted, the King James Version is public domain.
[2] My good friend Hawk said this to help me feel at ease about things I worried might offend another's beliefs.

nor do I want to be. Yet it influenced me, my life choices and my feelings about those choices to leave me living a life outside my soul.

I have rewritten the first of this countless times, color coded it in red reminding myself to remove it, and gone back to soften it trying to not sound so reproachful. I have lost sleep over what the two extremes of my divorced family might think of my reckless decision to use bible chapters and question its content. My father, who trusts in nothing but pragmatic science, would be proud and boast to his friends how he raised a factual, realistic daughter. But as much as I desire his approval, the disquieting reality is, if he is intrigued and continues to read, my truth includes unsettling memories about him. Then my mother's side is entrenched in Catholicism—confessions, Catechism, priests, and nuns in my step-father's lineage, might they disown me? Of course not; that is a fear of my own mentality. My mom and step-dad are loving, forgiving people. It's the part that pains me, knowing their forgiveness will ensue to exorcise my sacrilege.

To imagine my words might very well hurt them and their lifelong unyielding faith is one reason I needed such space. But it is only one reason I ran to a faraway land. I needed to force myself alone so I could hide and consider these boorish thoughts without hurting them or their beliefs. I needed to go through my journals, write things even I do not want to believe, examine it to piece together the patterns of my life and once and for all fix me and my relationship inability.

How did I end up resolute to write a book about religion, fairytales, sex, and indiscretion? All I can say is it was an obsession causing me to sell my entire life and move to a third-world country with little funds. I spent over a year putting sanity aside to pursue one big dream to write with hopes of self-discovery. That dream now seems like a delusion as publisher rejection after rejection manipulates my soul's illusion. If I lost sleep over the writing process, consider I am near broke with no way to go back, having let my credentials go to prove to myself I had faith in my dream. Only now do I question it all—the mid-life crisis some say I had, my purpose, and the faith in myself I thought I found. Perhaps my father was correct, and I have lost my mind. Maybe I am a therapist who needs a therapist. I do at times wonder if I should have been more grateful.

I had it all, a prosperous practice making more money than I as a small town girl with a trailer park heart knew how to handle. I worked my own schedule, traveled first class and drove a luxury dream car to weekly spa visits. Single and living on my own, I had freedom, having raised my son now off at college. I even owned a cute little home full of meaningful furnishings. Maybe I should have appreciated it more. Or at the damn least, worked longer to pay off my debt and do this crazy mid-life thing debt free.

But oh no, not me, not in the moment I found my calling. I had to go radically to prove faith in me. I was certain I could be a writer. Confident that security came on the path of dreams. I wanted to escape the lifestyle that infuriated me because I failed; I was unable to fit its idea of what I should be. I wanted to immerse myself in nature to spark creativity. Rejection letter after rejection letter, I worry, funds dwindling, while my father's insults circulate in my brain. It very well could have been a mid-life crisis. At present I sit on piles of debt, jobless with credentials I let expire because I had the wild idea if I renewed my licensure, I was doing what society had done to me—doubting my ability.

I grew up in the Bible Belt where faith in religion purported to be the foundation of all things worthy. That term "Bible Belt" just makes me cringe. The name comes from the region's strict belief in all things

·Christian, but with an over focused idea on church attendance and discipline. If you don't adhere to both, you are told Hell is where you will go! Any form of discomfort in our lives was automatically thrown into the massive groupthink idea redemption is needed with a cure found only in the Bible. Turn to church to find peace. The remedy is religion. But that idea leaves struggling souls having the most difficulty coming forward because the unhidden message is if you are suffering, you have not sought God enough. You are unholy. So rather than add shame to your shame, you learn to stuff your pain. Despite the fact questions were harassing my heart, I adhered to views I was conditioned to accept as true.

Those unanswered questions lingered although I put them aside, paid little mind, while taking for granted truth surrounded me, in confidence others knew more than me. I never allowed my questions space to breathe because I learned to believe. Believe despite the heaviness in my gut, gnawing away an all knowing spirit traipsing about as a little girl seeking relief from discomfort she could not even claim. Write it out all you want, but don't dare speak up nor let anyone read what your mind has thought.

From chapel in a Lutheran church as a kindergartener, Baptist church and Baptist camps as a young girl, Methodist on occasion, depending on which friend I was with at the time, I absorbed Christian religion from many angles. Oh, and the scare-the-fuck-out-of-you Assembly of God Church that told me to say "Jesus" over and over until it overcame my soul, turning the word into some form of uncontrollable tongues. Watching people shake and fall back in a spastic convulsive fit was the most confusing thing I have ever seen. Was I not holy enough because it did not happen to me? Or did it not happen because I secretly prayed to something other than God?

I was frightened to be overcome with this God's convulsive conformity.

To question those holier than I were faking it to fit in was committing a sin. It would be considered a lack in faith, but then why did they need to instruct me? When they laid me on the floor and tried to teach me how to do it, telling me close your eyes and mumble "Jesus" until overwhelmed, I wanted to run like Hell. But would the devil own me if I ran? People lay all around me crying saying "Thank you Jesus" and I went along with it just to be part of the group. There was an eerie awkwardness like I was caught somewhere between Heaven and Hell. I milked a few tears and murmured "Jesus" to fit in allowing the articulation to mingle a bumbled blend.

The sisters of the church told me the Holy Spirit had entered me and why I cried the language of tongues. But I cried to ease the fear while the words were my doing to mirror the assembly. When it ended, I admit to having immense relief—relief this holy nightmare was over and I could go home. My parents did not force me to go to these churches; I was following my friends. I even took classes to convert and fit in to my step-father's side of Catholicism exposing me to the guilt of "everyday" sin and the need for weekly confession.

One of my earliest memories in church, I caught my mind wandering off, staring at the bloody Jesus hanging from the crucifix. As I chanted the repetitive commands, I silently wondered why anyone would want to wear a cross around their neck when that's what killed him. No one wears a gun to signify how Gandhi died. Why must we be reminded of the suffering? But as soon as I entertained the idea I wiped it out of my mind quickly from fear of going to Hell for having such tainted thoughts. It was drilled in my head "though shalt not worship any other idols" so even the thought of Gandhi was disrespectful, especially in a Christian habitat.

Still, it just seemed so odd to me. Why would God put one person on earth for billions of different people? Weren't we all made in his image? So how can just one religion be right? Why put a white man to represent all races? And while I am at it, why do you even have to go someplace to worship if God is everywhere? If God is love, why am I scared of the statues, the blood, the building, the costumes, the judgment and the penance? Why am I scared of death if that's where I meet this loving God? And isn't it feasible God could be a woman?

The possibility man cleverly wrote Mary as a virgin to somehow taint our sexuality kept going around in my head as what an intelligent way for men in power to keep us small. To preach the idea we too should stay virgins in a world where the same men pushed to see us naked baffled my still innocent mind. I was alone in my questions, afraid to ask my fellow believers who appeared unaware religion was controlling them. No one allowed me to disagree because no one was brave enough to disagree with me. I inevitably thought I ought to believe, I must believe, or Hell hath fury on me.

I heard the stories of the Bibles from the various Christian religions I was exposed to and wanted to question them all. Discerning the difference between fairytales and religion puzzled me. The pages of victimhood, hardships, battles, disaster and ways to be rescued by none other than a man and his word parallel. Both appeared to embody a myth of unjust oppression ending in the reward of ever after. The Bible was the ultimate script with the rules on living. Society continued to develop scripts, fables and words with messages akin to the fairytales telling false stories to trick and control.

Fairytales, written by various adult males who determined it would be entertaining or better yet healthy mental nourishment for a female child. Get a fucking clue. What I really learned was be this limited certain way, look perfectly and follow, follow, follow the yellow brick road, to be rescued by a man who will inevitably give you happy ever after. Nowhere was there a story of a happy single woman, providing for herself, loving herself, rescuing herself. It is no wonder I began to look to men and only men as worthy of worship. I had to defend myself countless times if I said I was Catholic because in many minds I was worshiping a woman. Oh hell, then I began carrying the guilt for the guilt-laden Catholic Church for honoring women.

The Cinderella story my grandmother read me reinforced the idea women can't be trusted and do not deserve honor. It so eloquently programmed me to believe a submissive woman who obeys rules and "female" responsibility may be allowed to join the party. If she looks pretty enough (through godmother magic or by today's standards, the knife) she will meet the man that will rescue her from none other than an evil, not man, but woman. Snow White the fairest in the land according to a mirror, was rescued with a kiss from a woman's curse after eating what? Oh yes, yet another tainted fruit, the apple once again. It reinforced my childhood idea religion had already instilled— fear of being cursed for something as innocent as eating a freaking apple. Again presented by whom? Well, now that would be a woman. And the ever so lovely Sleeping Beauty was cursed by another evil woman and "awakened" by none other than the kiss of a man to break another wicked spell. All this rubbish burned in my little brain at a time when I had no interest in boys at all.

Then God made man in his image to rule. Growing up in a divorced family, that image can get thwarted; but I am here to say only because society and religion labeled it wrong. From the teachers bestowing pity on me, whispering to each other "her parents are divorced," to adults encouraging coupledom with questions of "who is your boyfriend" and "who will you marry?" Then the extreme old maid stories hovered over everything, instilling a fear you could never be happy, pretty, youthful, or successful without marrying and staying married. It was a message of how to be happy in the form of a prince and a palace.

Religion begets fairytales begets marriage begets happiness. After all, isn't that all religion and fairytales are—a myth with a lesson to be learned by the moral of the story? The idea hovered that I needed something or someone to be whole; being fed parables even my ribs were not my own. Life instilled early on that a female lacked value if she was alone. So let's see. Big picture: listen to rules set forth by men, be leery of other women (they are evil), look beautiful and wait for his kiss to live happily ever after. Programmed by religion and the fairytales it fueled, all I knew was guilt, fear, and to look outside myself for happiness in the form of a church, a mirror, a man.

This was a huge contrast to the world my soul craved. My childhood heart sat for hours outside with nature alone but never lonely. Although I lived in the drying up desert, I found remarkable life in the tiniest of flowers emerging from what seemed the most arid of cracks. It amazed me that from the waterless soil, life still begged to live. I had grasshoppers, caterpillars, lady bugs and countless other creatures for pets, but I never took them from their environment. We simply met up each day in my secret place where we talked and played.

Stray animals somehow always knew where I lived and I took great joy in their friendship. My childhood mind could not explain it then, but even the drying up tree outside my trailer house seemed to whisper to me as I climbed her brittle branches to sit with her silently. I could not stand to see anything suffer. Feeling the thirst of the earth, I often watered the weeds, the cracks in the dirt and left bowls of water under the trailer for whatever life crept out at night. Even the flies that frantically fought the sticky fly trap my mom had hung tugged my heart as I snuck to do my best pulling them off sometimes unable to save their wings. Watching them crawl away wingless, I wondered what their name now should be. I recall contemplating if I had done the right thing, but in my young soul knowing life should live wings or no wings. I loved to write poetry on the messages nature always seemed to send me. It soothed my soul to put on paper pieces of my mind, but over time I lost my voice to a fast paced judgment based society.

I just wanted to enjoy my animals, play outside in nature, get dirty and forget tomorrow. But similar to many young girls, I was molded for wedded bliss, made to look pretty and told to kiss. When we are repeatedly forced to do things we do not want, the lesson learned is we do not count. I would escape it all in my writing where my thoughts had meaning. I would write for hours about my love of being outside when they made me go in, about not caring how I looked when they made me curl my hair, about not wanting to kiss boys or some stranger I just met and as scary as it may be about not believing in the church. Needless to say, I hid my journal, afraid I would be caught and not fit in.

I learned what I wanted was irrelevant and my inner guidance was destroyed. I hear people tell those who are struggling to listen to their heart. How is that possible when no one allowed or showed us how to listen to our own voice growing up? I had an eerie sense nothing the adults pushed as "belief" seemed right. I didn't even believe in

Santa Claus, but did not want to hurt my parents so I went along with the story just to please and get the presents. I did not understand how a Bible full of stories by men, with the only memorable woman being a virgin, could dictate where my female soul would go. I most certainly did not consider a kiss by a prince would break a bullshit spell that could not exist. All of these ideas came from the mind of a little girl desperate to be accepted, spilling her truth on paper then hiding it out of shame.

Only now I see clearly the moral of fairytales and religion is to be rescued, leaving me waiting, wishing, wanting for a story of salvage to unfold. I was trying so damn hard to live a good life amidst confusion over religion and abstinence while social media flaunted feminine sexiness as happiness. I grew from a girl content with herself to a woman needing feeling from everyone and everything outside of self. This little people pleasing child heard her voice but rarely talked; afraid she was consumed with unclean thoughts. Over time, I lost that voice all together and inevitably lost myself.

As an adult, I worked with many a client who felt the same. I never brought up religion; it was not my place. But if it was causing them grief, and they brought it up first, then they were free to explore whatever thoughts they had in my office. A question I sometimes presented to clients who were condemning themselves for choices they had made by quoting the Bible was, "who wrote the Bible?" Every client I ever asked this would blurt out, before even contemplating, "God." Only after giving them moments of silence to reflect did they consider other options. I too was programmed to say God wrote the Bible. For many years I tried to trust this. From what I know and undoubtedly speak now, the Bible contains a variety of books written by more than forty-five men spanning thousands of years. Not God. Apparently the Holy Spirit inspired these men to come up with quite similar themes of hardship, sin and destruction with the only redemption being to obey and pray.

I am tired of holding on to such limiting beliefs. It is one thing to break a spell you are aware exists. But quite another when the curse convinces you of reason by capturing your consciousness daily, continuously and systematically leaving you in a state of amnesia unaware you are even under a spell. So this is my genesis, my tattletale fairytale of all the unspeakable hardships, sins and destruction to end my myth of unjust oppression.

In hearing my story, I hope others recognize the confusion I felt to find my identity and I hope they feel less alone. Some who've read this book prior to publishing told me they could not tell which voice I was writing from in the beginning. Many asked me to alter the first chapters. I did not. If you can't tell which voice I am writing from, I've portrayed my struggle properly. I could not tell which voice I was living from. It is symbolic to the way I was feeling—confused and angry. I never felt peace trying to be what others wanted from me though I rarely showed how conforming displeased me.

Religion, education, work, income, marriage, youth and any form of security are all gone from my identity. Am I the "American dream" girl next door with a pious picture perfect personality? Not if I publish this book and let my skeletons dance freely. Fuck it, I never was the person people labeled me. It was a heavy illusion to carry that untruth. As I peek down at my once pedicured feet now dirty as my past—one night stands, two week flings, a prisoner, a hippie, broken heart after broken heart leaving me alone dangling by threads of an unraveling dream—I smile feeling something you might not ever deem.

I am happy. I am happy! I am alone with worry and doubt swirling around like a massive storm brewing while I sit in the calm of the eye watching the hail, lightning strikes, and haunting gusts of wind that no longer frighten me. I smile, breathe, and feel immense love in my heart mimicking the tranquility of the storm's center. I am centered. An awesome life-altering storm shook me to the brink, displacing and discombobulating my everything while I beam eager to tell you how in God's name I got here.

I've angered many deciding to finally do things my way. It has been a dark journey but like all things it ends in light. I have come to realize many hurtful remarks are blessings in disguise. Even my father's demeans telling me I am living off the reservation are now comforting. I cannot go back. My father was correct; scientific fact has been traded in for feeling, medical journals for shamanic healing, and the church for Mother Earth's teachings. I am living off the reservation with people I feel I have known my entire life. My world is the fairytale. I have found my tribe.

Just as is in the end of Genesis where God's people are in a foreign land wandering about, I too wonder. Why can I not have my own moments worthy of a book? Why if I came from God can I not sense his voice, the Holy Spirit enough to write a prayer, a psalm, a Bible verse? Dependent on what religion you are exposed to, you get a Bible to instill restrictive ideas composed of whatever books that group sees fit and in varying order. So I have done the same, choosing my chapters as I see fit to tell my own history of oppression in search of my redemption. It is the skill I used in therapy on others; listening intently to their stories, looking for repetitive themes to piece together the puzzle with love, acceptance, and compassion for all they had been through. If I was really good at it, they would have an 'aha' moment, feel relief and acceptance. Often they would carry that unconditional love on in their heart motivated to make great change. I am turning this skill around on me, to break the curse and tell myself my story for my own sanity.

If you hold on through my attempts to find my voice and continue on this journey with me, clarity seeps in slowly. It is my hope one woman finds connection in my efforts to fit in a society pushing coupledom to feel love, whole and complete. If she can identify with my tale of kissing frogs seeking Prince Charming while confessing those kisses for the Prince of Peace, I feel my story worthy. Because you my dear sweet woman are enough.

The programming sucked the life out of me pouring a happy ever after recipe down my throat. I tried to swallow it for the last forty-plus years only to end up one very misplaced soul. In attempting to break the unspeakable spell, I discovered a deep desire to expose sins held in silence and express myself authentically. Similar to therapy clients who often went back to their original story when they felt comfortable I would still love them, my truth also revealed in layers. With acceptance of me, I added pieces I had deleted and or altered to portray myself in the best artificial light. I no longer need to modify reality to feel illuminated. I have seen the light. Once you see it, you can't un-see it. This is my truth, the ugly truth, often the ungodly truth. Shall it set us free? We shall see. [3]

---

[3] Truth is perspective; perspective changes. It is one reason I consider this fiction. None of this was filmed, it is my memory which I am learning rarely matches reality. Not much unlike the fairytales I grew up on—fictitious.

Exodus

Giving of the moral laws, or in my case, it would be giving in to the moral laws. Oh Exodus, the book of history and rules. Well, by my teens my history began repeating itself in an effort to appeal the laws before me. I am still seeking happiness outside myself, trying to gain acceptance with my immensely inadequate being. I have already had more serious relationships than a girl my age should according to the stories I am told. The guilt bestowed upon me for confusing sex with love pushed and pulled me from one extreme to the next. After all, church taught abstinence, while the priests I thought so Godly in costumes covering shame, played their mythical parts oh so well to abstain.

Rumors of sin dripped from my church walls like the blood of Christ who hung silently watching. Inappropriate behavior whispered gently like the incense softly burning odors that would linger to never be queried. Nobody questioned the Bible. Nobody questioned the rumors. Sin seeped not only from my small church but many. I heard talk of all the churches I attended where devout members and clergy hid their sexual secrets beneath their flawless image of weekly attendance. Even the "speak in tongues" preacher was rumored to have had several affairs with the "sisters" of his church. Creepiness lingered and the silence the adults wore masking their voice taught me to shut mine up too. Ignore truth.

Muffled by the rules, I put aside my soul's inquiry to seek happiness as the good book portrays in a savior. I began to buy into the idea I was not capable alone. I mean how can I be whole when even my ribs are not my own? At some point my entire meaning became redeemer seeking. I do not recall ever wanting sex. I wanted acknowledgement, to be understood and simply held lovingly but I fell victim time and time again to the "word" of men I so sickly learned to worship. Not a one of them protected me as I longed for. Not one of them cared if in the seducing of my soul they gave me a disease or got me pregnant. If they did, they did not act on it. I cannot recall one boyfriend putting on a condom or asking me if I used birth control. I had no clue how to care for myself; it was not in my script. I dared not talk to women about this. We had all been pitted against one another to judge and call each other names if sex was on our brains.

The shame pushed me from I'll never do that again to lying to my mother that I needed birth control for acne. The monthly guilt of reminding her for more cursed me to stop asking and try to refrain from sex. That and the fact my longtime boyfriend's mother caught us and went off on me with words I will never forget. "You are going to end up pregnant looking to heal your issues with your dad!" I was so hurt and mad having no clue what she was talking about. I had a good relationship with my father, though my parents had divorced. When I saw him we got along fine. Sure he has issues but none of which were mine.

Inevitably, I ended up pregnant. I told no one I had missed my period in hopes if I too ignored truth, it would dispel beneath my pleading prayers. Weeks of crying shame passed, pregnant with despair as my depression lifted momentarily when I began to bleed.

Petrified, I confided in my sister worried that a miscarriage ensued for penance to properly punish me. Mom found out and took me to a doctor who said it might be a miscarriage, none the less; an abortion would need to be done in either case. That same day they walked my confused sunken soul down the cold white hall where they put me to sleep and terminated the pregnancy and/or completed the miscarriage. I am not sure because like all defacing sin, no one ever spoke of it again.

I awoke from the medicated sleep with a soul destined for Hell now more than ever. To hold so much silent grief within, I was sure my heart would explode. I could go into greater detail but it is still so raw in my heart. To write and leave it in view for the first time in my life seems like all the detail needed. To bring to surface wounds that were pushed down deep is an agonizing release. I did find the strength to confess to a priest in another town, because our priest was practically part of the family. But I did not experience relief, only more shame as the priest on the other side of the holy wall, shocked me with no words. We sat in unnatural damning silence for what seemed like hours to my ailing heart. He followed his script breaking the quiet to sentence me to one rosary. I walked out dazed mumbling "that's it" under my breath as I knelt knowing it was not enough and he knew it. It is why he sent me away, to not have to deal with my unholy presence.

This is when I surrendered to the script of being the weak female victim now more in need of rescue than ever. I began a desperate search to fit the fairytale, appropriately marry in the church, redeem my soul, and live happily ever after. With insides burning from the blistering wound, I ended one relationship and began another that continued into college. Love on the outside was all this small town girl misunderstood.

So here I am eighteen, standing on the steps of an enormous university with a heart full of guilt, fear, and shame, stuck between a generation of married moms fighting to remain appreciated and women breaking the mold to be independent; my confusion grew. I witnessed the evolution of woman taking on more and more responsibility. Society's rules for women began to explode while the roles of men were imploding. The aged position of woman as a submissive, married slave to her husband and children had begun to fade. But I was caught in a hesitant generation fighting to hold on to the idea as acceptable and even touted as holy. My grandmother married young and so did my mother and her sisters. Everything I understood about being happy began and ended with a man. My mother even told me "college is not for everyone" as she dropped me off to a collegiate world I was terrified of. This worshiper of men, having not been taught to care for myself sought a savior to care for me.

I hated being away from my new boyfriend now off at another university. We continued to see each other a few more times on weekends. Trying my best to take care of my body, properly sneaking my sin to the Planned Parenthood clinic, I obtained birth control. I am not sure if the occasional missed pill, not taking it at the same time every day or being on antibiotics for acne is to blame, but I became pregnant again. Now beyond mentally sick, not understanding why this kept happening, I told him, looking for rescue. Instead, he broke up with me.

So lost, my soul was already doomed at a time I was trying to decide who I was. The only thing I identified with was a horrid guilt-ridden person on a fast track to Hell. All I wanted was love. How unfair another human can tell you they love you then leave you heart sick and lost down the darkest road to misery? One of his family members contacted me; she had the money and a place to take care of it. I was already going to Hell, I took the only option presented at the time and agreed. Even though days later his mom called to say they would send me away to hide, have it and give it away. I said no, I had made up my mind. But to this day that is not true. I never made up my own mind, I just followed. Alone at the clinic, I watched couples console each other, escalating the lonesome sting salting my open wound.

I thought it would be the same—sleep and awaken from the nightmare, never to speak of it again. It was not. They left me awake. I experienced the pain physically. It was on this day I learned physical hurt pales in comparison to emotional pain. The mental anguish sopped my heart as I cried for our demolished souls. I sunk into the deepest sadness. I did not leave my room for weeks. I do not have a clue how my young heart came out of that. Maybe it did not, and I simply did as we all have been taught—embellish the mask no matter how heavy, wear it and march the masquerade meekly.

I found escape in the college party life, where I began to numb guilt-laden memories the way my father taught me—Alcoholism. Not once in my life have I called it by that name because it dishonors a man the Bible pushed me to honor. I never wanted to admit he had a problem nor that I walked on his coattails of cocktails. Compelled to write about my wounds and confusion, I hid in my room when not partying and I wrote. Paper soaked with tears and bleeding words began to breed massively as spiral after spiral overflowed. For the first time in a long time, I got a glimpse of my soul that so easily comforted others, trying to comfort me.

It felt amazing to let her breathe. Still, so unsure of what to do with my effortless unpleasant expression, and afraid someone would find it, I started a fire in the fireplace of my apartment with the sin-stained paper. I prayed the pages of fiery words would save my burning soul. Believe in fairytales, do not question adults, and do not question the Bible, the priest, or men in general. They are here to save you if you can be a certain way. My words represented nothing they would want to save.

Scared to say anything my rebellious soul had put on paper with absolutely no faith in my ability to be humane, I continued to party, missing my college classes accordingly. I could not bear to look in the eye my own pain. My soul was lost beneath judgmental fog with every year passing pushing me down further until I was blind to see who I was. No one taught me to seek love inside.

At the bar, numbing my voice and pain, is where I ran into a childhood friend who began talking of marriage the first month we dated. Although a very faint voice inside tried to push me in another direction, thorns covered the path I was not equipped to cut down. My inner voice yearned for things I used to do that became wrong in the faction I was part of. Playing outside in nature, mud on my face, no shoes and dirt between my toes were activities of long ago. The only inside activity I longed to do was writing poetry and stories but that would be considered just as dirty as my feet. It felt safe to finally have a man wanting to commit. No woman in my immediate family had completed college.

To witness the past generations of "just a mom" fading left me baffled as to who I should be. Believing I might let down wives and mothers if I did not uphold that dying vocation, but at the same time failing future generations if I gave in to be "just a mom" and not succeed professionally, added to my confusion. My gut wanted me to be independent, but with no script, the yearning inside that I had never learned to listen vanished. Boys in my small town were asked what they wanted to be; I was asked who I wanted to marry.

Church and fairytales taught me to go outside myself for love while society taught me to acquire stuff outside my person to be happy. Consumerism, get more to be more. We obtain so much outside ourselves it becomes impossible to look in. My grandmother who read me fairytales appeared miserable in my eyes with the life she settled for, finding only glimpses of happiness and solace in her stuff. I never saw that woman happy with her life. It is sad I only recall her wanting; a bigger house, a pink Cadillac, her so called antiques. She had stuff piled so high she had a trailer in the back of her house, not for living, but for stuff.

I watched many female family members do the same. Countless out-of-town trips to shop then hide the bags of happiness from their husbands. Temporarily content with the new, excited with the secrecy, but quickly numb again looking forward to the next shopping fix. In addition to religious guilt, tales of women cursed by poison apples, victim to a sleeping trance, to be rescued by a man, the outer idea of stuff clouded my brain.

Days filled playing with teeny ass Barbie dolls with boxes and boxes of clothes, driving the best vehicle and living in a mansion. From "Brady Bunch" to "Leave it to Beaver," mom was merely the keeper of other's souls with not an ounce of time for her own. She must stay tiny, perfectly kempt, serving with a smile all the while wearing a string of pearls while she vacuums. Never mind that she has dreams, ideas, or needs. I bet that string of pearls around her neck is why she smiles while she cleans up everyone else's shit. It's no wonder women fall victim to consumerism. Happy ever after can only be achieved with the help of a man to attain your dream. Materialism keeps us addicted to every facet of American culture.

I measured my happiness with external means; looks, adornments, men, and things. I even attempted church again in a building built by man to kneel before others and take communion so all could see I had confessed properly going outside my being. Yet it all left my insides empty. Because nothing made sense on the inside I thought I fell in love with my boyfriend who wanted marriage. He was a familiar person I grew up with. I thought it was love. It felt like home, safe and fit the script dealt. It was the rescue I needed now more than ever. I tried to create the perfect scenario by telling myself since I grew up with him and met him again in college it had to be fate.

We both tried to stay celibate until we married, verbally agreeing to each other, but how two college partying kids do that is beyond me. It may very well be the reason we wanted to marry because both of us grew up believing sex a sin. Neither of us wanted to be sinners. So if we were going to have sex anyway, why not save our souls and marry? That and being terrified of getting pregnant unwed again can be quite motivating. I just wanted to fit the script and do it suitably this time in an effort to pull myself out of the Hell I'd been doomed. He would be moving for a job opportunity. It seemed like a lot of money and that made my already materialized mind fantasize. I told everyone he was the one. I had faith he would be faithful and that alone was enough given I grew up surrounded with infidelity.

So I did the proper thing and at twenty years old married to take the path of just a wife that would turn into just a mom. After all, this is the script I knew. There was an App for that. I dropped out of college and followed his work to what seemed light years away from the small town I grew up. I expected him to make me happy. I wanted everything to appear perfect on the outside so judgments from this point on would save my soul. Following the path laid before me, a year later I was pregnant and desperate to prepare my lost soul to raise another. I read every book on parenting I could find hoping to have a chance to be good at something.

At twenty two, his birth changed my view of life and my world. The experience, while only lasting hours, tore my core long enough to teach me how to live for another, in an almost movie-like encounter with suffering. That joyous day turned extremely terrifying in an instant as I faintly recall hearing something about no heartbeat. The anxiety intensified when they began running with my bed down the hallway, as doctors practically came out of the walls to save a life yet to be lived. I knew something was terribly wrong when I did not even get to see his face as they rushed him off to neonatal ICU. No heartbeat! Not breathing! I heard them say. It seemed hours passed as I tried to piece together what had happened. The joy turned pungent in my gut realizing he may be gone. I've never felt sickness like that. It was a thick black cloud of uncertainty ripping my heart apart.

My mind tortured me with thoughts of every mistake I had ever made to deserve this. I just knew the premarital sex, the abortions, had doomed me and this was my punishment. The only thing I ever truly loved was dying, and I did not even get to see his face. Suddenly, a moment of clarity came to me with a feeling I cannot to this day describe. There were no words, only a comforting sense my past choices were not all ending. The doors opened; I heard a cry that soothed my world as they held him up high so I could see he was alive. That baby whose heart was not beating shocked the team of doctors scoring a perfect ten on the Apgar. It was in that moment of clarity I knew all my months of preparing to raise a baby—the books, the research, the expert advice with all their knowledge on shaping children to fit our world—were irrelevant. I made a promise. Rather than change this perfect child to fit my horrendously imperfect world, I would change my imperfect world to fit this perfect child. Best decision of my life. My son has been my greatest teacher.

I learned how to live for another but still had no clue how to live for me. Being totally absorbed in mom duties left my own spirit drained. The fairytale expectation that my young husband coming home exhausted from work should fill my gaps with happiness must have drained him too. It is no wonder my marriage began to fall apart; within a few months of my son being born my husband had an affair. Everything I knew, everything I thought I was, instantly ripped from me with the shock of infidelity. Wife, lover, mother with a faithful savior husband; labels vanished leaving empty space filled with pain and shame. It had to be my body that made him stray. I gained more than ninety pounds (I am not sure the final number because I refused to weigh the last month).

Appalled at my own appearance, I hid more than ever. I never believed my body to be good enough. Even when it was perfect I hid behind huge t-shirts, not even letting my friends see me naked. Lights had to be off during sex or I would not do it. Now it was even worse. My huge stomach during the pregnancy exceeded the normal charts so my doctor thought for months I was having twins. My skin ripped apart from the fast weight gain so the scars were some of the worst she had ever seen. And now my faithful husband had chosen another woman's body over me.

He tried to lie about the affair. My gut knew it had occurred but my gut also needed so much uncovering to be heard. I needed clues, and I needed someone to be honest with me for once. That is when I pulled out the Bible once again desperately seeking truth. The only reason I did not believe him when he put his hand on our Bible and swore he abstained was because his story of the night was unrealistic and there were cum stains on his pants!

More investigation and a call to the woman named Cherry confirmed my idiocy. He moved out, not even trying to contact us for months. I say us because what killed me the most was how in the hell can you leave this precious child? Fuck me, how can you leave this precious child? For the longest, I hated everything Cherry. For years I couldn't even look at a box of pop tarts.

Totally playing the victim part well for the several months he moved out, I sunk. This is not how the fairytale goes, how unfair for life to deal me this hand. I did my best to hide my pain from my son and am so thankful my cousin moved in with me to help. While my son napped, I tried to fit the pieces of the puzzle together.

Who was this man I married, worshiped, and thought would never betray me? I gave up on college for this man. I kept a book with hand written pages and pages of timelines trying to discern where it went wrong. Was he always cheating? I called people I knew in the past asking them if they ever knew of him cheating. It totally consumed me because I had nothing else to live for. I did not read books on being single. I read fucking princess stories of females rescued by a man after kissing frogs that magically turned into Prince Charming. I did not want another offense of divorce on my sin card. Because my

28

parents had divorced I wanted to prove it could work. The church told me everyone makes mistakes, and why God tells us to forgive.

My grandmother consoled me saying this is just what men do and maybe I should not have another child, get fat and risk him cheating again. WTF! Even my so-called support system wanted me to take back my cheating husband. After months of literally dying on the inside, I did the only thing I knew to do. I went to church and prayed like Hell he would come back. I prayed for the pain in my heart to go away and when it didn't work, I prayed or more appropriately begged for simply a few hours of sleep.

I lost a ton of weight from the stress and trying to drastically repair my broken after-baby body. I thought skinny would fix the scars and loose skin but it only made me look like an old saggy lady. I remember the hunger and comparing it to the pain in my heart. The hunger felt better and so I continued to deny myself food.

Several more months passed. My son had his first birthday without a father and he began to walk a few days later on my birthday. It killed me that his father missed his first steps. This child was such a joy, my only joy. I just knew if his father could see this wondrous child he would snap out of it, come home and give me back my fairytale.

Leviticus

L eviticus is the book of offerings—sacrifices made to usher us into the kingdom. It speaks of more laws instilling more fear and often death as punishment. I was convinced my past sins were the reason for my suffering and to be forgiven, I too should forgive. The religion that burned in my background rose up to convince me exoneration need be. I became determined to get my husband back and make a perfect fairytale life for myself and my son. My cousin drove me to find him in the town he had moved. Never mind that when I found him, yet another young lady had moved in to comfort him. Deflecting facts as I'd been taught, I walked right past her and begged him to come back—literally begged, I got on my knees like a church coached clone and I begged.

I had been trained well to beseech my savior. On my knees, tears gushing from my face, I begged him to see me, to understand my pain and to do the right thing. I loved him if he could only see. "See me," I begged. He finally caved to end my shame. Tremendous relief swept over me when he agreed to come home. Days later, the relief diminished beneath images of my pitiful pleading as I realized I sold my soul. Still, I swept that pain under the doormat I had become to continue my life being stomped on.

For the next ten years, I tried to twist and mold him to fit the savior image now massive in my mind. A constant quest to push him to achieve my dream kept me busy focused on his inability. So much potential, I could not understand why he would not strive to be all I knew possible. In my eyes, he could have achieved so much more. The constant pushing him to pursue dreams exhausted me. The ammunition I obtained from his infidelity allowed me to degrade his choices when he failed to fit the dream. I forever brought up cheating, convinced he went elsewhere for the kind of sex I declined. All my years of growing this female body inside confounding principles of sin left me believing anything other than love making to be a sacrilege. I suppose that is where missionary position got its name because it's the only way guilt did not set in. Other positions turned on the words of society slapping me with labels like slut, whore, and cunt. Thus I chose the label prude because my mentality was so judgment stained; I rarely did anything resembling his mistress's way.

For more than a decade, I stayed with him trying to push him forward while keeping his head above infidelity. Countless times the nagging in the pit of my stomach suspected cheating still persisted but society and religion had taught me to shut that voice the hell up. I stuffed it deep under my rusted gut. At some point, I simply quit looking for signs and ignored even the sticky note with hearts and her phone number. I allowed my soul to become so weak; I was not even sure I had one. But to others my life appeared great. It all looked perfect on the outside despite being empty on the inside. I had my chance to go to college and be independent. I failed. The only other option was to fake this path like I faked my faith.

I put my entire being into raising my son. I stayed home to cook three meals a day, clean, and all the motherly duties. I attended school meetings, volunteered as room mother, and had a position on the PTA board. I even helped with sports. At home, I filled our time with games and neighborhood kids running in and out all day long. I myself played in the mud, played tag and joined in on all the sports. I even roller skated every week with the kids. I kept myself so absorbed not much time existed to consider myself.

My husband often commented that I did nothing and pushed for me to get a job. I wanted to be there for my son but also wanted to please my husband so I took occasional small jobs. Still he never seemed to appreciate my passion to be a good wife and mother. I often resented the feminist uprising, like we shot ourselves in the foot wanting it all. Even my husband could no longer respect me for the most remarkable title – Mom!

I did love being a mom. But at some point my son became independent and I totally sunk the day he asked me to, rather than play with the kids and skate as usual, perhaps I could go sit on the bench and relax like all the other moms. It's funny now to think of him telling me this because I recall being so taken aback, like I did not even comprehend I was the only mom playing. When I looked around and realized that yep it was just me, I knew my son was correct and I needed to get a life of my own. That day was not just a day of my son breaking away, but a day forcing me to focus on myself and the emptiness took me down once again. I turned to my husband hoping he would fill my gaps but in the end it was too much to ask.

I tried to focus on me but the questions that always seemed to get me into trouble started seeping in my mind. I questioned my upbringing, society and religion again. I began to dip my toe in what seemed to be odd guru things. Books on intuition, a bit of yoga, some meditation; I just kept hearing the queries in my brain. Without the distractions, I began seeing signs he might be cheating again. I confronted him with a note I found. As in the past, he denied it, but I did not believe him. I never believed him again after the first time he cheated. Even when he told me he loved me, my thoughts countered it with "yeah right." How unsettling it is to lay your head down beside someone not knowing you are loved each night.

We began to fight—not the kind of fights you see in passionate relationships; there was not much passion at either end of the spectrum. He was for the most part a very gentle man, but I did push him to punch a hole in the wall once as he cursed my jealousies. He never admitted any affair to me. And I still to this day am not certain if something else happened.

Unable to understand anything, I found myself being wooed by a much younger man who made me feel worthy for once. All my years of bashing my husband for being untrue led me to confess to him in an effort to save the marriage and prove my honesty. I understand why people lie; it would have been so much easier to hide and continue the false fantasy. I wanted to prove to him, to myself, and my inheritance of infidelity that honesty is honorable. I had not even slept with the guy yet, just some kissing but I was heavily partaking in flirting by email. My hope was my husband would be jealous, snap into Prince Charming, swoop me up, save me from my sinning to live happily ever after. I thought if someone else was interested in me, he would finally be motivated to prove his love. It did not happen. Every effort to explain saying "I am the one who told you" and "can you imagine how I felt not finding out from you but catching you" did nothing. I ended up sleeping with the guy and as programmed to confess my sins, I confessed to my husband. I wanted him to beg me as I had begged him but he didn't. Instead he found solace in his secretary and filed for divorce.

The life of lowly single mom began. Here's an excerpt from a journal I did not burn but hid inside an old box. I found it during a move years later. To read these words now still brings tears as the memory of pain surfaces.

My head feels heavy on my pillow as I peel my lifeless body up to face another day. Today my son comes home from his weekend with his dad so I have to somehow muster up the strength to pretend I am happy. He is my only joy and so far I have done amazingly well continuing to play, cook and be there for him despite my inability to be here for myself. The only relief I can feign this morning is in knowing in just two short weeks I can do it all again.

As he rushes out the door excited to spend the weekend with his dad, watching him jaunt happily down the sidewalk sets in motion the process: My heart begins to feel heavy in my chest sinking deep like a cold heavy stone that's been heaved over the edge of a dry empty well. I will cry myself to sleep and wake only momentarily to torture my broken soul with more wasteful thoughts of how wrong, unworthy, and unloved I am. Of course my marriage ended. Look at your past, look at your body. Stretch marks, sagging skin, drooping boobs. Not to mention you are broke, mentally, physically, spiritually and literally—eating rice and beans, living off credit cards, in a tiny apartment with not even a degree. What man in their right mind would want this? Certainly no Prince Charming.

I beat my psyche daily with brutal thoughts. All I ever wanted was to be married and be a mom. I had a nice house, car, and great neighborhood with kids who ran in and out all day loving the home I created. Perhaps my grandmother was right and it is just what men do. Maybe I am unholy and had I been more religious, I could have forgiven and stuck it out. Maybe I am a slut and had I had more faith in my husband I could have resisted temptation. Why could I have not been happy? Three home cooked meals a day, game night, movie night, and all the dress up and indoor tent building a boy could ever want. We did have so much fun. Every kid on the block wanted to be at my house playing. I created the perfect family home, but the hidden pain no one knew was that I was constantly lonely, unsupported, feeling cheated over and over again.

I must have taken the wrong path. I had to find a way to break free of my past. Go a different route all together. Just as I threw my whole heart into raising our son and creating the perfect home after the Cherry affair, I found a way to ignore my soul and dove into another project. I did a bit of crisis meditating, the kind you only do in times of turmoil. I had a vision of a piece of paper. I still had not learned to listen to my gut. All the years of living with what I deemed an unfaithful husband smothered my voice even more. Every time I sensed he cheated, if I confronted him, I was told I was jealous and had no clue what I was talking about. So I started to believe I had no clue what I was talking about. I over-analyzed the piece of paper vision and decided since the first option of family did not work, I would go for the second option and get a paper diploma via formal education.

I had no money. I used credit cards to live on and bank loans to go back to school. I would not even let myself stop long enough to think of my loneliness. I took as many hours as they would let me to not even have a moment to feel the pain gnawing a hole in my heart. I felt on the right track and this time I was not going to let myself get off the new path. I took so many hours I had to get the Dean's permission every semester. He would tell me it was impossible as I begged I could do it, touting "look at my grades." Every semester, he signed off, looking at me sadly like he knew I was running on desperation to fuel my dedication.

I took more than twenty grueling hours a semester. I took classes while my son attended school and online when he was out on summer vacation. I did not take a break, taking classes even on holidays, as well as summer classes. When the schedule only allowed me eighteen hours, I signed up for the eighteen and an additional three hour online class that would transfer from another university. I studied while waiting to pick my son up from school, while he slept, while he practiced sports, and even at his games when he was not playing. I had a text book on my being at all times, reading even while standing in the grocery checkout line.

I lost years of sleep and the only joy I experienced was the grade outside my soul given for each assignment or test. That being an A on most occasions and if not an A, it was a freakn' A+. I have A pluses on my transcripts because I feared if I did not push hard, I would fail again. I completed undergrad Summa Cum Laude and graduate school with a 4.0. I would not recommend anyone to try this. I had no life. I do not say this to stroke my ego but to demonstrate how over focused I could be, completely ignoring reality. I will never forget walking across the stage to get my graduate diploma and expecting to have something spectacular happen at my efforts to always make an A. The disappointment as they herded us like cattle and handed me the exact same degree as classmates who barely skimmed by made me feel like my efforts were futile. Not much unlike the feeling I had the day of my divorce and my perfect A + family life flashed before my eyes as my thoughts slapped my soul with the words "why did you even try?"

During grad school, I filled my loneliness with some online dating and met my next long relationship online. I did my best to do it correctly this time. He lived in another town making it easy to take it slow. We kept our dates to once a week most of the time. With so much energy going towards school, I did not see that relationship for what it was. At times I would drive over to see him and stop on the side of the road wondering why the nagging in my gut kept saying "turn around." But not once did I listen.

I continued to date him while finishing up grad school and opening my practice. He helped me tremendously with the finances and construction of the office building for my practice. From smothering myself with school, to the energy it took to open a practice, I never once looked up long enough to see the reality. I went from obtaining my license as an LPC, Licensed Professional Counselor to going full force into obtaining Board Certification. The licensure took more hours of study, travel for training, and countless hours of mentored practice and examinations. My wonderful son was totally involved in his sports and if I was not at one of his ballgames, I was working, studying, or off at another training conference.

It seemed like the right choice. No, it seemed like a different choice. With a longer courtship (we dated over four years) and pre-marital counseling, I thought being on a different path meant I was on the right path. This man was a financial genius and exuded more power than anyone I had ever met. He had achieved the status I pushed my first husband to attain. It was quite attractive in the beginning as he sucked me into his fantasy world seducing me with unbelievable dates, trips around the world and a family I love dearly. I stayed despite my unease.

I had no time for a relationship. I now see that is exactly why it was working. We moved into the house he built. Let me make that very clear, he built the house and just as I have made it clear to you, he made it clear to me regularly. It was his house. I begged for marriage to gain some equality but more importantly to not break the laws of my religious society. I mean after all I was a marriage counselor. I pushed to have it all this time: a professional career and the family image I was programmed for.

He reluctantly married me. He did not want to marry me. He had already been married twice and according to him they both only wanted his money. "Took him to the cleaners," he boasted. Still, he gave in to my ideas; we married and life settled for a year or so. That is until I began asking him to come to bed with me at the same time. He did not want to. Only then did I notice something was off. Living miles apart, only seeing each other once a week, and partying when we did, I never realized he left the bed almost every night. He would sleep in his chair and I slept alone. Most nights he would come to bed later but I did not realize it was nearly morning. I went to bed before him every night since I had school (I was also teaching at a university until my practice took off) and or work. He worked for himself so he had the luxury of sleeping later.

When I began wondering why he slept in his chair, I also noticed the liquor cabinet and how much alcohol disappeared. I confronted him with the issue. He said he could not sleep due to constant pain, so he slept in his chair, took prescription pills and drank to ease the pain. I tried to help him and at first he agreed. But it was too much and eventually the fights became horrific. I had never been exposed to such anger. He kicked me out of "his house" almost weekly. Just as I had in the last marriage, I repeatedly begged and pleaded for love, for him to see I loved him, to let me help him. I could see who he was beneath his programming. Just as my first husband had so much potential, he too could have been the man of my dreams if he could have just seen himself the way I could see.

The battles became increasingly malicious. A switch flipped in him; there was no turning it off. Somehow I began to meld into his behavior, like he brought out the worst in me. I found myself screaming and yelling just the same. I even tore his shirt on one occasion tugging at the sleeves begging him to stop and hear me. I quit drinking to prove it was not me and I was in no way provoking it. It happened on occasion when he was sober, always over money and/or my parenting that he believed was too soft. The sober rages would only last minutes. The drunken rages could go on all night. One night he screamed at me for more than four hours because my son had purchased dinner at the clubhouse without asking him. Never mind I was working late and had given my permission; this man wanted total control.

He made decisions without ever acknowledging my existence. He even sold my car, a $30,000 car I had paid for all but $4000 of, without telling me. He paid it off when we married and that just gave him the power he needed to control me more. I could not have a view, no voice at all. At one point the battle started, and I decided to record it on my phone so he could see the next morning how drunk and irrational he was. I told him I was recording. He did not care. He continued to mentally bash me. It became clear when I showed him the video he did not even remember the fights. I did not video it to hurt him but to help him. Looking back, it was the oddest relationship. There was not much time spent together at all. He even continued to go back to the town he originally lived when we met and stayed the night sometimes twice a week, for work he told me. Everything was always about work. I have never been lonelier than in that marriage.

I tried desperately to help him, but it seemed he began doing things just to make me leave him to his whiskey drink. When he refused my help, I just tried working on myself and filled out every psychological, self-help, marriage worksheet I could get my hands on. I was a damn counselor; I had access to the best help. If you can imagine how I studied in grad school, well that's how I began studying my marriage. I was not going to let it go. It was apparent my reciting "facts" and research drove him nuts as I tried to prove my point when he let me know my entire family disliked being around me and my "know it all" mentality. As much as it hurt for him to tell me this, it was true. I lost my voice to science and spoke it freely unable to believe in me; I became a research dictionary. I did my best to stop the lectures to fix us. I was going to find a way even if it meant me drastically changing, stunting my voice even more and becoming the submissive wife he needed.

That is when my dad got very ill and I spent a month helping him recover. I had been staying in ICU with my father overnight, and driving two hours back and forth to work. After weeks of being physically and emotionally exhausted, I finally decided to drive the two hours home to sleep in my own bed. It was late when I arrived. My husband had already settled in his drinking chair. I suppose my coming home unexpectedly set him off. He never liked anyone to disturb his routine. His script was set in stone. He marched my exhausted body up the stairs to show me my teenage son, who thankfully was not home, had left a milk carton in the movie room and the small amount of milk had gone bad. My every effort to calm him was met with even more rage. All I wanted was to come home and get some rest.

Emotionally exhausted, I just needed sleep. He kept me up most the night to play his abusive part. That's the night I shut down. Nothing mattered anymore. I had tried everything. I quit crying and lay in my bed numb as he stood in the doorway screaming, demeaning me with every subject that came to his alcohol drenched mind. A few months later "get the fuck out of my house" was thrown my way for the last time. I knew all he wanted was a fight and I was programmed to beg but that last get the fuck out had somehow bore the script. I never again begged for his love. Instead I filed for divorce. Watching my father battle to live forever changed me and in many ways saved me as I watched him save himself. Here is an excerpt from my blog about his battle and how it changed my perspective.

It is said the mind gives up long before the body. I have found this to be true on more than one occasion. At work I understand all too well how the mind can wane. Emotional and mental pain is much more damaging than physical pain. It hurts like no hurt on this earth. But if we can find a small sliver of hope, allow ourselves to feel the pain, and simply allow tomorrow to be, life heals. In a strange way, I am often inspired when suffering comes our way because I have come to know change is about to occur. It is as if the pain rips a hole in the soul long enough to let inspiration in, and if we bear the pain, that insight can steer our spirit to new heights.

From a very personal place, a brush with death opened my heart to change when we nearly lost my dad. My amazing, traveling, marathon running, triathlete, nothing can stop him dad, was hit hard with some mysterious form of Meningitis. Bacterial, Viral—who knew? They had to treat for both. Over 30 days in ICU, I watched him fight a battle that sickens my soul. The pain was writhing. His spine was so inflamed he could not lie down, but only sit straight up for days. He could not sleep or eat, and his brain was being beaten with infection so bad he literally lost his mind. No one has ever recovered from the extent of infection he had, and we all knew he was supposed to die. Even he knew it as the tubes down his throat, his nose, his back, and other unmentionable parts drained the last of his courageous soul.

I held his hand begging him to stay longer as tears rolled down his cheeks and he whispered "Honey, I've had a good life." All the memories we made together began to flood my mind; our first cruise on the very first Carnival Mardi Gras ship, Hawaii, Cozumel, camping, hiking, treasure hunting, panning for gold, reading every Historical Marker from here to Kalamazoo and oh yes, the snake pit. I wiped his tears knowing it would be selfish of me to make him stay just so I could have him by my side making amazing memories. I was just about to tell him goodbye, when in that moment of letting go, the tightness in my chest expelled and I knew what life was about. "Memories"—It is what you take, it is what you leave.

As the days passed, he somehow held on. He amazed the Doctors who said he may not walk again and/or have brain damage. Not live? My Ass! Not walk? Pffft—he runs, competes, he rappells freakin' waterfalls and his brain is as brilliant as ever. Lived a good life... HA! Not my miracle Dad. LIVING a good life, making memories with me that fuel my soul. Dad, thank you for giving me my competitive spirit, traveling gypsy heart and unconditional love for all people, animals, nature, life!

While Dad has spent the last two years recovering, I've spent them soul searching. I've realized the majority of my adult life has been exhaustingly spent chasing love. Something in me changed as I dedicated my life to loving myself and my world. I stopped the madness of wondering why love had eluded me. I began focusing on growing love within rather than looking outside myself for it. I quit seeing what I lacked and focused on what I have. Love of a man? I have more than one heart deserves; my father and my son. I very well might be the luckiest girl in the world having not one great love, but two. Of course it's not the romantic love we long for, but maybe something more, something better and perhaps, just perhaps, it is enough. I've taken to heart the revelations I had. I've learned loving life means you are going to have to face your fears and be OKAY with the unknown. I'm choosy about who I spend my time with. We only have so much life—be sure whoever and whatever you're engaging in is not draining you, but energizing, creating many a soulful memory—because in the end, it's what you take, and my friend, it will be all you leave!!! ~ Juls ♥

Numbers

The point of the book of Numbers, as I understand, is instruction and preparation on how to enter the Promised Land. It discusses a census, thus the name Numbers. I took my own inventory as the divorce raged on gathering new data to change my course in the hopes of entering my own Promised Land. I did my best to pick up the pieces I exploded into. I worried I would never find anyone to love me again after my first marriage ended; now I simply worried if I even understood what love was.

I truly believed I had given my heart completely and been extremely good at wifely duties. But I also watched couples sit in disbelief at the activity I often had them complete. I would give them a piece of paper and ask them to write down every single thing their spouse did wrong. I would say "This is your chance. Get it all out." I could hear the tension engrave harsh words describing the one they loved. They easily etched the other's flaws sometimes asking for more paper to fill passionately with ugly faults. After, I would hand them a clean sheet of paper and have them now list their own wrongs. Silence, blank stares and a look of pain washed their faces as I watched their attention turn inward hesitant to tattle their own mistakes. Sometimes they would come up with a few self-flaws but not once did anybody ask for more paper or even fill a page like they had when blaming the one they apparently loved.

So I understood my own blindness contributing to love always ending. But I did not comprehend the specific issues I myself had. I battled myself daily to overcome my heartache while trying to redefine who I should be, if not a wife and mother. My son moved off to college, and that left a gap in my home and my heart, begging to be filled. Able to absorb myself with work for a while, my practice became a huge success. As I had in the past I dove right in to hide my pain by focusing every ounce of my soul on others. Even though it felt as if my fucking guts had been sucked out at the end of each day, it did not hit me until the work day ended or if there was a long break between clients. If I had enough time to switch my mind to me, the pain seeped in. I had learned from my clients grieving that pain whether it is from death or divorce comes in waves. I knew the heartbreak would come and go. The first few waves are huge; they knock you down and submerge you so you feel you may never come up for air. But if you can hold on it will subside. Every time you battle a wave it gets easier. You may not notice it at first, but little by little you will begin to see the waves are not coming in as often and they are not as forceful. You may get a wave of pain daily in the beginning and then once a week, a month, etc. There is no set pattern but you will see the days between blows will grow while the blows will soften. I held on to this knowledge and tried my best to ride each wave. I learned heartbreak is energy just as joy and I learned to use it to my advantage. People get things done when their energy is fueled by joy. Why can't we do the same with hurt? So I did. I got things done despite the waves of pain washing over me.

I gave myself Sunday to deal with the pain and prayed to my gods. I decided not to go to church this time but question it, even out loud if I needed. I went back to studying other religions and philosophies some of which I had been introduced to in Grad school and others I simply sought on my own. I read up on Buddhism, Taoism, Hinduism, and watched a popular Christian preacher on TV because his stance appeared guilt free. I had never been exposed to religion that did not instill shame. I liked the positive stance coming from a place of love rather than fear.

I dove into meditation and yoga daily rather than on a crisis-only basis. I was still after all these years of on and off meditation struggling with what I was supposed to do. But something in me said it was the only way to gain my strength. I stayed strong all week but then on Sundays I would close myself off from the world. Sometimes stay in my pajamas all day. Cry all day if I needed, eat chocolate and/or ice cream, pizza, or whatever my body craved. I took as long a bath as I wanted and I cried. The tub was always my cry spot. When I went through the first divorce, I learned I could hold a smile long enough to tell my son I was going to take a relaxing bath, where he knew not to disturb me. I would run the water, play music, and cry. The sound of water and music hid the sound of my cries. It was perfect because I could ritualistically wash it all off and tell myself to let it go down the drain at least until the next bath. It was my space to be a basket case. I recommend everyone create a space to be a basket case when you are mourning.

I continued being consumed by my work. In fact, I was maybe even better than before the divorce. Counseling others was definitely a gift, at least from my end it always felt each person or couple left my office better off than when they arrived. I was often surprised at the words of comfort I was able to give and at times looked over my shoulder in my subconscious wondering where such beautiful advice came from. I would sit after session and absorb what I had said in an effort to get myself to take my own advice. It was still so much easier to help others than it was to help myself.

My relationship with my clients grew even stronger. As I began to be more myself, it was as if my clients became more themselves. On one occasion, a client I had seen for years decided to tell me a secret they had been harboring and had even lied to me about from the beginning. I remember feeling an overwhelming connection as they began to open up. They looked up with tears in their eyes and ask "Do you still love me?" I broke down in tears as well, feeling a connection that tugged my heart and said, "I love you even more." I began to hug my clients and wondered why I had not in the past. It was some ethical rule but at this point I just wanted to comfort and comfort hard. I know I was damn good for them and they were damn good for me.

I began to write and sit with my questions allowing them the space they craved. And little by little, I began to voice my opinion rather than stating other's people's facts. There was something happening as many of my clients began to question religion as well even though I never touched the subject with them. I only followed my clients where they wanted to go, delving subjects they presented. I could see the fear in their eyes when they would say something like "I am not even sure if I believe this or that" as they waited for what they thought my response would be, reprimanding them in some way for questioning faith. I never judged anyone and the space I gave for them to explore doubts was exactly what people need. It was so refreshing to see the relief that would overcome them when rather than reprimand; I would say "I am not sure either. It's okay; we can question it here."

Many clients stayed stuck in horrible patterns of relationships, or hiding their true being out of fear of religion. From people struggling with homosexuality but never acting on it out of fear of going to Hell or disappointing their pious parents, to people staying in abusive relationships or wanting to kill themselves out of guilt for something that occurred years ago. So many people struggled like me trying to be and remain holy. How sad to never experience love out of fear of religion. Do you see how ironic? It makes me angry we are raising children out of fear. God is supposed to be love, yet we taint it with fear. People choose to stay in unhealthy even abusive marriages because divorce is a sin. It's as if living Hell on earth will spare us Hell thereafter. The one that hurts me the most is the use of the Bible as an excuse to spank a child. In my opinion, it is barbaric abuse.

Nevertheless, at work I could not ethically speak my opinion; I could only listen. So I simply allowed a space for them to explore without judging their own voice, their own beliefs. I did my own personal exploration. What is a Bible but a set of beliefs? A belief is just a thought ruminating long enough to become a belief. I had an extremely rigid set of beliefs stemming from very negative thoughts. Not ever being able to live up to the Bible's idea of holy drew unholy to me time and time again because it was what I believed me to be. Whatever we accept as true always comes into view.

I believed myself unholy from the beginning when I was labeled as sin; as a child of divorce, with questions burning in my brain that if I asked would sentence my soul with shame. And God forbid I write the polluted words for others to read sending them to Hell along with me. This unholy female with gawking body parts, growing femininity, and ungodly feelings towards men did not want to have pre-marital sex. I wanted love. I wanted love so desperately I would succumb to the touch of a man just to have that moment of feeling worthy. To feel whole briefly with hope he would stay. But even if he did, I was unable to sleep due to the guilt that overwhelmed me.

I would desperately push to make something out of the sex I just had to not feel like a whore. It is one of the reasons I married so young. My immature mind so wanted to be right in seeking love outside of self, I sold my soul, not to the devil, but to the word of some god. No matter how much change was evolving around me and how I wanted independence, those rigid fixed beliefs kept steering my choices—leaving me believing I was wrong, always going to be wrong with no salvation in sight. Deep-seeded beliefs that came true for me time and time again. I did not believe myself worthy of the fairytale, it is no wonder I never got it.

Although I could barely breathe myself, I trust I was a good therapist. My heart could so easily connect to others' pain. I believe simply sharing that tender space with them was enough. I am positive they never knew I was hurting too because so many of them wished for my joy. It was not a fake joyfulness, it was real. I felt immense peace when I was focused on another, like our connection or maybe just sharing pain was what was needed to ease it. The amazing thing about the human heart is it is possible to console another while you are dealing with your own suffering. I fully understand how powerful emotional pain is. It does not matter that we suffer different pains; the way it feels is exactly the same.

I did not want to be a hypocrite expressing joy only lasting momentarily so I worked on me immensely. It was painful. Turning my attention inward when I got home at night was the most difficult thing I have ever done. My heart was already heavy from the sometimes extreme stories I heard leaving me grieving for our shared heartache. Maybe if I could have gone home to someone holding me, comforting me, I could have been stronger. But I was alone often crying, with no one to calm my effort to carry the world. Some nights I wanted to scream but instead, I washed the day away climbed in bed, gave love to my dog and stared at the ceiling just trying to breathe.

Breathing, the first marriage sucked the breath out of me a little at a time while the second knocked it out hard and fast. Breathing, seems simple enough, yet I so many times felt I was laboring to take in what always felt like limited thin air. Being a therapist and doing biofeedback, one of the first things I teach all clients is how to do diaphragmatic breathing, yet I was forever feeling depleted of oxygen. Meditation began to be my only free breathing moments, but I was still not dedicated to it. On the nights I did get lost in meditation, I slept well but it was like I wanted to avoid the peace and, in some weird way, enjoyed the crying spells. So I found myself choosing activities to make me cry over meditation.

So here I am absorbing myself in work. Sulking my lonely ass at home and trying to redefine who I am. Despite the prosperity, I could not shake the feeling I was on someone else's path. I began my now sporadic crisis meditating to find some peace when I would come home to my lonely little house after my taxing work but it was difficult as those damn questions began to resurface. Questions about religion, about who I was, what I was doing with my life, if it was even my life. I tried hard to focus on myself and my issues that had contributed to destroying my marriages and demolishing my dreams; those dreams that now I am not even sure were my own.

How do you get over a broken heart, yet again? More importantly, what do you do when your world gets swept out from under you?

When all hope you ever had of happily fn' after has been sucked right out, leaving you dreamless. When you grow up defining happiness as the "happily ever after" in the books, television, and fairytales you dreamed, it is excruciating to wake up one day and realize its bullshit. No one is going to rescue you on a white horse, no one is going to wake you gently with a kiss making all your troubles fade and no one is going to take care of you, unconditionally loving you flaws and all, not even if you do it properly and marry in a church.

I went back and forth from being terribly mad and feeling cheated out of my religion-fueled idea of happiness, to beating myself up for apparently doing something wrong, unable to fit the idea. I was not sure what I had done wrong, but it had to be something. By this time I realized it was me attracting the unavailable men, whether they chose other women or they chose whiskey, it was all the same, leaving my needs unmet. There were desperate broken me nights I would call my ex crying, to ask for an honest opinion of what was wrong with me. I am a counselor for God's sake. I should know how to fix this shit. At one point, he did send me a text that gave me some relief stating "it was not you, it was me." And for at least one night, I was able to sleep. But the sunrise brought light and the realization I must take responsibility.

None of us can see our own flaws. Just like the activity where I had couples write all their complaints of their spouse, I knew very well I was only seeing faults of another and not my own. I made my first husband miserable because I could not forgive him. I made sure he knew he was the reason my dream was not as written. It's no wonder that marriage fell apart and then I immediately rushed into another relationship desperately seeking my knight. I thought I was healed of my past but apparently not.

Deuteronomy

Deuteronomy is similar to Exodus with more history and laws to abide. So trying my damndest to make different, better choices within the laws, I turned my work around to be used on me. One of the techniques I often employed was to ask the client what they sought looked like? If what they wanted was happiness, which is what everyone first said, then what does that look like? A better job, a loving relationship? If you do not know where you are going, you will never get there. When asked, most people sat with a misplaced appearance on their face, which is exactly why they were lost in the first place. It always baffled me how we can easily say we are not happy but then have no immediate answer to define it. On very rare occasions people discovered they already had it but were not seeing it. But most people did not have a clue what they were seeking.

So taking my own advice, I sat in the silence questioning my own idea of happy. For me, happiness was a loving relationship. I wanted love. Seeking it consumed me. I pulled out a worksheet I had developed in Graduate school on finding the perfect soul mate. I filled out the worksheet as if it was going to magically bring me Mr. Wonderful, holding back nothing and asking for everything my heart desired in a mate. Take the time to fill out the worksheet for yourself, even if you are not looking for a mate; just go with me here before reading any further.

LOVE COMMANDMENTS

It helps to write down specifically what we are looking for out of love. A positive relationship with someone is the key to happiness, but you have to know what you are looking for. Imagine getting in your car and driving aimlessly never knowing where you are going or how to get there. Just like taking a trip in your car, where you first need an idea of where you are going, you also will need a map to get there. Think of your soul mate. Dream big and fill out what qualities that soul will possess.

Education:

What type of degree? Be specific and remember to dream big.

Career:

Type, What level to reach in a career, financials, etc?

Family:

Parenting, Traditions, etc? What do each of these areas look like?

Attitude:

What type of attitude? Personality, morals, values, etc.

Physical:

Athletic, yoga, dance, eating habits, etc.

Pleasure:

What they do for fun? – Hobbies, interests, etc.

Add any other important factors that come to mind.

I wrote everything I thought I would want in a man. I was still harboring the idea I wanted love outside myself. In addition, my friend and fellow counselor told me I needed to "kiss a lot of frogs" to find my soul mate. Yep, here we go again. Kiss the stranger, kiss your mother's second cousin's great uncle, kiss the boy, kiss the man, be rescued by a kiss, awoken from a spell, break the curse, kiss the bride and by all means kiss the frog. It was still so much easier for me to listen to others and so I did just that. I set a goal to kiss frogs, letting another fairytale myth drive my decisions.

I had never dated, having gone from one long relationship to the next. It was not proper according to my script to date more than one person at a time so I set out with the intention of burning that script and dating to get to know people, lots of people. I had to fight myself constantly because inside I still wanted one at a time and one for a long time—a committed long time, like ever after. I knew I had to be stern sticking to my list because I always see the potential in people. Never seeing them as whole, as who they are now, I fall in love with who I think they can be rather than the reality.

As a counselor, I understood the only way to critique others is by their behaviors and not their words. But I don't take my own advice well. I love words; I believe what people say. I was taught to have faith in the word. Whether it spilled from lips or ink of pen, something in me adhered to verbiage like commandments etched in stone. I decided the list would be my way to keep it real and judge based solely on behaviors, what is presented to me, plain and simple. If they say one thing and do another, I am going to have to ball up and move on. I had listened to a few lectures on dating and found one idea funny about looking at dating like shopping until you find what it is you desire. When you see a flaw you cannot live with, you have to buck up, and put it back on the rack. End it and tell yourself "NEXT." I joked with my girlfriends about this. It became our humorous mantra.

I did not want to fill out the worksheet and then crumple it up only to be found years later in one of my many moves, so I took the main points from the worksheet and created a list on my phone notes to be readily available. I read it daily to drill the qualities I was looking for in my brain. The entire idea is to get you thinking in the direction of where you want to be, to get you looking for these qualities in others and simplify your search for a soul mate. Make a roadmap and go. I wholeheartedly understand how the past repeats itself, how life's lessons are repeated until learned. Whether we continue to attract people who push us to feel the same feelings as childhood to heal or it's some vibrational energy we project or both. I really don't care. I just want it to STOP. I know I have to feel worthy to attract my prince and so the journey begins.

Here is the list, I shall call "**The Commandments**:"

Higher education at least a master's degree and interested in continuing to learn

Financially stable in a professional career

Family oriented

Crazy about me

Reads

Writes – journals, poetry, love letters, etc.

Honest

Display affection daily, kindness, and respect

Romantic

Loves to travel

Athletic

Handsome

Tall

Hairy Chest
No tattoos
Loves to dance
Loves music
Crazy about me
Loves animals
Loves even my flaws
Loves to touch me because he is crazy about me!!!!!!

As I made the list of what I wanted in a man, I began to wonder if I had ever really been in love. I have met women who describe the love of their life and the overwhelming attraction. I hate to say it, but I have never felt something as intense as they describe. At least not with the men I formed long relationships with. If there was an immense attraction, I got nervous and avoided them. You know that weak in the knees, sweaty palm feeling? I clammed up and turned away if that energy thing came over me. Not once had I pursued a relationship based on attraction. It was not lady-like to feel those feelings so I had only been in relationships with men who wanted me. They pursued me, I was simply grateful someone liked me and so I stayed with them. I had never really even looked for someone based on what I wanted. I laughed that I wanted someone crazy about me, not realizing I wrote it more than once until going back over it. I wanted someone to beg me as I had begged my last two relationships. See me for whom I am, all the flaws, love me anyway, beg me to stay.

Next step was to begin dating. Ugh. I want the comfort of knowing someone. I hate the feeling of trying to get past all the games. We all put our best foot forward in the beginning and even though I made a mental note to just be myself, it is easier said than done. I took another piece of advice I often give single, lonely clients and that is to get online. Even if it is just to look at all that is out there, it gives hope you can find someone. I totally ignored the fact I had met my second husband online and convinced myself online dating was much like the courting of old days where you begin by writing letters to each other. I created a profile and at night when my heart was aching, I would have a glass of wine, look at pictures, and pretend he was out there in digital land.

It did make me feel better to see everyone was just seeking the same thing, love. I felt connected with others. One night, I got an email and decided to respond. Our conversation took off and it appeared we had so much in common but that was a brief first go. It turned out to be nothing romantic. Again I love words and he had a way with them. But in person he behaved differently. As long as I was listening to him which I was great at, I had been trained, then he was happy. But if I discussed myself or my own needs he interrupted with his own issue like he had one up on me. He needed me more than I needed him. I did not feel heard.

I examined the online process mentally and decided it was not for me, realizing to be online was forcing the situation as I always had in the past desperately trying to make a relationship out of nothing. Since I am trying to break my old patterns, I decided to cancel the account and trust in life, letting the universe place people on my path, rather than me forcing it. That and the countless "dick pics" I received made me think the online process had lost all chivalry. Later I would discover it was not just meeting someone online that enticed men to message their member. Nevertheless, I do not want to see it even though sometimes I said "sure go ahead" just to see if they really would. And yes, they really will.

I looked at the list almost daily to reinforce it in my brain. I set a goal to listen to my gut this time. If it says "turn around" then I better do just that. I briefly dated another man. It did not feel right from the moment we sat down at dinner. The way he flaunted his status by treating the waiter poorly made me cringe. The man sent back my food because the sauce was not a proper, well I cannot even recall the name of the sauce, it was some French name, but the point is he took it upon himself to make a decision without my consent.

The second he saw my plate he pointed it out abruptly ordering the waiter to take it back as I calmly whispered "It is okay, I don't mind" and "I really don't even know what kind of sauce it should be." It took all my guts to walk away because I would have never done that in the past. I always stay. I always give two, three, a million chances, but I left. It felt good to honor myself. Yep, listening to our gut does just that, it takes all our guts. I altered the commandments to reflect what I had learned I wanted—respect and to be heard. And I said, "NEXT."

The Commandments
Higher education at least a master's degree and interested in continuing to learn
Financially stable in a professional career
Family oriented
Crazy about me
Reads
Writes – journals, poetry, love letters, etc.
Honest
Display affection daily, kindness, and respect
Romantic
Loves to travel
Athletic
Handsome
Tall
Hairy Chest

Loves to dance
Loves music
Crazy about me
Loves animals
Loves even my flaws
Loves to touch me because he is crazy about me!!!!!!
Respectful of others
Listens to me

Joshua

Lonely months passed. Going home to my little dog, I did my best to appreciate the joy she gushed on me. It is the kind of love we all crave. Free to do and be what we want, make a million mistakes, and still come home to someone who only wants to love. I tried to figure out how to love myself that way, be with myself and enjoy my time alone. I spent weekends working on my house and took momentary pride in many accomplishments. Momentary because the inner dialog in my mind trumped every achievement with a yearning to be appreciated by masculinity.

Still, I did alone many things that would have in my past required the help of a man. While putting together a fireplace I had ordered, clearly stating "two person assembly required," I cheered myself on with every step while it began to come together. As the weight of the massive piece grew, it seemed impossible to maneuver, but somehow I found a way while vowing I would never need a man again. However, upon completion, my brash pride sunk as I looked over my shoulder wishing someone had seen what I had done. Not just anyone, a man. For a moment, my mind conjured up the image of a man saying "good job, Juls," but it broke my heart even more to realize no one was really there. I lay down on my cold wood floor next to my newly assembled fake electric warmth to cry. I wanted someone to be proud of me, of my accomplishments, of me and my being. I sat in the sadness trying to love myself in the moment, asking why it is not enough you yourself be proud. Why can you not give yourself enough love? I know love comes from within but by this point I am utterly sick of hearing this, of facedly telling this to my clients when I had no clue what it meant.

I swung from happy moments to low sad stints more often than not. Work still gave me satisfaction but when I was low, it was the lowest I had known. At the end of the day, I stayed in my therapy chair, trying to absorb the advice my comforting heart had given others doing my best to cheer me on and keep it up. But there were many situations at work that made it extremely difficult to go home alone, from the abuse I often heard about to a tragically horrific satanic story that left me sleepless many, many nights. Counseling is a difficult job. Graduate school taught me how to refrain from transferring clients' issues, how to debrief and not take it home but I am human.

Many nights I cried for my client's pain, searching my mind for ways to give them relief. On the nights I did not cry for them, I cried for me; wishing someone would relieve my pain. Then guilt would sweep over me for being so weak when my pain was nothing by comparison to what others had been through. And the shame still snuck in to convince me my sins were the cause for suffering of not seeking god enough. I would remind myself that we come into this world alone and go out alone trying to toughen up. I searched my soul for release. Just letting the tears gently fall off my cheeks wetting my pillow with cold felt different enough from the weight on my heart, that I convinced myself the tears were comforting.

My family's annual cruise was approaching so I used the upcoming vacation as a fuel to keep me going. More than ready when the moment arrived, I promised myself to have a good time and get out and kiss some frogs. The very first night of the cruise I mustered up the courage to go to the singles gathering. Immediately, my eye found a man who looked close to my age. He was already talking with another woman so I ordered a glass of wine and turned my attention to the young boy playing a video game sitting to my left. We began to chat and to my surprise his father, the cute man talking with the other woman, came over to introduce himself. He sat down and began to ask a million questions about me. I was in shock I had immediately met someone showing interest. Yes, this is my pattern. Be impressed someone notices you and be grateful if someone likes you. I know—sad, insecure, unattractive, but oh so true.

So the story unfolds. We discussed our lives and found commonalities in our love of wine, travel, and music. Each night we met at this same bar and continued to grow our friendship. During the day we often bumped in to each other, on the elevator, stairway, and in my cabin hallway. I can admit now I found it odd he somehow found me every day on this huge ship but at the time I told myself it had to be fate. After all, I was letting life steer me now, and this is where it drove me. He seemed to fit everything on the list I created. The fact he smuggled on his own rum and boasted about it to my entire family was not even a concern since we all had done this. Alcohol is extremely expensive on a cruise ship so if you can get a bottle in your bag and not have it taken away at customs, you are cool in my book.

The first romantic night we spent together, I awoke the next morning to a long letter under my door from him. As I was reading it, the phone rang. Words! The man writes and speaks his feelings openly. It is exactly like me. I love to write what I feel but I hide it; this man was brave enough to slip it under my door and call to make sure I saw it. As vain as it may seem, my excitement over the words was confirmation I needed that my body did not gross him out and he was still interested. Now keep in mind the lights were off. I do not let anyone see me. But still, you can feel the scars and my belly mush so my mind keeps me small reminding me during intimacy.

Not only was he interested, he was giving me attention like no other man had. Hmm, he is romantic, he writes, he was educated, and financially stable with a love of travel. He had an athletic build and was family oriented having brought his son with him as I had mine. The trip continued to unfold and although there were odd things like me catching him staring at me intently across the room so hard it made me uncomfortable. I ignored it, telling myself this is attraction. I mean it was the kind of stare I often caught my exes blatantly giving to other women; this man was giving it to me. Maybe this is why I run from hot men because it makes me uncomfortable to be the object of their glances.

So I convinced myself I should not run from physical attraction as I had in the past. He continued to write me notes daily and give me gifts. We were all partying so the bottle of rum he kept on his person fit right in. The words he was so passionate about followed us into the bedroom and I discovered it to be a huge turn on as he described what he wanted to do to me, was doing to me and wanted me to experience. The last night he gave me a pair of diamond earrings and although I felt a bit uncomfortable accepting them I told myself, "This is what you ask for, to be treated like a princess, now go with it."

When I returned home, I had to be at work early the next morning. I was surprised to find a card from him in my office mail. Somehow he mailed a card quickly, and it looked as if he must have done it from the ship. The cards continued to come daily along with gifts and flowers. Multiple texts on a daily basis and even pictures of the meal he was eating kept coming my way, "wish you were here," countless "I miss you" and pictures of me he had taken, without my knowledge, while on the cruise. I told my co-worker it was a bit much, but she said "you are just not used to attention. This is what attention feels like." Well okay, maybe so. I know when we break past patterns it is uncomfortable and so if I was going to break the pattern of men choosing women and whiskey over me then maybe I was going to have to feel uncomfortable.

When he told me he had a plane ticket, I let him come. Never mind that a few days prior to his arrival, on my birthday, I received a package of M & M candies with my face on them. He had taken a photo of us from the cruise and paid to have our faces printed on the candy. The other side said "I love you." Okay now I worried, but I decided to try and see the humor in it.

Picking him up at the airport was about the time I really started thinking it was bizarre, as I got out of the car to hug him and he put his hand on my ass in front of everyone. Not a playful love pat, no it was a full out grab my ass, squeeze and grind. Then the bottle of rum came out of his bag while he rooted for approval. He looked at me in wonder of where my enthusiasm went. It was funny and cute on the cruise ship where they want you to spend tons of money on their alcohol, but here we can stop at any corner store and purchase a cheap bottle.

We went for dinner and I offered to pay as I always do and yep, he let me pay! Hmm, where is the princess now? I pushed my gut feelings aside because what was I supposed to do now, he is here and I have to make the best of it. That is what I do. Ignore the truth of a man to see the best in him. Besides, the sex was good and for that, I could not wait. I was prepared, even willing to get completely unclothed, letting the gown come completely off, well as long as it is totally dark. Maybe it was the fact I was losing confidence he was the man for me, or maybe it was the rum I drank to try and keep up but I was at a complete loss for turning on sexually. His words of passion began to feel like commentary as he announced every play and cheered me on to reach my goal that sadly never came.

By this time, I am glad it is just a weekend trip. We met my coworker and her husband for dinner and the way he looked at me just kept getting more and more overbearing. My friend who said "this is what attention feels like" noticed the odd way he looked at me, but did not tell me until after he was gone. Stating "I thought for sure the way he looked at you, he was going to roofie you."

Later that same night we were alone drinking wine and listening to music on my phone. When I returned from the bathroom, I caught him on my phone. He looked up like he had all the right in the world to be on my phone, calmly asking who the guy was messaging. He insisted he was just trying to turn my music down when the text came over. But the text was old from a few days ago so I knew he was going through my messages.

Not sure how to respond, I mean after all this is my first shot at single, I did not respond at all. Sometimes we just have to let things fizzle while we ponder. Is it okay for someone to like you so much they check up on you? I have to admit, in some odd way it felt good to have someone that in to me. I understand why people stay with controlling people. Even though it is a violation of boundaries it feels uncomfortably comfortable to have someone be um, dare I say "crazy about you." I took him back to the airport the next day, knowing in my gut it would end.

In a panic when I got home, I looked over my list and immediately marked out the crazy about me! Still, it took a few weeks for me to let the relationship go completely. I did my best to honestly explain during several phone calls his attention was too much. I told him he was an extremely intelligent, handsome man and had no reason to be so insecure. Time and time again I was sent letters, songs, emails, and texts often saying just what I thought I wanted; "I am crazy about you." Countless texts that continued to seem stalkerish eventually died when I ignored him completely.

Oddly, I still felt heartbroken. Being single is tough and having someone even if just for a weekend filled that space I had yet to learn to fill on my own. I studied the relationship intently and tried to determine what it was about me that had attracted this to my life. I looked over my list again and added some of the great things I discovered I did like in Josh while deleting the crazy part. I loved that he was bilingual, he was very sensual, loving travel, good food and wine and he was a good father. It was perfect that he already had a child and did not want more kids. I added confidence to the list because that is obviously what he lacked. I said "NEXT" hoping now that crazy was off my list I could get it out of my life. Oh, do be careful what you wish.

The Commandments

Higher education at least a master's degree and interested in continuing to learn

Financially stable in a professional career

Family oriented – maybe already with a child since I am not having more

~~Crazy about me~~

Reads

Writes – journals, poetry, love letters, etc.

Honest

Display affection daily, kindness and respect

Romantic

Loves to travel

Athletic

Handsome

Tall

Hairy Chest

No Tattoos

Loves to dance

Loves music

~~Crazy about me~~

Loves animals

Loves even my flaws

Loves to touch me ~~because he is crazy about me!!!!!!~~

Respectful of others

Listens to me

Proud of me

Confident

Loves good food and wine

Sensual

Bilingual

Matthew

If you are trying to follow my chapters according to the Bible, don't. The Bible originally did not even have chapters. Someone came along much later and divided it up into sections as they saw fit depending on the version you use. There are countless translations and versions. It has been interpreted over and over. It is, as my son would say, "the oldest game of telephone." I am taking some power back to do the same.

So let's talk about Matthew. He was a longtime mutual friend of mutual friends. I had always found him attractive, mainly because he was tall. Yep, tall is on my list. If you are going to be my rescuing prince, it is necessary you be bigger than me. I suppose in looking for someone to save me, as in the fairytales, it is embedded in my head he be larger than life. I mean he is going to need to carry me.

Matthew kept quiet all the times I had been around him so we never actually had much of a conversation. But my longtime friend, Phoebe, thought we might make a good match. Again listening to others comes easy to me, I do not trust my own instincts. He asked me out to dinner. It was not a spectacular evening, but nice to go out and be treated like a lady. After all, he did pay for everything. At the end of the night when he dropped me off, it was terribly awkward standing there waiting. Was he going to hug me? Or kiss me? It was not flowing at all and it seemed he was nervous. Or hell maybe it was me. I was nervous. He did finally kiss me and it was okay, I suppose.

I can only imagine how obvious it is to my readers this is not the one but we all can easily see what's best for another before we can ourselves. That right there should have been my sign, but you can't read the book when you are in it. I was in it.

I waited for him to call as the days passed. He did not. My girlfriends said guys often do this; they wait several days to keep from seeming desperate. Three days passed before I heard from him, which drove me nuts. If you like someone, say so. Funny, I say that now because I should talk—I am not comfortable calling a man. I mean, my script says "ladies do not" and so I don't. He contacted me, but did not call, he texted. Um, why am I even surprised? He asked me out to dinner via text and I reinforced it by going on the date. Of course he is not going to change his approach. Who am I kidding? I pushed my nagging mind aside over the issue because no one is perfect. Weeks passed. Occasionally I would get a text from him and or run in to him when our mutual friends would get together.

We made out a few times and continued to go out on occasion, dinner or a movie over the next two months. On one occasion we sat outside my house as he dropped me off talking about where this was going. I found it odd he said more than once, "I am not good enough for you" and "I cannot compete with the doctors you work with and mingle with at conventions." I explained that I am not a physician and I liked him just as he was. I could not believe this tall handsome man was feeling insecure. That one line kept running through my mind, "I am not good enough for you," but I am the insecure one so I did not listen to the deeper meaning.

We continued to see each other, but it moved very slowly; still I began to think we might have something because our make out sessions were hot. I decided to be an adult and go to my doctor to get reassurance I was okay after my last fling and get on birth control. I lost sleep over how to explain to her I was thinking of having sex with my "boyfriend" and appalled at my ability to be so immature at the ripe old age of forty-something! Nevertheless, I headed off and prepared my body for the wishful encounter. The texting continued but it was nothing like Joshua's over the top texting. Matt sent brief, "how is the princess today?" texts. I assume he did not need to say much since he was calling me princess. It fits the fairytale fantasy I still believed in.

I tried to adjust my expectations going from a man who texts me his entire day along with pictures of his dinner to this man texting every third day very brief, keep me on the line tidbits. I counted down the days for our next date since I would be prepared for sex physically. I say physically, because the mental part did not exist. It felt so evil. I at first deleted the word evil as I wrote, but then put it back because it is exactly how my mind felt about sex out of wedlock, evil. I continued to battle that thought and watched countless "Sex in the City" episodes to open my mind to being single and okay with sex. The texting from him was limited the week I was ready to sleep with him. There was an occasional "hello" and "how is the princess?" but no date. By Friday, I just knew he would text me, so when my girlfriend Phoebe called that evening to see if I had plans I explained to her I was waiting on Matt. She wanted me to go to a party with her and insisted I call him to let him know I would be out. Disinclined, I threw my script aside and called. This is how it went –

Matt: Well hello, how are you beautiful?

Me: I am great. I just wanted to see what you were up to and let you know Phoebe wants me to go to a party with her.

Matt: Um, okay. (And then silence)

Me: Yeah, well I felt like I should let you know.

Matt: You don't have to tell me where you are going.

Me: I thought I should since we are dating. (More silence)

Matt: We are not dating.

Yep, my heart hit bottom hard. Every moment we had been together and every word he said and or texted to me swung through my mind like god speed fastballs. In an instant I tried to reevaluate what had just been said as I pulled the phone away from my ear to look at the number I had dialed. Surely I had called the wrong number! Nope, it said Matt. I had called the man I thought I was dating, that I wanted to sleep with, that I was prepared to sleep with. Damn it! And he just informed me we were not dating! My silence must have spoken loudly through the phone because he said "don't be mad" and in an instant I felt my script change. I normally would act like I was not, that it was all okay, you know be that stepped on, walked all over doormat. But instead I spoke my mind, told him I was mad, and I hung up.

I went to the party, cried to my girlfriend on the way and knowing full well alcohol only intensifies the underlying emotion; I still partook in the drinking. I drank until I was sick. My girlfriend Phoebe had to take me home. She stayed with me, consoling me with her wonderful "I won't let you drink alone" intoxicated pep talk, while she became inebriated and called him up. She handed my drunken ass the phone and all I recall is crying to him. I am not even sure what I said, but he came over. He came over and with the relief of having a man console me, I sank and we had sex. I hate to say I had sex with him because as a young woman we spread rumors about others saying horrible things like she's such a whore or slut. Now I only talk to me that way. Thank you female support system. Thank you.

I am not even sure how it was. I know I always feel awkward. Like the clumsy girl who is trying to turn a cartwheel for the first time or that feeling you get when posing for a picture wondering "where do I put my hands." (Maybe it's just me. Am I the only one who feels that?) It just feels fucking awkward to me, drunk or not. It's like the times I have gone to Zumba class and everyone around me is popping their ass all sexy, while mine just aimlessly shakes, arms flailing all about as I sheepishly look around to make sure no one is watching. Yep, that's how I feel during sex. Awkward as shit! Add to it he left, and I did not hear from him again for a long time. I was very hurt. When he eventually did text weeks later, I did what I have never done and ignored him. He did apologize some months later by showing up to my office because I would not return his texts.

I never told him the steps I went through, that I was prepared to sleep with him or I had mentally made room for him in my future. Nor that my period was late and Phoebe took me to buy a pregnancy test that thankfully came back negative. I just took my ass whooping and moved on. Welcome to the world of dating. Getting over a broken heart is one thing but getting over the guy you were not even "dating" well fuck, now that sucks. Not only am I dealing with confusion over why my heart hurts but confusion over how someone with a 4.0 graduate degree could be so stupid.

The dreadful days after seemed unbearable as my heart tore open and shut. There was a burning in my chest like my heart was screaming for nourishment. I know now it was just me trying to make sense of it all and it did not add up until weeks later when I discovered he had been seeing someone else, not just someone else, a former stripper all along and I was just plan B. I was still playing the part of the doormat. Now the fact she was a stripper has nothing to do with judgment of her but judgment of me because to be a stripper you have to have a rocking body and well you know what I think of me. So it hurt to consider my body was the reason he did not choose me.

I don't understand why a man cannot just be honest. When I discovered the truth, although disheartening, the sense it all now made helped my heart stop beating up on me. It is a huge disaffection to conceal the truth from another. You may think you are not hurting them by hiding it but what you are really doing is making them question their feelings, their inner being trying to guide them authentically. Listening to my inner voice was still so damning and I blame men for the misunderstanding. My exes had taught me I was just a jealous bitch. I believe cheating is one of the most torturous destroyers of our inner voice. Just tell the truth, let us have our emotional outburst and move on. At the very least let us have back our intuitive power by confirming what we are feeling.

I suppose Matt was able to live with his cheating heart as long as he continued to believe he was not dating me. The night Matt told me he was not good enough for me, I mean c'mon. If someone says they are not good enough for you, LISTEN! There was a gnawing in my heart the entire time we dated, well no did not date, whatever the hell we did, my heart was heavy trying to tell me something. Again I altered the list, marking out tall and hairy chest. I decided if I was going to let go of the fairytale fantasy then maybe I need to let go of some of the macho labels that go with it. Besides, from what I recall of the sex, not all things are proportional. I added enjoys conversation since it annoyed me he would only text and I added um, single. NEXT!

The Commandments

Higher education at least a master's degree and interested in continuing to learn

Financially stable in a professional career

Family oriented – maybe already with a child since I am not having more

~~Crazy about me~~

Reads

Writes – journals, poetry, love letters, etc.

Honest

Display affection daily, kindness and respect

Romantic

Loves to travel

Athletic

Handsome

~~Tall~~

~~Hairy Chest~~

No Tattoos

Loves to dance

Loves music

~~Crazy about me~~

Loves animals

Loves even my flaws

Loves to touch me ~~because he is crazy about me!!!!!!~~

Respectful of others

Listens to me

Proud of me

Confident

Loves good food and wine

Sensual

Bilingual

Single

Enjoys conversation

Mark

After Matt the bullfrog devastated my hope for fairytale love, I decided to start dating myself. I wanted to avoid the lonely the weekends sucked out of me. I contacted my friend Abigail who I have known since we were three years old. She is the most beautiful, witty, funny person I have ever met, and she is single. I was delighted when she too had had enough of the frogs and could travel with me. We headed off in November for a week of spoiling. I fell in love with a country that would forever change my life. Our driver, an older gentleman, probably my father's age, was so kind. From the little Spanish I knew, he began to refer to us as his daughters. He wanted to be our driver the entire trip. We agreed. He took us zip lining and to his friend's restaurant for dinner. After dinner we were allowed to explore his friend's garden. The magical garden filled with massive foliage and humming birds as big as parrots reminded me of a fairytale book with odd plants and animals my eye had never seen.

The days continued to improve as my need for more nature grew. I loved the people, the outdoors, and the rain. I began to feel like something in me was coming alive for the first time in a long time. We drank wine, danced in the rain, and sang songs by the pool. Our driver took us on long adventures to see other parts of the country in his little toy car. Other than one night that ended in a satisfactory kiss from a frog, there were no other men on this adventure and despite my script calling for men to be happy, I felt happy. I felt peace in my heart and since my practice was going well and finances were good, I decided not to spend another weekend moping and to head out as much as I could.

One month after my return from paradise, my stories of nature's adventure had made my father, step-mom, and sister want to travel with me so we headed out this time to the coast of paradise. The resort where we stayed was beautiful. I honored my goal to date myself and on the first night after my family went to bed, I took my anxious lonely to the disco. The bartender spoke limited English but knew enough body language apparently to see my awkward attempt to fit in. He immediately told me this was a lovers resort, lots of families and honeymooners and if I wanted to meet someone I would need to go elsewhere. Wow, I cannot even fake confidence. Clearly, his words offended me. I mean good goddess, do I look that desperate? I rebutted with "I am not looking," as any well-established single girl would while I silently damned my circumstances. I decided to make the best of it and do what I would do had I had a date. I danced alone despite the unease.

We had amazing adventures; scuba diving and white water rafter. I had never been rafting. It took great courage as the guides explained the rapids to be level five. Apparently that's bad. Ignorance is bliss. Knowing what I know now, I am not sure I would do it again, I am glad I did because the last plunge over that thirteen foot waterfall was enough to shake some of my programmed soul free. I emerged from the pounding waters grateful for life. Something more about that adventure opened my spirit.

We drove over an hour through rough winding dirt roads lined with tropical forest to finally reach the river that would take my breath away. Although the exhilarating rafting holds space in my mind, the part of the trip that grasped my heart was the multiple stops the guide made to pick up trash along the road. On the last stop, he came back inside the bus to properly place each piece in his tiny recycling bins. I watched him look up from the bin and stretch his arms wide as if to give a hug to the outside land, while he proclaimed to the somewhat perturbed tourists now looking at their watches, "she is my office, I work best in clean spaces." I smiled knowing he knew something I used to know, and I wanted it back. I knew his soul well—a reflection of mine. It was on this trip I began to hear whispers in the wind again.

Each night I headed to the bar alone with more courage as the week progressed. I danced alone or with the dance instructor and on one occasion a man who told me he was gay. Then he walked me to my room and tried to kiss me! I was bewildered as he told me I might be able to turn him straight. I said "no I don't think so, but thank you for the compliment, I think." I pouted my ass back to my room, lying on my bed talking to my gods and pleading with them to let me know what it is I need to learn. How can what just happened be a lesson? I went to sleep telling myself I was fine and needed no one.

On the next to last night, late for dinner, I ran to the lobby to meet my family when I saw this handsome man standing at the hotel entrance steps overlooking the sea. He turned to me politely asking my name, as he reached to shake my hand. He was good looking. Dark, thick wavy hair dusted in powder gray and a manly body he had dressed in elegant linen to perfectly fit the tropical scene. I told myself there is no way he is single but he surprisingly invited me to meet him for a dance after dinner. I said, "Sure, I have been dancing alone all week." I headed off to dinner battling my head that kept trying to halt the excitement growing on the inside.

After dinner I sat in the lobby with a glass of wine wondering if he would show up. He did. We headed to the bar and danced the night into the day. We ended sitting out by the pool where he read me poems he wrote. He not only reads poetry, he writes it. Oh yes, I was wooed. He sang a sultry sexy song called "Besame Mucho." Had the singing out loud not made me a bit uncomfortable, it would have been perfect. Still, I did as the song instructed and kissed him a lot. He asked to take me to dinner the next night. We kissed good night and I went to bed with dreams in my heart again.

The next day was my last night so even though I looked forward to dinner I feared what the evening might bring. Dinner was great but awkward. I kept questioning what in the hell this attractive man had in store for me, what had to be wrong with him and all the things we think when we do not believe we are worthy. He said he was single and buying land with the hopes of moving here some day because he loved the nature. Writes poetry, single, financially stable, love of nature, it just kept getting better. We went back to his room to continue the kissing and making out while listening to sultry music. I had to leave knowing my taxi was taking me to the airport at 4 am. He was nearly asleep and did ask me to stay but I did not. I was disappointed he did not offer to walk me to my door only a few feet away but I have so much trouble deciding if one red flag is enough to cut myself off; the answer is no, I go and go. I expected to hear from him the next day but I did not. I had given him my email and although I can fool myself into thinking I need no one, I checked that email more than one should. I went back to life and work trying to make sense of it all.

It was over a week before I got the email that made my heart jump. He said he had been thinking of me and wanted to see me. I wanted to see him too, so we began talking on the phone to see how to make it happen. I decided to fly back to paradise for a long weekend since he was still there looking at land. It was a wonderful time, with horseback riding, hiking to waterfalls and simply resting in hammocks. He cooked almost every meal for me. We became intimate and the struggle to relax made my enjoyment nothing in comparison to the guilt and shame. I hid my body for fear of the scars. I cannot stand to look at them. How can someone else? I have stretch marks all around my waist, even on my back and down the inside and outside of my legs. The front of my stomach is covered all the way above my navel. I have tried every fancy cream out there. I am just going to have to learn to love them. I will put my body in a bikini at times but I have to find a way to stop caring what a man might think.

I can never tell if it is my insecurity about my body that makes me not enjoy sex or if this is just how it is. I have never felt good about my body and never felt free enough to just let go. I hate to say it but I have been a faker for years sometimes out of sympathy for them trying so hard and sometimes because it starts but something happens and it just does not finish. So things were just okay on the intimate end at first. Then one would think the more we got to know each other it would be more comfortable but the more at ease he became the more uncomfortable I became.

Despite his sultry music and poetry, there was a mysteriousness to him that grew in oddity. I tried very hard to make a connection on a deeper level but there was an eerie coldness at times. The sex was not emotional at all and his out loud fantasizing was simply not doing it for me. I had already been exposed to Joshua's commentary that went from sexy enticement to annoying announcements. I wanted to find a way to talk with him because everything else was pretty perfect, but I put off discussing it because we only had a few days together.

On the last day he told me he had an ex-girlfriend in a rehab he still talked to on occasion. Despite the ex now in the picture and the sex being off, I blamed myself for being a prude and focused on the rest of the trip which was pretty spectacular. I returned home. We talked on the phone daily. Our conversations were very encouraging, and I even opened up to him I was having difficulty with sex and his ex. He assured me she was out of his life and the more we got to know each other the better sex would be. I decided I wanted him to visit me.

We began to look at air prices. He explained since he just bought land it would be difficult, so me being the giver or door mat I am, I paid for the ticket. He arrived, and I decided to throw him to the wolves introducing him to my friends and family. Some of them loved him and some of them felt there was something off. None of them knew I paid for him to get here. That would have probably tipped the lovers over to the other side.

We spent five days together. He began to tell me he loved me. I could not say it back. In the past I had said it back to anyone who said it to me first. I was determined to not say it until I felt it. Whatever it was, I don't even know what I should feel but I know I will not say it this time until something feels. At this point I was not even sure I had ever been in real love. Every time he told me, and I did not respond the agitation grew. I could feel the tension. I explained it was too soon. I was simply not ready. In protest, he told me his ex was calling him. Obviously he was trying to manipulate me into feeling inferior. Like someone else wanting him back was somehow going to push me over the edge to love him. (Hmm, who has done that before?)

Then there was his preoccupation seeking opportunities to make money with a salesman attitude, I do not buy. I had a ring to sell so I showed him to see if he had any idea its value. He offered to take it home with him and sell it for me. I would only have to pay him ten percent commission. Really, this, after I paid for his plane ticket and most of the meals?

But probably the most agitating thing was the more comfortable he became with me, the more the sex grew in oddity. Even after I had discussed it with him and he assured me it would get better, anything I said I did not like, he listened changing his approach but to something even odder. It went from talking dirty during the act with very odd fantasies about people watching, to changing his approach when I said it did nothing for me, now talking out loud about other people joining. I mean telling me who else he would like to be in the room with us and giving me details as to what he would do to them. When I said I did not like it he stopped the dirty talk of other people and started talking about exhibitionist shit during the act. Yes, I like words but talk to me about what we are experiencing not some fantasy. I have to remain in the moment to enjoy it. My mind already drifts like crazy, I need someone to help me stay here now. I know I am a prude and all, but this was off the charts.

I took him back to the airport feeling confused. The phone calls and texts continued always ending in I love you from his end. He sent countless texts proclaiming his love for me and a picture of a puppy saying "do you love me now?" On our last conversation, he tried to make me jealous by telling me his ex was out of rehab and coming back to live with him. I did not know why I was so hurt and why I cried so hard to him over the phone. I pleaded with him, "How can you say you love me? You do not even know what it means if you are back with her."

I think I understand now it was not I wanted him, but I wanted to believe in love. I wanted to believe it would grow. That love grows until we can no longer contain it. And I wanted to believe that in him telling me he loved me he really did. But no, there it was in black and white. He was not in love with me. He just wanted someone, anyone to fill his holes the way I had begged people in the past to fill mine. He was, for a brief stint me, and I was him.

I wanted to remain in his life to learn from this but his poetry online began to be about me, and I felt it best to set him free. He still had an unhealthy idea he loved me even though he was now back with his ex and he was posting it for all the world to see. On several occasions he messaged me to make sure I had read the poems and to confirm I understood it was about me. I ask him to stop and eventually he did. But the damage or lesson was done and now all that was left was for me to alter my list. I have gone from a man passionate with words and a to go bottle of rum, to one with no words and a stripper on the side now to one with words so twisted it's absurd saying he loves me with his ex in the room. Writes poetry, needless to say, got nixed. Not that it is not okay, it is just not a deciding factor. I added able to remain in the moment because he was off in dreamland either fantasizing about sex or fantasizing about ways to make money. Lastly I included "over past relationships" and said "NEXT."

The Commandments
Higher education at least a master's degree and interested in continuing to learn
Financially stable in a professional career

Family oriented – maybe already with a child since I am not having more

~~Crazy about me~~

Reads

Writes – journals, ~~poetry~~, love letters, etc.

Honest

Display affection daily, kindness and respect

Romantic

Loves to travel

Athletic

Handsome

~~Tall~~

~~Hairy Chest~~

No Tattoos

Loves to dance

Loves music

~~Crazy about me~~

Loves animals

Loves even my flaws

Loves to touch me ~~because he is crazy about me!!!!!!~~

Respectful of others

Listens to me

Proud of me

Confident

Loves good food and wine

Sensual

Bilingual

Single

Enjoys conversation

Able to remain in the moment

Over past relationships

Luke

Back to working my week away and hating the lonely weekends, I asked my friend Abi if she would join me for a New Year's Eve trip to New York City. We knew it would be expensive, especially booking it last minute, but we opted for the trip of a lifetime attitude and booked it. Everything flowed; from our upgrade to first class, to our room being perfect. We arrived and hit the first bar our eyes found emerging from the subway tunnel. Then hopping to every bar thereafter all the way to our hotel. I could tell immediately this would not be a site seeing adventure but merely giant rock out party. With only three days and a holiday, we didn't even worry about making time for anything but fun. We did not stop. We partied all day, all night, and had a blast piecing together the night's events with receipts, pictures and a few sketchy videos to jog our memory of where we had even been. The next night was the eve of eve.

We slept our hangovers off just in time for dinner reservations at my favorite Italian restaurant. We arrived to standing room only. The hostess was perplexed trying to please all the rude people rimming her for their reservations not being on time. They all griped they had plans that would be missed. She apologized to me, as I pushed my way to the pulpit. She explained the kitchen was running way behind, an hour or more. I saw her brace for my response. It is in these moments I am so glad I am beginning to learn to let plans go, so I smiled sweetly, comforted her, and told her to not even worry about us because we would do what we were best at and find a seat at the bar. I told her she could seat us whenever the others with plans were taken care of.

Our kindness was quickly reimbursed as the couple sitting at the bar next to us engaged us in humorous conversation. We laughed and toasted and drank not even caring how smashed our bodies were next to the bar as the crowd continued to roll in. The couple crammed next to us enjoyed the toasting and began to order drinks and join in. They asked us our plans for the big night tomorrow and our "no plans" quickly turned into an invite from them to a party at a VIP hotel club overlooking the stage and ball drop. Talk about Karma paying off because he was talking about the place I looked into and I knew the tickets were outrageous. It is unbelievable how life works, when we let it. He told us where to pick up our VIP passes and police blockade passes the next day.

We eventually got seated, ate, and rejoiced even more now that we have something grand to toast to. We are ecstatic. It feels unreal. The next day we again slept until our heads could hold themselves up. Off for a late lunch, pick up our passes and then back to the hotel to rest for our big night. Despite our resolve to eat then nap before the best party ever we began drinking in the pub around the corner from the hotel party we would soon attend. We met a few cute men, no wait let me rephrase that, one of them was hot. The kind of hot that makes me tremble and run away. Up until now I would describe men as attractive, cute, or handsome but hot, that comes with a feeling. A feeling I am not too accustomed to because it scares me. In this case, I did not run away because I fooled myself into thinking he was not available and if he was, he was not interested.

I visited with him. When he asked our plans for the evening we told of our encounter with the dream maker and our VIP passes to the upscale bar around the corner. The sexy men asked us to come back after we got ready because they wanted to attempt to go with us to the party. It seemed like a complicated adventure but nothing at this point had been impossible. We have had the grandest luck with upgrades and unexpected wishes granted so we quickly left to get ready saying "screw the nap."

We adorned ourselves back at our hotel trying to make the best of what outfits we had although we never intended to attend a VIP party. It is a good thing we were day drinking because we really didn't care our attire may not be appropriate. We headed back to the pub now blocked off by security but our passes worked and we got through the blockades. We discussed with the hotties how to get them in. We decided to act like we were staying in the hotel. Abi gave her pass to her cutie. He took her hand as if he were her date quickly passing the guard. I held on to my pass worried one of us may not get through and I was going hot man or not.

As we approached the blockade it hit me, this is just a piece of paper and the police are overwhelmed with the crowd so I grab another piece of paper I found in my purse handing it to Luke, my now hot date. Luke did not even look at it as I had hoped. I anticipated the police would do the same. We approached the guard. I shoved my paper first as Luke showed his with all the confidence in the world. I made small talk to the guard trying to keep his eyes occupied. He let us pass.

Luke grabbed my arm whispering "how did you get another pass?" I showed him it was not a pass, but my hotel receipt. We both laughed. I felt clever, young, rebellious, and maybe a little bit worthy of my hot date. We made our way to the hotel entrance requiring yet another pass that looked like a hotel key. We only had two. We walked on by security as if nothing. Abi and her man again made it past. I showed my pass, got through, but Luke was stopped. In an instant I got the idea to act like he is my husband and do as bossy wives do. Sharply I walked back to the standoff pointing my finger at Luke and spouting "What? You left it in the room? I told you to get it." The guard immediately felt sympathy for Luke who was now playing the degraded part well, looking up sadly with his big beautiful puppy dog eyes. I continued saying "I told you" and "See, you never listen." I suppose being a wife twice has its perks because I was spot on.

In an effort to shut me up, the guard let us pass telling Luke to go straight to the room, get the pass and please don't forget it again. I was so proud of the rebel I seem to have found. We all laughed at our luck and headed to the party. There were elegant decorations, lights, people, food and drinks. We indulged in the fanciness for a while but soon agreed the party was stuffy. I was so glad we left because the elevator music was boring and I wanted to dance. We went right back to the place we began not even caring we let high dollar tickets go.

Back at the pub, the Irish music was invigorating. I kicked off my shoes to dance like the river dance I had always dreamed to be a part of, not even caring who was watching. "I am the best dancer in the world," I thought and the Japanese ladies confirmed it with "yoo good dancer" time and time again as the night unfolded. Luke danced with me on occasion but I continued to tell myself he is too good looking. I mean he was a hunk, so New York, oozing rough and tough hotness. At times he flirted with other girls and since I felt I had no chance, as usual I did not even try. To my surprise he grabbed my hand to pull me from my Irish jig dance-a-thon, yelling "it's time", dragging me outside into the street.

The song "New York, New York" was playing and fireworks were exploding as people crammed streets sang the song in celebration. He kissed me gently but it was only a peck reminding me he was taken, or too cute, or just too everything. We enjoyed the countdown and then went back to our pub to dance it off. Luck would have it, a bottle broke on the dance floor and my clogging bare feet got into it good. Luke came to my rescue and since the night was ending or better yet day beginning, he said "I just live around the corner. Let me take you there and get the glass out of your foot." We followed him up to the cutest NYC apartment. I knew right away he was brilliant; the place was spectacular with art and books everywhere. He doctored my foot and then complimented me tremendously leaving me feeling perplexed, like I didn't deserve his attention. He jokingly said to counter the compliments "but you are a bad dancer." We laughed, knowing it was not much of a joke. Still I wondered why I had so much difficulty with compliments especially coming from such gorgeousness; it is as if his joke about my bad dancing eased the tension of the positive attention.

Abi passed out on his couch; it was nearly morning and so I said "Thank you, we should go." He insisted I not leave yet, asking to cook me breakfast. In one swift move he picked me up and sat me on the tiny kitchen counter. I watched the beauty before me seduce my cravings with his kitchen skills. I did my best to take it all in as he conjured up the sexiest waffles this girl has ever indulged in. We ate and because the perfect night had weakened my resolve to leave, I simply followed when he grabbed my hand to take me to his room.

The first thing I noticed was the structure on his floor. It was a huge wooden statue covered in rosaries, more rosaries than I had ever seen. I too collect rosaries despite my religious confusion. It is my rebellious way of somehow revolting against my past. But maybe it is more about me hoping if I collect enough they will let me back in the club. I took a mental picture of the structure as he laid me down and kissed me with more passion than I deserve. He stopped periodically, and we talked. He told me about the rosaries and where they all came from. Some of them were very ancient and worldly. He was passionate about his faith, his family, and his city. He said he could never leave New York. It is part of him.

His family is part of its history and a few of his deceased relatives were even in the mafia. He told me about his breakup with his ex and how he was taking a break from dating. He had not been with a woman in a long while. I could tell it was part of his spirituality. He was no heathen. He was honorable, moral, and looking for more of a connection than sexual. I knew this even before I told him I did not want sex, but verbalizing it and him agreeing was very freeing as I allowed him to kiss me feeling safe this was enough.

We kissed a lot and I could not help but think how this man was so much more beautiful than I. I told myself "you could never get naked in front of this specimen." He was perfect. I loved the way he cuddled me because I just wanted this, nothing more. Totally satisfied with the love I had received, I decided I must leave. I woke Abi who was still out on his couch and we caught a cab to our hotel. The sun was coming up as was Abi's alertness to ask me in the cab how it was. She was lightheartedly appalled I did not sleep with him, scolding me in her way that always makes me laugh hard. "He was fucking hot! I will never let you live this one down sister."

He texted he missed me the next day as we left for the airport. I considered going back to see him. But the periodic communication fizzled, despite my efforts to make something of it. His texting ended. I consoled myself to let it go, while rejoicing the bar on attraction had been raised. Hotness is never again going to be deterrent but rather major criterion. I looked at my list and added what I liked. Spirituality, and beside handsome, I added hot. I need to learn to accept maybe I am worthy of not just a handsome man but a hot one. One that makes my temperature rise in the way that used to make me flee because I defined the feeling as fear. If I am going to live my life fearless, then I damn well better burn through the fear of passionate romance with all the hot I can handle.

I myself decided to make my own statue of rosaries including other religious artifacts, celebrating my history because I am beginning to see it as history and merely that. Not necessary a way to live but to honor as the way it was. I found a tall crystal candelabra to hold the end of relics and allow my rosaries and beads to hang in harmony. To this day when I travel, I purchase rosary and mala beads or some other artifact to hang in celebration to love of all. It is my way of honoring a combination of religions, not one being better than the other just being. I delighted in the fact my small town mind is expanding and I said "NEXT."

The Commandments

Higher education at least a master's degree and interested in continuing to learn

Financially stable in a professional career

Family oriented – maybe already with a child since I am not having more

~~Crazy about me~~

Reads

Writes – journals, ~~poetry~~, love letters, etc.

Honest

Display affection daily, kindness and respect

Romantic

Loves to travel

Athletic

Handsome and HOT

~~Tall~~

~~Hairy Chest~~

No Tattoos

Loves to dance

Loves music

~~Crazy about me~~

Loves animals

Loves even my flaws

Loves to touch me ~~because he is crazy about me!!!!!!~~

Respectful of others

Listens to me

Proud of me

Confident

Loves good food and wine

Sensual

Bilingual

Single

Enjoys conversation

Able to remain in the moment

Over past relationships

Spiritual

Daniel

I want to return to Paradise again and again. And so I do, almost monthly. There is something about the country that pulls me in. I feel something. Something different but not unknown, like a familiar friend I forgot. It is as if there is a treasure to be sought. Every time I visit, I find more and more reason to go back and I want to start looking for property. I am not even sure how much things cost or if an American can even own property but it does not matter at this point. It is as if I am playing a game; pretending to own a vacation home is even plausible. So I play and I search online. I know I want a place in a town without tourism destruction. I want off the beaten path. I want nature. I search online and discover a little beach town that seems to fit me perfectly from the few articles I find. I contact a realtor online even though I have not even been to this particular town and ask to see property upon my arrival. I research how to purchase property and even though it seemed impossible, things begin to unfold.

I returned again with my dad and Abi because we all decided to look at real estate. I had been emailing the realtor quite a bit, and he was very helpful easing my mind because there were so many loopholes; like you need lots of cash, a lawyer, possibly residency, a corporation, etc. It seemed overwhelming, but I reminded myself, I am playing.

I arrived and scheduled an appointment with the wise old realtor. I had constructed an image in my mind of an intelligent older gentleman, sun damaged and overweight with sparse sun-bleached sprockets of hair coming from his freckled balding head. We arrived to the town I had only read about and I instantly felt a belonging. Something in me connected with the energy, the people, the nature, with myself. We walked the beach and ate before heading to meet the realtor. Totally sweaty from the heated humidity we were not yet used to, Abi joked about our melting looks as we spotted the real estate office "what if he is cute?"

I shrugged my shoulders, throwing on my hat to cover my sweaty head knowing full well the realtor had to be a jolly old man. I impatiently opened the door to escape the heat, only to lose my breath at the sight behind the desk. I took a step back to escape but it was too late. I silently wished I was not covered in sweat and secretly asked the universe that this hunk of a man not be him. I sheepishly said I was looking for Daniel. He smiled his brilliant white smile responding, "That is me."

"FUCK" is all that went through my head. Abi asked for the bathroom, beating me to the punch. I know she merely wanted the mirror as did I. The guy was the most beautiful man I had ever seen. Dark hair, bluest, blue eyes, tall, and well built. FUCK, FUCK, FUCK! This is the feeling I run from. Luckily he was ready to go look at property so I escaped to the back seat of his car, and we are off looking at houses. I was still unsure how I would make buying property happen but I knew I wanted a vacation home here.

That evening we went to dinner with Daniel. His personality was as adorable as his looks. Everyone else was tired from the long day so they retired to their room, leaving me alone with the most beautiful man in the world. He was funny, smart, and had somehow managed to make me feel at ease. This place and his presence had me feeling safe. I find it odd to say I felt safe, but for some strange reason, safe in a situation I would have normally left. I would have said goodbye when everyone else did because I would have felt inferior next to this gorgeous specimen.

As he discussed his family, life, hopes, and dreams, I wondered what I was even afraid of. Earlier in the day I discovered the sign on his arm and I knew I was where I needed to be. He had a sand dollar tattoo. I have always found sand dollars to be a sign from the universe I am on the right path. I wanted to believe maybe it meant he was the guy for me, but I had also discovered how young he was. I decided to see it as another lesson reinforcing the one Luke taught, that maybe I am worthy of hotness. We had a fabulous time together. The night did end with a wonderful kiss therefore he gets to be a frog even though his influence in changing my life would not be romantic. I knew he would be in my life somehow. As a friend maybe, I was not sure at this point.

During dinner, a friend of his had approached and Daniel introduced us. "David," Daniel explained "is a local surf instructor and the best." If I wanted lessons, he said, this was the man. We set a date for the next morning. Surfing is so much more difficult than one might imagine. The lesson was more intense than my forty plus body was prepared for but I braved the waves and did my best to impress my unwavering instructor and the two hot guys who spontaneously signed up to take the lessons with me. I could tell David took his job very seriously and safety was of utmost importance as he commented time and time again "Julia, we got a problem" when I did something incorrectly. He would quickly explain how dangerous it could be.

I apologized over and over to him as my body tired and I could see his concern for my safety grew even more. He did eventually get me up. It was exhilarating but my body could take no more as the wave crashed down. I recovered but my board went flying toward David because I was of course holding it wrong. He scolded me like a father scolds a child fearing they could harm themselves in a firm but loving manner saying, "Julia we have problem; look here, this is so very dangerous, Listen to me." I admitted how spent I was. I hugged him and complimented his long hair to bring him back to smiling, rubbing it with my hand and saying "I love you for being so concerned, but I must stop." He smiled with a look of relief saying, "Yes, Julia maybe you will do better on the beach, looking pretty and enjoying a drink." That would be my last attempt at surfing but my first encounter with having a man I can honestly call a friend. I instantly loved this guy. He oozed Paradise. He was the kind of guy you can't help but love—cool and chill. I wanted him in my life forever though we had barely met.

I visited him often. He is joyous, funny, and soulful. He instructed me on everything from riding a bike to simply living in a foreign town. I loved his accent; it is not typical but reminds me of a Spanish conquistador. The way he went into great detail telling stories put my mind right there in it as if I was watching a movie. I laughed hard when he tried to describe his efforts to get a visa to the United States. He repeatedly told me his "appliances" were all rejected in an attempt to get me to understand. We both cracked up when he realized the word was "applications" and I told him "well I thought you were trying to bring over a refrigerator or something."

I adored him for letting me laugh at his attempts to communicate. It is not like I have any room to talk. I have struggled for years to speak his language. I think he is brilliant. He often calls to check in on me, gives me tons of advice on things to do and introduces me to all his amazing friends. I wanted his Tiffany blue bicycle with a basket, but he would not sell it; instead he put together a more appropriate pink one for me. He laughs with me when I make fun of his bag he carries his things in. I teasingly tell him "don't forget your purse, D."

Over the next few months with me coming back and forth, our friendship grew. We talked about everything, including sex. He often came to pick me up at the airport, sometimes staying with me the first night to make sure I felt safe and then would call me as soon as I returned home to make sure I was okay. His wisdom is brilliant. He is Zen and does not even know it. He has told me time and time again to listen to my heart, while warning me of who to avoid when it comes to men. He has been my greatest ally in explaining to me how this beach town works. Men here only want one thing. It is their way of life. They have grown accustomed to weekend romance. It is all they know. They enjoy love briefly with the beautiful girls who come in to town just as fast as they go out. The local men are so good for female confidence. They are very complimentary and love women of all ages, color, and sizes. The local men love women. But keep in mind "women" is plural. The joke is "you did not lose your girlfriend; you just lost your turn."

It helps tremendously to know this and keep my head in check. I realize all the flirting is just an attempt to get me into bed. I count my blessings I have made two wonderful friends. One who worked his ass off finding me the perfect property and one who made me feel at home.

Over the next week, we tossed around ideas on how to make buying a vacation home happen. Dad and I decided to split it since it would be a vacation home. The beach house we wanted ended up going up in price so Daniel found us a property that was the best bargain we had seen. Little did I know the house would be so perfect. We bargained and before I knew it, my dad and I owned a home in Paradise!

Daniel and David both are a huge part of the rest of my story and how my life would begin to unfold. I changed my list to reflect many of the things I had learned I liked from them. For David, I added Zen even though it is his effortless state of being. It is one of the reasons I love him so. And I marked out Master's level education because I am beginning to wonder if my formal education was not one of the reasons I am so arrogantly scripted. David is one of the most brilliant men I know and although he attended university, it was not graduate level. I crossed out the "in a professional career" and added "doing what he loves" in honor of my new found friends.

Daniel put me in a house that was perfect for me—the location, the neighbors, all magic. I added adventurous because the story Daniel told me of how he moved with only one suitcase was the most adventurous thing I could think of. I marked out my original wish of "No Tattoos" because Daniel was very attractive to me and he had beautiful tattoos. Maybe it was another one of my pompous programs put in my mind when the spell was cast. Plus he helped me burn through my anxiety over being next to a hot man! It is a great lesson because little did I know I just bought a house in the land of man candy. If I am going to kiss frogs here I better learn this lesson first.

The Commandments

~~Higher education at least a master's degree and~~ interested in continuing to learn

Financially stable ~~in a professional career~~ doing what he loves
Family oriented – maybe already with a child since I am not having more
~~Crazy about me~~
Reads
Writes – journals, ~~poetry~~, love letters, etc.
Honest
Display affection daily, kindness and respect
Romantic
Loves to travel
Athletic
Handsome and HOT
~~Tall~~
~~Hairy Chest~~
~~No Tattoos~~
Loves to dance
Loves music
~~Crazy about me~~
Loves animals
Loves even my flaws
Loves to touch me ~~because he is crazy about me!!!!!!~~
Respectful of others
Listens to me
Proud of me
Confident
Loves good food and wine
Sensual
Bilingual
Single
Enjoys conversation
Able to remain in the moment
Over past relationships
Spiritual
Zen
Adventurous

John 1

I met John back in Paradise to close on the house we purchased. Being the first time I had traveled to the little village alone, anxiety exploded. I worried about driving in a foreign town, since I hate to drive in any town, making friends, eating alone, how I would spend my alone time and countless other things. When I arrived at the house, it was nothing like I expected. Most homes here come fully furnished. I should have asked more questions, but I acted on my gut and bought a place on a whim with my dad splitting the cost for our vacations. This home I had purchased did not even have appliances. It was tragically hot, no air conditioning, had only two small chairs and one moldy bed that stunk to high hell. Exhausted from travel, I could only stand to clean the bugs up, throw down the old chair cushions and sleep on the floor.

The next morning I got up, went for a run and paradise began to unfold. I went to the market for a smoothie and met Angel who owns the organic market. The place is fabulous with fresh fruits, vegetables, quinoa and almost anything a vegetarian heart could desire. She was kind as is everyone in this little village. She even invited me to a dinner benefitting a health fair later in the week. I said I might go and went on about my way.

A few days later a stranger sat with me at lunch so I would not have to eat alone and invited me to the benefit dinner. We continued visiting. It was as if I had known this wonderful woman my entire life. She was absolutely stunning with looks like a movie star. Miriam shared with me her amazing life stories and her move to Paradise. We had wonderful conversation over lunch. To have a woman simply ask to sit, visit, and be interested in me was so unexpectedly welcome. We both had an immediate connection as we opened up during lunch about our pasts. She is an incredible strong woman who moved on a whim to run this restaurant. She asked me about a boyfriend and I went into my long single explanation. There is a vast contrast in this country to women being alone versus what I am used to. I mean it is not an oddity as it is back home. In fact, many of the women I have met here are single. It is so refreshing to be surrounded by beautiful, successful, adventurous, single women whom dare I say, are happy.

Miriam confirmed what my friend David told me earlier about the men here. They get so many women in and out they are used to loving and leaving. Then the women go home. She explained "you would be surprised at the gifts these men receive from their so called international girlfriends—computers, iPods, and even cars." All too often they end up getting a girl pregnant. Many of them have children overseas. It is just the way it is and has always been. I tell her it is okay because I need to focus on me and I do not want a man. I say this out loud but I really don't believe it. I want a man but I want one forever. We made plans to go to the benefit dinner together.

When we arrived, it looked like we would be the only ones there but all things in this country run on "local time," which pretty much means things happen when they happen. We took the table with the best view overlooking the sun setting into the ocean and moments later John joined us. His smile was captivating but more than that was an energy bouncing off him making life seem easy.

Other guests finally arrived and the wine began to flow. We called our table the "happy table" because we so joyously enjoyed our wine, food and each other maybe a bit loudly and more so than the others. We toasted often as the other tables looked on, apparently not having as much fun as the happy table. It was great laughing with my new friends. We danced salsa after dinner and then I left with Miriam. I met up with John again at a local dance club where we danced and kissed for the first time. Let me clarify, I did not kiss him. He kissed me. I was not comfortable with it because people were watching. Never the less, I enjoyed his company.

He explained he was a yoga instructor and bam there it is. I just changed the list to include Zen and the spirituality running off him was intriguing. I think it was about this moment when I realized the list was becoming more than a road map; everything I wrote, began to magically appear. So I let him kiss me. I mean it must be okay to give in to a man of such deep spirituality, right? We enjoyed more dancing and I invited him to my house. I wanted to go with the flow and a good flow it was. He reminded me of the Dalai Lama, even looked a bit like him, all meditative and yogi but in a hot Dalai Lama way. We swam in the pool and kissed more. We ended up in the bedroom no doubt and again I battled my brain over whether or not this was right. I gave in to the touch telling myself it was alright because this man was spiritual. I must say the positions he put me in were physically – no, make that mentally – uncomfortable. It was dark but still I worried what my body might look like and the worry always ruins it for me.

Preparing to leave for home the next morning, he asked me again what I did. I explained I had a private practice as a therapist and I was Board Certified to do, "simple brain stuff" I joked. He smiled saying he knew all about it because his father was a neurosurgeon and his mother a doctor as well, although she focused on research. I was overjoyed to have met someone who might be able to understand my work and converse with me about it. I left back home unsure of where we stood as the case always seems to be but we continued to message periodically.

When I returned the following month, an earthquake had hit. We arrived to a town that had been evacuated for fear of aftershocks and/or a tsunami. I was with my dad and step-mom and even though none of us had experienced an earthquake, we decided to stay. We had limited damage, so it confirmed our decision to ride it out. My friend David was house sitting next door and also staying to keep an eye on his family who would not leave. I messaged John I had arrived. He asked me to come over for a glass of wine but I declined saying I was with my parents and we were going to sit on our front porch and have a drink. We listened to music and drank wine not feeling much fear at all.

Around 10:30 pm a loud crack burst through the earth and a vibrational buzz surged throughout my body that I had never experienced as the ground began to fiercely move. I describe the sensation like when you put your tongue on a battery to see if it is alive only my entire body felt the buzz starting from my feet quickly moving all the way up growing in intensity. We panicked, running around outside the house trying to decide what to do. There were mixed reports to evacuate, so I called John who said he would be right over. He settled us with his calmness and gentle smile. We all looked at each other in disbelief for a while then I made the comment maybe we should stop drinking. John walked to his jeep and returned with a huge oversized bottle of wine announcing "no we should not!" We all laughed and continued to party.

The atmosphere evoked an unexplainable ease rather than fear as one might imagine at the thought this could be it. Realizing just how small we really are is a wonderful release of control being at the mercy of Mother Nature. We stayed up most of the night, drinking wine, listening to music and allowing mother earth to shake us free. John and I slept together but did not sleep. It was nice to feel another amidst the chaos of nature. The ground continued to shake throughout the night while he continued to make me laugh with his calm wisdom. I worried he should move his car parked in the neighbors path. I said what if they need to get out? "Yes," he calmly smiled, "if they need to get out, I will move it." I laughed hysterically knowing he was right and I need to learn to stop trying to predict and prepare for the future.

The next day he left but came back with a healthy juice mixture for all of us to soothe our drunken stomachs. We made plans to visit one of the most beautiful beaches near town. When we stopped at the store on our way out I noticed all of my money was missing. I had seen it just before the big aftershock hit and knew I had been running around with my purse. I figured it must have fallen out at the house. We went back to look for it and John asked the gardener in Spanish if he had seen it. I did not want to blame anyone knowing full well the shock of the earthquake and my drinking could have left me ditsy enough to let it fall out on the road somewhere. I let it go even though it was a rather large sum.

We headed off to the beach with only a slight gnawing in my gut. We spent the day swimming, lounging, feasting on fruits and drinking beer. We ended that evening with a promise to attend John's yoga class the next morning. It was wonderful to have my dad join me in yoga since I have been trying to push this alternative exercise on my family for years. During class when our eyes were supposed to be closed I opened one eye to see this amazing yogi clang the Tibetan bowl with his naked muscle filled chest staring back at me and I remember telling myself "oh no you don't fall for him." But it may have been too late. I had never been with such a spiritual being. It was nice to feel secure in his superiority.

At the end of class he touched me like many instructors do as I lay in shavasana. I did not want it to stop. After yoga he joined us for breakfast. We discussed the class and my father mentioned the nice touch. I joked, "Wait, you mean you touched everyone?" knowing full well he had. Still, I wanted it to just be me. We spent the rest of my time there together kayaking to an island right over the fault line, feeling aftershocks and laughing. It was fabulous. We had deep discussions about life and his family. He told me he had one brother and a daughter but he was not married. I was so glad he had one child. It was perfect because I do not want any more kids and do not want to take that gift away from someone who does.

I began to see him as human. He told me about a trial he was involved in. He said a few years ago he and his daughter were abducted. Two men had tried to steal his car in the capital city and held him at gunpoint forcing him to drive out of town. He offered them everything but they insisted he keep driving. He began to feel they were going to kill him so he reacted on his martial arts training received in China (his mother was Chinese) and wrecked the car into a cliff. The gun fell to the floor. One guy ran away. John said he went off on the other man telling him "you will never hold a gun to anyone's head again," as he proceeded to break every bone in the man's arm and hand. He explained to me the trial for the two men was why he needed to go back to the city. He was a bit worried because the man he fought was from an influential wealthy family. They were trying to counter sue him for medical expenses claiming it was excessive force since the gun had been knocked out of his hand by the crash and there was no longer a threat. We walked down the beach to a secluded area and sat under a palm tree leaning into each other. I had a million questions but instead of asking I just sat in the warmth of the moment comforting him, comforting me. I told him goodbye and put my heart on hold.

We began to video phone almost every day. He was very open with his feelings towards me, telling me the night of the earthquake he was disappointed when I at first declined to have a drink with him. He said he went to bed with his phone just in case I changed my mind. When the big aftershock hit and I called scared asking him to come over, he hung up and said "Thank you Earthquake." We laughed and he continued to say "thank you earthquake" periodically during our conversations. As the days passed, I grew fonder and fonder of my time with him online. He was always making me laugh and encouraging me to practice meditation and yoga. I added practices yoga and meditation to the commandment list.

The Commandments

~~Higher education at least a master's degree and~~ interested in continuing to learn

Financially stable ~~in a professional career~~ doing what he loves

Family oriented – maybe already with a child since I am not having more

~~Crazy about me~~

Reads

Writes – journals, ~~poetry~~, love letters, etc.

Honest

104

Display affection daily, kindness and respect
Romantic
Loves to travel
Athletic
Handsome and HOT
~~Tall~~
~~Hairy Chest~~
~~No Tattoos~~
Loves to dance
Loves music
~~Crazy about me~~
Loves animals
Loves even my flaws
Loves to touch me ~~because he is crazy about me!!!!!!~~
Respectful of others
Listens to me
Proud of me
Confident
Loves good food and wine
Sensual
Bilingual
Single
Enjoys conversation
Able to remain in the moment
Over past relationships
Spiritual
Zen
Adventurous
Practices yoga and meditation

Judges

Back home, I awoke not feeling right. My senses were missing the mystical morning sun, the howler monkeys screaming a wild song, the gecko chirping, the horses outside chomping and neighing, and even the occasional squashed bug under my feet. Work was still enjoyable but something was missing. I practiced with a friend I met in graduate school. Looking back on how the practice even started was quite another one of my "lost faith in myself moments" totally leaning and listening to others. Ruth was one of the strongest women I had ever met. By strong I mean tough, opinionated and stern in her positions. Again not believing in my own strength, I felt I needed her to build a practice. We shared ideas and office space. I always felt her strength overshadowed me. I quickly learned to stand down to her. She was not one to easily consider another's opinion but that is not to say I ever felt she was wrong. She is brilliant. I shared my world with her. She was a great comfort and pillar of strength during my broken moments.

I had a wonderful opportunity with work to visit California for an Ayurvedic medicine and meditation conference with a very well-known physician. I was excited to deepen my spiritual practice while introducing my coworker, Ruth to the gifts of yoga and meditation. I knew she was a bit apprehensive about the whole "guru" idea, and in particular, going without meat. The center only serves vegetarian dishes. Her uneasiness was apparent as the trip approached and she joked repeatedly that she hated yoga pants and would want a burger. I was simply happy she was willing to challenge herself and her ideals. It dismays me that with all the research on relaxation, yoga, meditation and healthy eating, so many Americans still choose to see these practices as alternative, odd, or guru. At least my little town was behind in the times, with only a few yoga studios, and two recently new health food stores.

I shared with Ruth I was considering moving to Paradise in a few years because of this. I loved the connection to nature, yoga on every corner and healthy foods were the norm. I was not sure how it would unfold, I was simply dreaming out loud. At that time she knew my entire life and her straight forward approach to things had helped me tremendously get through the divorce. She tells it like it is and although sometimes her words burn, for the most part her brilliance was spot on. Since she was my business partner, I felt it necessary to keep her in the know with what was going on in my mind so she would not feel left out if the opportunity to move arose in the next few years.

I had no clue how, I just felt a pull to this tiny rugged country and at some point in my world I would like to try and make a life there. Every time I was there I felt complete—out in nature and writing in my journal for hours. I had hope the deep meditation workshop I was about to attend would help clarify things. I was so tired of feeling lonely and drained after work every day. It made no sense that I struggled so at home when I had a plethora of knowledge on dealing with change, healing the past, living single, finding joy in the now and remarkable biofeedback equipment I used on myself daily to relax. Here I am with access to countless tools at my fingertips to seek the path to happiness, yet I was simply not feeling, well, myself.

We arrived in California. The instruction on Ayurvedic medicine was fascinating. Meditating with the masterful physician was mind-blowing and yoga in the mornings soothed my soul. I talked of Paradise often because this center evoked a similar peace in me. I could feel the tension bounce off Ruth like a slap in the face when I brought it up. It was simply on my mind constantly with all of the talk on yoga and meditation. The town I now have a vacation house in is full of people who believe this lifestyle. I thought if I eased Ruth into the idea, by the time life led me in that direction, she would have come to terms.

She rebutted my every joyous statement with some form of negative feedback. Like "you just want to move there because it is a tourist town and every day is like a vacation with you having no responsibility." It stung to hear her say that as did many of her words. But I tried hard to take in her knowledge, to question my desire and hopefully find some resolution. Her sharp, direct comments continued to mull in my head so I talked to John one evening about it in the hopes he would be able to put it in perspective. I was shocked and hurt when he said "She's right." He paused longer than I find comfortable as he always does to let things sink in. I sat with the words trying to decipher his wisdom amongst Ruth's sharpness. The grueling battle going on in my mind ceased when his laughter finally broke the silence. He giggled "Yes, she is right. A life that is like a vacation; yes, Julita, she gets it." We both laughed as I realized that is exactly what I want and exactly how life should be. Perhaps, I could make this happen, maybe even sooner than I believe.

That night I began the mental process of moving. Worries I had yet to consider began to emerge but only one worry deemed me sleepless; the fact; I was truly considering this. I tried to set aside my worries for the rest of the conference over what to do with my practice, my friends, family, and the biggest worry of all, Ruth. Although she tried to be impartial it was clear from the energy and under her breath comments she was so not in favor of the idea now or ever. I mean it would take years to manifest a dream this grand. So I told myself someday I would find a way to make it happen and it would not interfere with Ruth's happiness. I promised myself to let life work because if I am meant to be there, I will be.

The meditations at the conference were pushing me in a direction I did not understand. I kept feeling the need to write but I was not sure about what. During the conference breaks, there were many booths set up with health supplements, books, oils, and potions. Ruth had found a table with aromatherapy where she purchased a concoction she said helped with menopause symptoms. I decided to visit the table the next day to see if there was anything to help with my hormone issues. The young eclectic woman ask me to look at a group of small spray bottles each with different scenes on the label and to choose the label appealing to my visual sense. My first thought was "and we are at a scientific conference?" but I hushed miss analyze and did just that.

I found a green label with a lush fern like design catching my eye. Although I was unsure if I was doing it correctly, I simply said "that one" as I pointed to the spray with the verdant green picture on the bottle in order to appeal to the lady's mysticism. She acknowledged my choice by simply saying "hmm." I felt I might have made a mistake by her lack of response. Then she asked me to place my hand over a group of oils and use my sense of touch to feel the energy coming off the oil.

Ruth was standing in the background watching. At this point I cannot believe brilliant, science-driven Ruth even considered doing this. I placed my hand over the oils and to my amazement actually felt something as I grazed over the oils. There was a gentle pull over one particular bottle, as if the bottle was emitting heat. I pointed it out to her. The lady told me I had made a surprising choice and asked me what I did for a living. I said I was a counselor, just as the bell rang for us to go back into session. She said she wanted to talk to me further but needed more time. "Go on to the meditation session while I mix the oil with the spray you chose and come back to visit during the next break" she told me.

I was confused wondering if it had something to do with my hormones or maybe because I had surgery a few years ago leaving me with only one ovary. Maybe that was the confusion, I mean I thought this was for hormonal balance, but then why did she ask about my job? I tried to forget about it and went into the session. We were meeting for a lecture with the center physician. He gave a witty lecture on the benefits and process of meditation. After the lecture, we sat for thirty minutes in meditation. My mind continued to think of Paradise, the spiritual people who live there and living each day like a vacation. I would be surrounded with people who love yoga, meditation, healthy eating and playing outside all the time in adventurous nature. I thought of John but told myself that he is not the reason. My heart was steadfast on doing this for me, if I ever find a way to do it. I felt as if everyone in the room disappeared, I saw the ocean before me and the waves were calling me in. I asked over and over who am I, what do I want and what is my dharma.

I was doing so well in my practice, the years it took to complete school, all the extra training and studying my ass off, left me confused as to why I felt change ensued. Not to mention, all the time it took to build the practice with an entire year of me bringing in no income at all. I found the building, purchased the building with the help of my ex and spent grueling hours repairing the old house. I designed the company logo and even built the website. I had the calling to learn about biofeedback and I built a separate website to educate people on the alternative practice. And now here I am thinking of letting it all go to move in a few years. A few years, that was my safety net. I just kept telling myself a few years and it will work itself out. I continued to try and divert my mind to my purpose during the meditation and every time I saw blank, I saw white, I saw blank white pages. I got lost in the empty pages knowing full well they were missing words. The time flew and all of a sudden the bell dinged us out of the meditation for a five minute break. My feet were asleep. I didn't even care, it was so peaceful. A bit disoriented as to where I was and amazed to see others in the room around me, it took a moment to come back.

I felt alone during the meditation, like they were gone and even the room, desk and chairs were no longer there. It was an alone but it was a very powerful alone if that is even possible. I looked at Ruth as she described her meditation telling me someone in the room was annoying her. I felt agitated because I so wanted her to discover the peace in this beautiful practice. I wanted her to love it, not feel annoyed with it. I told her the more she practices the more those outside noises will not annoy but draw you inward into your meditation even more. She rose up from her chair abruptly and I could see her annoyance now with me. I drew inward and braced myself to prepare for the energy slap coming toward me. She is very opinionated. I have learned if I have any idea other than what she thinks, I get hit with a bolt that makes me feel like a reprimanded small child. It almost caused me to quit our practice when we first opened but I learned to just agree with her. So here I am ready to shelter my heart because I have apparently just told her information she does not like.

She threw her cold shoulder to turn away from me and snapped "Oh yes, of course I am doing it wrong," as she stomped out of the conference room. I sat like a scolded child wondering if I had used a condescending voice. Did I sound like a know–it–all? My peaceful heart that had just seen glorious white in my meditation was now lying low in my chest as it pumped to the beat of hurtful silence. I thought to myself *this is one of the reasons I want out. I love her but I feel so voiceless. It is not always like this and it was much worse in the beginning when we were trying to make business decisions but now I just say "whatever you like" and the business runs smooth.* We were very busy at work and rarely saw each other, so that smoothed things as well, but still on rare occasions I got the cold and it hurt. Since I purchased a house in another country and began visiting frequently, her coldness returned. She is exceptionally patriotic and at some point made a snide remark about me wanting to give up my rights as a US citizen. I tried to explain I would remain a citizen but explaining to her was not easy.

I took a deep breath to get back the peace I had moments ago. Then I remembered the aromatherapy lady and jumped up knowing I only had minutes to go to the booth where my Ayurvedic spray waited. I took my scolded heart into the exhibition room. More disappointment hit when I saw she was busy with another customer. As I was about to turn to walk out, she saw me and gently told the customer speaking to please excuse her because she had something very important to discuss with me. At that moment in my peripheral vision, I saw Ruth walk into the room. More frustration hit because I wished I could just have this moment to myself. Ruth stood in the doorway. I wondered if she was close enough to hear.

The lady asked me again about my profession. I told her I love my job and feel I am very good at it. She said "I do not want to give you this spray then because you have chosen a spray that works on your dharma."

I said "well, I feel my dharma is to inspire and help people find happiness and that's what I do at work."

"Yes that is your dharma," she proclaimed "but the oil and the spray you have chosen come together to help change the way you express your dharma. Your dharma will remain the same but the way you use it will change. Do you want to continue in your practice? Are you burned out?"

Tears began to fill my eyes. A warm pulse rushed over me putting my heart back in the peaceful state Ruth plucked from me. I felt heard. Somehow this lady who knew nothing other than what my job is had heard my struggle. I was overwhelmed as I told her I was going to cry. I put my hand over my heart to muffle it because it shouted "yes!" The tears began to drip. I told her with my crackling voice, "I have been so confused. I think I want to write. I think I want to move and write. I don't know what to write about or how it will happen; I am so lost but I feel so much relief in your words."

She hugged me tight and I could see tears in her eyes too as we pulled away to look deep at each other. It was one of those moments where you can feel and briefly glimpse where God lives. She said "your heart, allow your heart" as she handed me the spray. "This will help you find the way".

I took in the air of the moment and tried to hold the joy my heart was feeling. But it quickly dissipated as I turned to see Ruth still standing close by. I thanked the lady and said goodbye, wondering if I should talk to Ruth about what just occurred. This lady somehow gave me confirmation the nagging going on in my heart wanting me to change was accurate. I decided to tell Ruth because the interaction made me feel confident that maybe now she could understand me.

I asked Ruth if she heard what the lady said to me. She coldly said "No, I was not listening." I tried my best to describe the discussion. I told her my dharma expression would change if I used this and it confirmed my desire to want to do something different with my life.

Ruth retorted with "that is not the way I interpreted it!"

My heart sank as I thought, "Ha, she was listening." But do you think I confronted her? Absofuckinlutely not! I just listened like her puppet as she tried to convince me it was not about my job but about the changes going on in my life and me adjusting to being single. I didn't disagree with her; I said nothing else at all. I just followed her back into the conference room silent and unheard.

For the ending session, we were instructed to sit in one last meditation together. I began as always with asking myself, "who am I, what do I want and what is my dharma?" We were told not to answer the questions but simply send them out to the universe and listen. I began my mantra we were each given on the first day and then I listened. I do not know at what point in the meditation it happened, but the white I was seeing in past meditations now had words. I saw my life on paper. All the rules I tried to follow and all the guilt from failing. I saw people wearing black robes; judges, nuns and priests all laying down the law with gavels in their hands. I saw myself being born into this judgmental society and turning into a judge myself. I pictured a gavel in my hand as I slammed it hard, not at another but at my very own reflection. All the distractions modern day had simplified us with came into view. Not making life easier but lonelier, keeping us from connecting to nature and our self-fulfilling self. There were images of prideful politicians spilling their guts on us to keep us busy cleaning up the mess, while they preached patriotism to control and detach us from the rest of the world. I saw me kneeling before a God outside myself that is no God at all.

Then I had a vision of every man I was ever in a relationship with and I saw me kissing them as they turn not into the fairytale princes, but frogs. It occurred to me to write about it all and to focus on the men I have dated trying to kiss the frogs to find my prince. A book title came to mind. "The Year of the Frog" emerged in my head as I saw an old antique looking book with religious symbols. I heard Ruth's voice telling me as she did after my divorce, "you have to kiss a lot of frogs." We were told to take a deep breath. I was surprised it was over. I made a mental note of everything that just occurred because I worried if it is like sleep, I may quickly forget what was envisioned. I did not even ask Ruth about her meditation nor did I tell her about mine. I just wanted the peace to remain.

The center team gathered on the stage for closing remarks. One of the female staff who instructed the morning yoga sessions discussed how to continue sharing what we learned with our clients and how to keep up the work on ourselves. She jokingly said in reference to happiness, "you have to kiss a lot of yogis." I nearly fell out of my chair!

John 2

When I got home from the conference I began to dabble with the idea of seriously writing. I started a blog to get my creative juices flowing. I wanted to see what kind of response I would get from others since I never felt confidence in my often controversial words. I kept it very realistic and gentle for the most part editing out any off handed comments. Upon completion of the first blog I felt energized and passionate. The feedback I received made me feel there was a possibility I could uncover the girl I used to be, that writer somewhere lost inside of me. I felt for once I had a voice. I was being heard and it was simply me, not quoting, not parroting others' scientific findings, just typing what my heart said. I was no longer referred to as so and so's wife or my son's mom (although that boy is the love of my life, it was time for me to be me). I was slowly beginning to get my identity back. There were nights I could write for hours and hours not knowing how much time had passed. In day to day life, I began to notice when people were smothering my voice and it began to irritate me tremendously.

I was overwhelmed with the need to find my words now and in the past. I searched old computers, old USB drives, an ancient floppy disk, journals, and boxes of keepsakes. I found only two of the books I had started but never finished; I calculated there were at least six. I found a few letters I had written and a journal with pages and pages scribbled through, so no one could see my words. Then there were the missing pages I had torn out to burn. I continued to blog trying to get my old spirit back and slowly a confidence began to emerge. It is difficult still to say that and fully believe it. But where there was no confidence, a seed was planted. I guess I will always question my talent as do most people. Talent comes from the soul. I believe since our souls have not been nourished properly, not exercised or allowed to come forth we stand back questioning anything coming from that deep down place. My clouded soul began to emerge on paper and the responses I got were enough to get me started on this book. I spent some time going through the reasons I quit in the past. I used to begin with an idea for a book and then something in life would occur. I would stop always questioning this silly dream to be a writer. It was so easy to cover that dream up with programmed responses of how difficult it is, how hard to make money, how publishers will not be interested, yada, yada. I found files of books I started over a decade ago and never finished. I began to recall other ideas I had for books on computers that had crashed and because I was not confident in myself, I did not care my voice was gone.

I planned another trip and this time I wanted to take my computer, the old files, my journal, and just write. I was also excited to see John, do yoga, and meditate with him. We continued to communicate and discuss our lives. I told him everything about the conference and my meditations, my hope and my dreams. Anytime I came home from my stressful job he was there ready to appease my yearning soul. I loved seeing his smile and his response to any of my stressful complaints. He touched his bare, buff chest and breathed the most refreshing deep breathe, telling me to "just breathe, Julita; just breathe." And we did. Over video chat I took deep breathes with this man and it felt so very good to swim in his calm. I have never in my life met a man with so much awareness. He knows all about consciousness, yoga, meditation, Buddhism, Taoism and several other ancient eastern philosophies. I listened intently to his serene knowledge, just absorbing every peaceful bit trying to make it stick in the space between my programmed thoughts.

He discussed his dream of opening a yoga studio on the beach, telling me he wished I could somehow be a part of it. For a moment I pushed my analytical mind aside and dreamed the dream. The idea of moving there sounded so peacefully wonderful for the brief moment my "Controligion" allowed me to dream. (Since I began writing freely I have come up with a word "Controligion" to demonstrate how I feel about the spell cast on me. I define it as a group of power hungry people whose main focus is to exercise restraint, dominate and command with the illusion of a moral code implemented to keep the soul small.) I sigh, maybe someday I can do that but now I don't know how to make it happen. He was confident if I allowed life to work, it would. I was in awe of how quickly his dream was unfolding. He told me the very next day he found a place for the studio he could also live in, but it would not be ready until the first of the month. He was looking for a place to stay until then. I offered him my place since it would only be a week or so and the house was empty until I arrived. He was very grateful and moved in immediately.

During our conversations, rather than comfort me, there was tension. I knew it was concerning the trial he had told me about and the wealthy family's threat to sue him. Over the next few days when we would chat, he would tell me how he partied and how late he had stayed out. I wondered if it was the stress from the upcoming trial he was trying to escape. Nevertheless, I began to feel insecure, which always happens when I start liking someone.

I spent countless nights with a pain in my chest. I could not figure out why I was feeling so stressed. It was the same pain I felt when Matt, whom I thought I was dating, and wanted to sleep with, was off sleeping with someone else. I began to think maybe John was sleeping around. I was having so much trouble deciphering my intuition. I imagined him bringing girls to my house and it infuriated me. I tried to meditate to see what was so heavy on my heart. I decided to tell him. He felt I was pushing him away and became very defensive. I look back on it now and yes I was accusing him of cheating. It is understandable that he became defensive; we all do when we are attacked.

He said, "You have to learn to trust." He explained to me how he is always going to be around people, it is his job to lift people up. He told me the negative feeling I have is low energy and it was not healthy. Wherever there is low energy there is a path, he said and it was not fair for me to be feeling this way and it was not fair to him for me to put my low energy off on him. He said I do not want that energy.

I felt hurt. We had our first disagreement. He said he would go for the trial and then he would move out of my house. It was not like him. Or maybe it was not like me. I don't know. I lost more sleep. He sent a few texts the next day of encouraging mantras; "Hari om tat sat, mucha luz," were his words. He always sent me chants to meditate on. And so I do. But I cannot help but be confused by the feeling in my heart.

I guess I pushed again in an effort to control and know it all. I have begun to see this is one of my biggest issues. I have so much trouble with the unknown. I see this same thing happen in my practice with persons with extreme anxieties. Anything that occurs out of the ordinary can send them into a panic. We are always trying to fill in the blanks and with our brains being wired for survival, we fill those blanks with worst case scenarios to prepare for destruction. I know this, I tell my clients this, yet I too fall victim to this mental wrath time and time again. We do not like the unknown and that is why we push to be know-it-all's so we can predict what's around the corner before we go around the corner. Part of my new meditation practice is teaching me to be okay with the unknown. I am doing my best to stop predicting and start accepting. Despite my attempts to meditate myself into peace, I awoke the next morning feeling like crap.

Something was wrong but my conditioned past just wanted me to think it was unfaithfulness. After talking to him that evening, I felt confident it was not him cheating but something else. He soothed me with his words and I convinced myself he was honest and I was just going to have to believe him. He told me he was stressed over the trial and his humanness wanted to escape. He agreed he needed to stop partying. I let it go and focused on comforting him because the trial was the next day. Certain it would be okay, he boasted "good things happen to good people." Still that night, I lost sleep, with a pain in my chest so bad I was concerned I might be having a heart attack. We talked via text as he went into the trial and I sent him love and positive energy. I waited to hear the good news. I heard nothing from him. I told myself sometimes the legal system runs late in his country and I knew his phone could go dead or run out of minutes so I just tried to sleep.

I awoke desperately looking at my phone hopeful for a message to soothe my confused aching body, but there was none. The pain in my chest had moved to my gut. The day passed while my insides reflected the uneasiness in my mind as it all became more and more twisted. Something was not right. Even when John's phone was dead or out of minutes he would find an internet café to send me a message or ask to use a friend's phone. I had not heard a word. I went over in my head his words about the trial again trying to understand and construct a timeline. Yesterday morning's text was brief but the night before he said he was going to the verdict at ten in the morning and if it is all over quickly, he was hoping to catch a bus at noon. So I expected to hear from him last night at the latest.

Another day passed and I was up off and on all night looking for his text. When I heard nothing, I decided to contact a friend of his. John had called me from his friend's phone in the past so I had his number. He knew only a bit about the trial which seemed odd to me since they were apparently best friends. I did not say too much because I had been programmed to remain confidential. He had not seen him and said he was worried too. He said he was going to the gym where John taught yoga to see if they knew anything. I did not hear back from John's friend until the next morning. My worry exploded as he explained to me he was going to the police because no one knew anything. My mind raced with concern over this so called wealthy family and what if they harmed him? What if they kidnapped him? John had told me a story about his uncle who was kidnapped and killed years ago.

That evening I could see John was active online. I sent a message "let me know you are okay." I was shocked to see a reply coming.

"I am not John, but his sister."

Now I was even more confused. John did not talk of a sister, only a brother, and she was spelling his name Jon without the h. She told me John was put in jail on "preventive detention" and she would sell her house to pay a lawyer if she had to. She said John told her to contact me for money and I could have his house as a pledge! She said trust her which made me not! Then she gave me her email to correspond. Why did she just not friend me? So I asked her name and friended her because I was worried he was hacked!

I studied her profile and could see she was a real person, well by the little reliability of the internet but it at least gave me hope. Still, I had no idea what to think. I began to question everything he ever told me. I went back and forth from caring about him and worried sick to angry at myself for falling for someone who may not be who they presented themselves to be. At times it felt as if I were dying inside. I had a cry fit begging every powerful god, saint, prophet, ancestor I could imagine. Anybody out there in spiritual land who might help, I pleaded for their assistance. Then I blamed myself for drawing this into my life. Is it because I am not open to love? Is my heart so damaged I project tragedy on others? Or is it life trying to protect me from a making yet another detrimental choice; allowing in another broken soul. That is what I have been told. I fall in love with broken souls.

The next day I talked to his sister but still answers were not there. It appeared I had more information about him than she did. I wondered why they needed money from me if their parents were Doctors. She confirmed she was his sister but her mom and dad were not even together and they had no contact with their father. She ignored some of my questions, skipping over them but I could see she was in tremendous agony so I did not push. She said her mom was very ill and they had no money. She did not know why John was in jail. She said he told her to ask me. I was the only one he told. I began to explain what he told me and she blew off the handle when

I mentioned John's daughter was in the car when they were kidnapped. It was an intense moment and with her grief over her brother and my confusion, I simply stopped talking and let her absorb the information. She was so upset, I could feel her pain, though oceans away. I opted to not say anything more or ask any more questions because I could tell she was on the breaking edge.

It appeared we were both very lost. She gave me a number to call him for answers. It was the phone number to the prison. She told me sternly to call right on time and if I got through I would only have ten minutes at the most to talk to him. She told me to say "Puedes Hablar Jon Moor Sanchez." Or something like that. Here I am not even sure of the language and I am going to try and communicate to a prison. Never mind he told me his last name was Le because his mom was Chinese and that was the name he chose to go by. Okay so maybe that is true because locals have several last names. At this point I just want answers.

That evening, I was a nervous wreck trying to call him. I rehearsed my Spanish in the moments before. The phone was busy as my heart pounded and time depleted. At last there was an answer. "Hola" came over the line in a very gruff tone. My shaky voice spattered "puedes hablar con John Moor Sanchez?" and then there was silence. Moments later it was him, exclaiming "Julita" in a forced attempt to sound joyous. My heart melted to hear his voice and in that instance, I did not care if he had lied to me. I knew there were rumors of local men lying to foreigners' in an effort to impress, find love, sex, whatever. I briefly thought of this and did not care if I was a victim.

He tried desperately to console me and apologize in the now three minutes we had and somewhere in the conversation, I made a commitment to help no matter what the story. I did not ask him any questions but instead put myself on a comfort mission because on the other end was a human soul aching more than my distressed sheltered heart could ever understand. He gave me a time and a number to call the next day. And so I did daily at the exact same time. I called and we talked about life, about suffering, about meditation, yoga and we laughed. We often laughed as strange as it may seem, we found moments of joy despite his suffering.

I just wanted to be a support. Many people feel I am a pushover and time and time again I have fallen for people others tell me have taken advantage of me. I have loaned money to a dozen people and never received it back. I do not say this to boast but to try and make sense of my own self. I have been called gullible, softie, push over. I just want to be a good human. And somewhere in my soul I feel I have not loved too much, I have not given too much and I am not too trusting. I struggle between whether others are correct and I should learn I do not have to do a thing to be loved, but I honestly only want to relieve the suffering of others. On the contrary I feel I have not learned to love enough because if I did, I would not even question my actions. I think when it's all said and done I will be proud I loved as hard, gave all I have and lifted others. I think what others see as gullible, I see as faith. Not in a Bible or a church but in the idea God is not outside of us. That I am part and you are part and this man I care about is part. The person asking for money from you on the street is part. The one that made you angry and the one that pained you part, as well.

For the next week I called every day. It was amazing to me how positive John remained, often having words of comfort for me. He encouraged me to stay optimistic and keep my mind busy just like he has done by meditating and reading books. He apologized over and over for getting me into this. He confirmed his mom was sick and he had a sister. He said it would all make sense one day. I did not question him further; I was set on being a compassionate friend and by now had pretty much pulled myself away from the idea of ever being in a relationship with him other than friendship.

John explained the influential family of his abductor had immense power. He and his lawyer had no clue this could happen. The original case was to sue him for medical expenses. He felt sure it would get thrown out, and it did, but then the judge snuck in this preventive detention for six months as punishment for nearly killing the guy. He admitted he did go off on the guy out of fear and his martial arts training just kicked in. He told the courts this. He said he went too far in defending himself. His lawyer had no clue preventative detention was even on the table and was not prepared to defend him. He said he is sure it was a money under the table operation.

Our daily conversations were very brief and most of the time only a few minutes once the call finally got through. Over the days, I pieced together information from the modest visits. He described the horrendous prison with a gruff voice. His throat hurt from all the smoke and drugs in the air. He said the prisoners even did crack they made themselves. Rather than cry about it, he proudly told me how he was figuring the system out. He had to meet the "boss" to pay for things. The meanest guy in the cell is the boss and if you want anything, you pay. He paid money to get to answer the phone if I called, not to a guard but to another prisoner! He had to pay $50 to get to sleep in a bed and this is a luxury because many people slept standing up or in the bathroom. All of our conversations got cut short and often I heard ferocious screaming in the background as fights broke out. John said there was a fight almost every night. There were often deaths from fight injuries and sometimes drug overdose.

John told me his father had been contacted and he was hopeful he might help. He asked again for my help just in case and said he would give me the title to his house until I could get paid back. He was in the worst jail in the country, often referred to as Hell. To grasp his peace over the phone and then hang up to the gruesome knowledge of what was happening in that prison, kept my emotions in extremes. As the days passed, I felt helpless. I often cried begging all the gods. One is not enough given this horrendous situation. I said I would do anything just to have him safe. The unbearable overcrowding pushed people over the edge. He described the fights, the rapes, the way they taunted the new men. It was beyond my mental comprehension that this calm, meditating, free spirited yogi was now restrained to a nightmare. I tried to remind myself I just met this guy a month ago. One month and here I was trying to save a soul I barely know.

I turned to any form of meditation I could find to try and give me comfort. During one of my meditations, I tried to mentally construct all of my options and sit with them to gauge how I felt. Leaving the situation was one option but I knew I could not just walk away. It did my heart no good. So I began to put a plan in motion. I searched the term "preventive detention" and a story of a lawyer who was wrongfully jailed came up. My initial thought was to contact him but I procrastinated, telling myself I did not even know the facts, or maybe this lawyer is too busy, the wrong type of lawyer to handle this case or too expensive. I was not even sure if this particular lawyer was even out of prison because the story I found was published while he was still trying to get out.

I talked to John. After learning his lawyer did not show up the day before and there was only fifteen days to appeal, I frantically searched for a way to contact this lawyer—no number, no contact, only story after story of how he was screwed over. One story looked like it was written by him in a jail cell and gave an email for people to contact him while he was in prison. Apparently people of higher power; doctors, politicians, wealthy people and lawyers, get sent to a jail that is "more comfortable" and they have internet access! My heart said just try. I sent an email in English not even knowing if he spoke the language. Only moments later he emailed back with fees and the process steps. I called via internet. He was positive and said he would go see John today. I told him I would kiss his face; pay him for his time, anything! I felt so much positive energy and my hope was restored with faith that maybe this was just some peculiar wrongful imprisonment. After all, John kept telling me to have faith this would all make sense one day and so I did.

I packed my bags a bit uneasily not knowing what to do with myself this trip. It always unnerves me when my expectations are shattered. I rushed out my door with suitcase in hand to head to the office prior to catching my plane. I watched my fellow Americans driving their usual morning routes with stern determination on their faces as they blankly stared into space like lost souls. I sat at the stoplight deliberately trying to force a mood different from my counterparts. I breathed deep and closed my eyes momentarily to see the dirt roads of Paradise and people walking or pedaling by, stopping along the way to hug and greet each other. My new best friend David's only possession was a rusty old bike and he was happier than any of these bodies driving luxury to their modern day monetary captivity. "I want to be like David," I whispered as the light turned green and the eager to be a slave robot behind me honked impatiently. I mumbled under my breath as I looked in the rear view mirror, "I'm so tired of being you," knowing full well I was both talking to my person and to his. I walked in to the place that used to be so peaceful simply wanting to be done with the day. The tension felt heavy as I told Ruth goodbye, assuring her I would be back in just a few days.

I had not spoken to Ruth about the things going on with John or with me. I quit telling her anything after we returned from the conference and one last attempt to discuss my yearning to move ended with yet another hurtful remark. She said "you will be surrounded with uneducated people, much like your family." I walked out of her office shocked at the words but knew all too well she and I both had fluffed our egos on more than one occasion over how educated we were. It used to make me feel accomplished but now I felt different; like my education made me better than no one. I thought of the times I was frustrated with my family and tried to help them with my so-called knowledge. It always ended the same. I would get frustrated that they would not listen. I could tell they were feeling inferior with my attempts to explain how the brain works. Boy had I became a know-it-all or what? I walked out of Ruth's office knowing I did not want to be that person anymore or anywhere near the snob I had become.

Diaphragmatic breathing in the lines, meditation on the plane, and before I knew it, Paradise is in my reality again. It was beyond beautiful, in the rainy season and oh so lush and green. The house felt odd as I walked in to some of John's remaining things. He did not know he would end up in prison so he left some belongings—mostly clothes but I was delighted to see his guitar, mala beads, and an old Indian blanket. I set up a writing station with his blanket as a tablecloth and the mala beads near. I have ten days to myself and other than going out to visit my friend David who put my pink bike together for me, I planned to stay in most days and write. I continued to try and call John in prison daily.

The lawyer I found did visit and John said he liked him. I told him I would pay and he graciously accepted the offer. I emailed the lawyer to get details on how to wire the money in the hopes he might fill me in on some of the case details. He told me it was a good case but he could not give me more information. He said, "I can only say I believe no crime was committed." And I wired the money feeling good John's story of self-defense and his "Julita, one day it will all make sense" were relevant. I did tell the story to my friend Miriam who eased my disturbed mind even more by saying that she had heard similar stories where people defending themselves were put in prison. I felt better about helping.

That evening after I wired the money, I walked into my bedroom and ventured to the side I did not sleep on to discover a pair of big earrings on the night stand. They were the same color as the nightstand so I just did not see them when I arrived. I immediately thought of the huge cheap earring I found in my second ex-husband's bed and I just wanted to kick my own ass for being so freaking stupid again. I sent a large sum of money to help a man I just met and let stay in my house while he was apparently entertaining in my bed! What have I done? What am I to learn? With all the dishonesty, infidelity and fighting I see, I sometimes wonder if monogamy is outdated. Is this jealousy I am cursed with some weak primitive feeling to keep a man faithful for survival of the species and help me raise offspring? Are we supposed to be so open to each moment and love whoever is in that moment then let it all go? I even read the

"Kama Sutra" trying to open my views on love and sex. The last chapter is about threesomes. Is this just a weak human feeling I have to want one person all to myself? I would never want to make another feel insecure and if I did I would want to make damn sure I made it right. But is this selfish? Am I supposed to love someone so much I am open to them finding happiness however that is with another or not? I so desperately want to contact him but I also just want to be different. I cannot even tell at this point if this is different or not.

I decided to just ask him tomorrow when we visit. I have always had such difficulty asking people tough questions; it's as if I fear the truth. I want to believe people are righteous and so I stuff the truth down just as religion taught me. I mean isn't that the truth. We are lied to by religion and thus we learn to lie and accept lies. Sleep was again lost but I found some peace in my morning meditation as I realized we had not known each other long enough to even discuss being faithful and no matter what answer he gave me, I am in this as a friend. I decided to see it through to the end. After writing all day, I called him and gently mentioned I found a pair of earrings. Without any hesitation he said "yes, I found them outside and thought they were yours."

"They are not." I said calmly.

He laughed. "Good because they are ugly."

We both laughed and I wondered if he was being honest or if he was a psychotic compulsive liar because that was the best comeback I had ever heard in all my years of being cheated. I did not push any further even though my gut was gently agitated. I ignored it and wondered why I never push for more answers, why I accept what is spoken. I just don't think we should have to make people confess. I was torn down by lies my whole life and maybe a small part is I too have lied and thus feel the guilt not wanting to expose another. I settle for the answer and move on.

I told myself I did not care about his past; I wanted him in my future as a friend. I had already altered my perception of him from possible dating material to simply a friend knowing full well I would help any of my friends. So I made a commitment to put my unanswered questions to rest and love him through this. It was the only way for me to feel better about what I had already done and so I committed to help.

The next day I found delight in riding my pink bike up and down the dirt roads waving and saying "hola" to everyone I passed. I loved riding into town to the organic market for breakfast or lunch. I visited with one of John's friends Allon who works there. We discussed John's situation. To meet such kind hearted people who love John reinforces my idea I was doing the right thing in helping. It made me think maybe John was who I wanted him to be so I forced myself to put him back on the pedestal I had previously placed him. I altered the list, simply adding "free."

The Commandments

~~Higher education at least a master's degree and~~ interested in continuing to learn

Financially stable ~~in a professional career~~ doing what he loves

Family oriented – maybe already with a child since I am not having more

~~Crazy about me~~

Reads

Writes – journals, ~~poetry,~~ love letters, etc.

Honest

Display affection daily, kindness and respect

Romantic

Loves to travel

Athletic

Handsome and HOT

~~Tall~~

~~Hairy Chest~~

~~No Tattoos~~

Loves to dance

Loves music

~~Crazy about me~~

Loves animals

Loves even my flaws

Loves to touch me ~~because he is crazy about me!!!!!!~~

Respectful of others

Listens to me

Proud of me

Confident

Loves good food and wine

Sensual

Bilingual

Single

Enjoys conversation

Able to remain in the moment

Over past relationships

Spiritual

Zen

Adventurous

Practices yoga and meditation

Free

Isaiah

The next day after writing, I decided to end my day at one of the beaches down from my house. As the sun set, I sat on a rock meditating when a man I had met earlier in the week pulled me back to reality by calling for his dog. A bit embarrassed to be caught meditating, I gathered my stuff and began to walk the path back to my house. Controligion left no room for something so alternative, thus I hid the practice. I could tell he was following me as the sound of his bare feet on the dirt path grew closer. I decided to turn around and say hello to end my unease. He pointed to a fence covered in vine, asking if I would like to see his house. I did not even know a house existed behind the brush so out of curiosity I took the tour. It was an extremely cute rustic house with the most amazing garden. The trees were overwhelmingly huge making the house feel small and secluded. He offered me a glass of wine and I of course said yes.

We sat outside and enjoyed the twilight, the wine, and his spectacular garden. He then said "let me cook for you," and I just laughed as my answer of "oh no, thank you though" was met with a very Italian "si, si es no problemo." Without further ado, he entered his kitchen to begin the process. I sat there drinking his fabulous wine smiling and thinking of one of my favorite movies where a similar response comes from the Greek mother when her guest refuses food and she cooks anyway. I laughed to myself at how wonderful life is. He yelled from the kitchen "you must stay" and so I did, eager to see how this story unfolded. He was not as tall as I would like but he was a very handsome man. I only saw him on occasion around town. He was always barefoot and wearing swim trunks. He had a few tattoos which I was learning to like and even considering getting one of my own. He kept his long hair haphazardly pulled back into a pony tail.

I was glad I decided to stay if not for anything other than to cure my curiosity about this mysterious man. I went to the bathroom and on return there was a lit candle on the rustic outdoor table. The gesture made me apprehensive; now that it appeared he was trying to make this romantic. I quieted my nerves by focusing on the wonderful sounds of nature, the frogs, chirping birds, and crickets. He served me a dinner of coconut rice, cabbage, pasta, bread, and eggs from a nearby farm. The food was really good even though I was not sure what the cabbage-looking salad was. He talked about Italy and his family. I admired his garden and asked what the platform below was. He said it was for yoga. Then as I remarked "what a lovely surprise this evening has been" preparing him for my exit, he mentioned he had yet another surprise. He went back to the kitchen, and I went to the bathroom to coach myself on how to say goodbye. When I returned to the porch there were now candles on the wooden platform and a mattress laid out!

I suppose he could see my fear because he quickly said "tranquila" to calm and convince me it was just to lie down and observe the night sky. I had just enough wine so I determined it was simply a friendly dinner with great conversation and as long as we just look at the sky it should be fine. It was enchanting as I lie there taking in this sky one must just see for themselves to appreciate. The stars and moon were so brilliant they did not even look real. For a long time we just talked and I continued to drink his Italian wine to numb my nag that just wanted to go home and fall asleep in my own bed. He sat up and I continued to lie there taking in one last moment of night sky thinking this was my cue to leave when all of a sudden he grabbed my bare feet and began to rub them. He cleverly had stashed his homemade coconut oil nearby. "Relax, it is just a massage," he wooed.

Hmm how appropriate and ironic I had tried to book a massage earlier in the day but the masseuse was out of town. I decided to quit being such a prude and let the man rub my feet. After all, the night was perfect and my feet being pampered can in no way be interpreted as sexual. I began to unwind as it appeared he was staying way south but just as I relaxed, his hand ran up my leg. I sat up saying "no" but then calmed my startle with a laugh so not to appear prudish. He was persistent remarking "Julia you cannot enjoy pleasure? Relax." In his very deep Italian accented voice. It was true. I could not relax as I went through in my head the men I had already tried out and failed with. I did not want any more trials. I just wanted one. I just wanted the one and my gut said this was not him. I missed John whom I connected with already. Again Isaiah went to run his hand up my leg, I stopped him for the last time and got up to leave. He again proclaimed in a now disturbed voice "Julia you are afraid of passion, you need an Italian Stallion." I thanked him for the beautiful evening and walked home.

My best friend David stopped by just as I was escaping my suitor and we sat outside on my porch to smoke. I had for the first time in over twenty years begun to smoke pot. I had tried it a few times in college but never experienced it properly. I was afraid and did not really inhale. I know this because my son pointed out that I do not take it all the way in and so when I finally did, I found out what all the fuss was about. I knew people who smoked a bit to help pain, and

I had secretly been researching it, not as I had in the past to find proof for my clients it was bad or wrong, but to find proof that maybe it was helpful. The research I came across was more and more seeing it as a positive.

In addition, the clients I saw that used it were nothing like the hard core drug users I counseled that were stealing, breaking laws and breaking hearts. But were, on the contrary, peaceful loving beings I just adored. It is from Mother Earth, it is natural, and well that is what I convinced myself anyway. Reality is I am stepping out of a very cramped box and laughing my ass off feels fanfuckintastic. I give all the credit to my son whom I caught smoking it with his college friends and my attempts to lecture him had failed repeatedly. After a hard day at work, I walked in my house to catch him yet again as I began my programmed response that sounds something like Charlie Brown's teacher mumbling scientific brain facts on how bad it is. With every mumble I saw the new research in my head not condemning it, but advocating it. My imagination said "just stop the freak'n lecture, you know nothing" as I proclaimed out loud "Fuck it, do you have any more?" We had the best laugh ever and he showed me how it's done, proper inhale and all.

David and I too had the best times. He was so very insightful even when I was not high, but on this night we laughed hard as I told him my recent experience with the "Italian Stallion." Sitting outside in my big wooden rocking chairs under the night sky, he schooled me in his unique Spanish Conquistador accent. "Yes Julia, men just want sex" he said as he exhaled the potent plant. "In fact," he proclaimed, "if you were to research it, I bet most men would take it up the ass just to have sex with a woman." We laughed hard as he demonstrated in his scientific voice his findings "statistical research shows nine out of ten men will take it up the ass." We laughed even harder, if only you can imagine, when his dog tried to hump me and David proclaimed again with his hand on his stomach and his head tilted back in between the hysterical laughs "nine out of ten men, (insert boisterous laugh) one dog, (as he reprimands his dog that will not quit humping me), and one Italian Stallion would take it up the ass just to have sex with a woman." We laughed until we cried and then cried because we laughed so hard repeating this astonishing fact our hemp saturated brains had just discovered. We ordered pizza that so fucking cutely gets delivered on a motorcycle, munched our little hearts out, and crashed in my huge king size bed side by side as we often do.

He is my most remarkable male friend who will lie beside me as no man has, never touching me. I love him for being in love with my soul. I do love him so. I awoke first to make my green tea and then we rode our bikes into town. He stopped at his street to go home. David hugged me, saying we are proof a guy and girl in this town can really just be friends Julia. I kissed his cheek telling him I loved him and rode off as he yelled back "me too."

I rode my pink bike smiling from ear to ear down to my favorite strip of beach where not many people go. I wanted to catch the morning sun and meditate on this nagging in my gut to move, to write and simply what in the hell to do. Many of my friends here came with just a one way ticket and suitcase full of hope. I have met more spiritual people who had the same almost secret drive inside that says break away. Live life differently. Get off the beaten path. I spent ten glorious days for the most part alone, writing and enjoying nature. I love riding my bike into town along the beach, the yoga classes and the organic market where my friends Angel and Allon make spectacular healthy food. I sat on the sand near the shore and probably spent about ten minutes with my eyes closed when I felt the urge to stand and look at the beautiful place one last time before I headed home in the morning. Something in me said "sometimes you need to have your eyes open to see the answer." I got up and walked to the ocean to baptize my body in its waters hoping for answers. I let the ocean rock me with its gentle morning waves as I lay on my back looking for signs in the sky. A bit disappointed that I felt nothing, I began a walking meditation along the beach to dry off as my soul whispered over and over "how wonderful would it be to live here, to absorb yourself in nature, to get back to whom you are and to write."

I asked for answers as to what I should do, should I do it soon, should I take a risk and put every single thing into following this voice I am just learning to hear? I thought "how ironic I have discovered this soft soulful voice wanting me to abruptly risk it all, and yet I feel at peace at the thought. If I sell everything then maybe I can get by for at least one year and focus solely on writing." At that very moment, I looked down and there was a broken sand dollar. I bent to pick it up and whispered to its broken spirit "oh sand dollar, you might be my sign but if only I could find a whole one I would know for sure I should move." Then my soul spoke to me loud and clear saying "yes, it is a sign but it is just like looking for love, as soon as you stop looking, it will find you." I made a promise to stop, to stop trying so hard and to trust life would lead me. I closed my eyes and took a deep breath to suck in the sea salted air one last time.

It felt so peaceful to be alone on this huge strip of beach and to cherish everything my senses could extract; the humid salty smell, the sounds of the seducing waves, the feel of the moist sand beneath my feet. I recorded every incoming experience to try and take it home with me. I opened my eyes with the intention of getting up off my knees and I will be damned if sand dollars did not appear everywhere around my kneeling body. They emerged from the sand and I swear to the goddess in me there were twenty or more surrounding me, in front of me, behind me. They were all around me. Perfectly whole, perfectly placed, and I understood I had to stop living life and let life live me.

After I completed writing that miraculous event, I wanted to end the chapter there and made a note in my journal to maybe not include the evening's events because what happened next was not so magical. It ruins the mood. But it is how it happened. I come and go from peace to frustration because I am trying to learn my soul. So I decided I should leave it because this is how it goes when the soul only gets a portion of my time and I go off on another as I do placing my energy in business that is none of mine. So my peace was short lived because my mind began to worry about John.

I packed up then rode my bike into town. I had not talked to John in a few days. The phone was busy every time I tried to call. I decided to have pizza at the restaurant John and I went to last month when he was free. It was a pitiful picture of me sitting alone there contemplating what my future holds, while watching my watch as the 7:40 call time approached for me to call John. I rushed to finish my meal because I realized the time was near.

As if lonely could not get any lonelier, picture a long dark muddy road with me and my leftover pizza in a box in my bike basket, walking my bike with one hand, while I anxiously dialed the prison over and over with rain pouring down drenching the charm out of my once spectacular day. Busy signal after busy signal, my frustration grew. Then with only a moment to spare there was an answer. My relief was again short-lived as the stranger on the line gruffly tried to explain in Spanish some nonsense of "John no esta aqui para" and something about "trabajar" maybe. "Injury" sounded to be his last word to me but the thunder crashed as he hung up on me. I wanted to throw my phone, throw my hands up and scream. "What the fuck am I supposed to learn? Mr. perfect is not so perfect" I mumbled to myself, while life met my dirty mood with a perfectly placed mud puddle to trip me up and cover me in muck even more.

My brief encounter with Isaiah made me think about what I want. Since he had pointed out that "Julia, you are afraid of passion" I added that and only that to the list to prove I can handle it. House in man candy town, with hot men all around; Yes, I can handle it.

The Commandments

~~Higher education at least a master's degree and~~ interested in continuing to learn

Financially stable ~~in a professional career~~ doing what he loves

Family oriented – maybe already with a child since I am not having more

~~Crazy about me~~

Reads

Writes – journals, ~~poetry~~, etc.

Honest

Display affection daily, kindness and respect

Romantic

Loves to travel

Athletic

Handsome and HOT

~~Tall~~

~~Hairy Chest~~

~~No Tattoos~~

Loves to dance

Loves music

~~Crazy about me~~
Loves animals
Loves even my flaws
Loves to touch me ~~because he is crazy about me!!!!!!~~
Respectful of others
Listens to me
Proud of me
Confident
Loves good food and wine
Sensual
Bilingual
Single
Enjoys conversation
Able to remain in the moment
Over past relationships
Spiritual
Zen
Adventurous
Practices yoga and meditation
Free
Passionate

Ruth

Sitting in the airport awaiting my last flight home, all I could think about was how badly I missed myself. Miss myself? How strange to be so misplaced, my body is not my home. I was going back to a society I dreaded trying to be a part of. To find happiness inside the American faction that now seems oddly like the cold concrete walls my friend John was trapped in, escaped my mentality. I left my insides in Paradise—the part of me that flies free, sits in amazement at tiny creatures crawling on trees, connects to people with unrealistic dreams, and writes despite rules and creditability.

I did not want to follow the system anymore: get up at a designated time, drive to work like a robot, make money to pay taxes to fuel a dead economy that only thrives during war, supporting a hypocritical society spouting freedom while generating power through control, manipulating us to believe it's about peace when we readily go to war. I no longer cared to play into this materialistic fictitious idea of happiness, pretending I was holy, pouring my heart out to console people I may never see again, pretending to like people I disagreed with all to go home alone, not even seeing my family living within driving distance of me. They were the one thing I would hate to leave, but we rarely saw each other. I can rarely see them from Paradise. I tried to rationalize that it was not just the loneliness; because I did still have lonely moments in Paradise but they were alive lonely moments that dimmed in comparison to the joyous moments with nothing but a bike and bare feet.

I wanted to escape a country where marriage is praised yet broken by unfaithfulness and lies for a country that is still unfaithful but is as honest as lies can come. Everyone says they do not want relationships. You see people go from one to another, bouncing like beach balls in this beach town. My heart so yearned for love, but I knew I had to learn to grow it within. It was just a feeling I needed to learn to create despite outside circumstances. What better place to learn to love myself than to throw myself into a town where finding someone interested in a relationship was rare?

It would force me to stay single despite my programmed yearning. Because I did not trust my past choices, I do not trust my future. There was a belief in me running so deep still pushing me to seek outside love. Then there was the feeling that who I had become in my practice was not reflecting my true authenticity. I wanted to write. But society told me I had to earn a living. I hate being told what to do. I didn't want to earn a living. I didn't care about money. I am tired of being too busy to have a thought of my own. I wanted an adventurous life worth living. It felt like I was following someone else's path. No, I knew I was because I did not trust myself, I did not trust a path uncut. It did not feel good to be so confused. In fact it is scary. I was frightened.

I had to speak to Ruth about everything. She used to be such a wonderful support, but it seemed near impossible for her to listen to me now. She simply began defending her stance, her beliefs, and I crumbled. I had enough confirmation from my gut and the signs that had come my way; I felt confident I could stand up to her and hopefully explain in a way she could understand. I wanted us to begin a plan together for the future we both could feel good about. We had plenty of time to work it out. I prepared for the encounter full of confidence but as soon as I walked in the office door, there was a dark heavy feeling making me want to run away again.

Everything I rehearsed to say escaped me as I went to hug her and she spuriously said "glad to see you" with her arms locked in hard to her sides. It was so obvious she did not want to hug me back nor was she really glad to see me. I muttered "the trip was good but I still feel like I need to make a change at some point." I tried to explain again that I did not know how or in what time frame but I just want to let her know where I stood. I told her I planned to return for the Holidays in a few months and stay two weeks this time. She looked away from me the entire time indicating my presence was not wanted before her words confirmed her coldness. "If you do not know if you want to be here, then I do not want to practice with you anymore and honestly, I do not want to practice at all." She scolded.

I did my best to calm the tension and tell her again I was in no hurry. I was not even sure how or why. She said she felt betrayed, and she heard me talking about building a website for the school in Paradise. She remembered when that was us, when we were starting a business together. I could tell she was as confused as I was and thought I had this all planned out. I explained I was not starting a business, I was only volunteering my time to help out the school with a simple website. "They are not paying me; it is my gift to them," I explained. She replied that if I did not want this, then she didn't either.

This was her controlling way and I knew she was just trying to make me feel guilty. It was working. It always worked. I did not know how to make her understand I had no plan. I was confused. "What if this is a mid-life crisis?" I tried to consider out loud the possibility. I begged her to please just give me some time. Then as if to add salt to the wound she attempted to pull some Zen manipulation on me from the conference we had attended by saying "this practice is my dharma." I knew not to say things back to her but I could not help it and blurted "if this is truly your dharma, then it is your dharma with or without me." The tensions rose to a peak. You cannot argue with this strong willed woman, you simply cannot. She was now as close to yelling as one can get and still remain a lady. "It is your dharma too" she demanded. "We built this together. It is like a marriage. I feel betrayed by you." She became even more agitated when I mumbled, "Well, now I feel manipulated."

Ruth snapped back like a mother would scold a child in her ruthless teeth clenched voice "don't go there!" I could tell she knew she had reached a level of aggression not appropriate for her Christianity so she did her best to chill the heat by saying in a forced calm voice "You see your life so empty. You are running away from love. I love you." I heard the words but the energy swirled like a storm bringing much needed rain in its path of destruction with an aftermath feeling nothing like love. I should have shut the hell up but a transformation was going on within and that voice wanted to speak. I told Ruth I was not running from love but rather seeking, just not outside myself anymore. "If anything, I am running from society. It is simply not important for me to fit in it, as it is you."

The look in her eyes told me I said something terribly wrong. She yelled and yelled loud, "I am not doing this for society!" She even stomped her feet. Then she did a little dance mocking me with a forced smile, jumping around saying "you get so excited about Paradise and the possibilities." The scene before me seemed like a bully mocking his prey, it was unreal. I tried to calm her and apologized saying again that I am confused and I am sorry to be confusing her as well. Maybe I should have said nothing. I know all too well not agreeing with her every word ends in a lecture with my words getting twisted. She calmed a bit to firmly disagree with me that she is in no way confused, she is unsure. I thought to myself same difference but did not dare say that out loud. I asked her to please give me time and not force me to choose now because I was doing my best to trust the universe would find a way that is best for us both.

My words did not soothe her at all. She became upset again and proclaimed how hurt she was. She said it is such a deep hurt caused by me, she did not know if it could heal. I felt sick, horribly sick, because the energy had changed and this emotion she was expressing is real. In realizing my confusion has made another human hurt, I genuinely tried to put my defense aside and comfort her. "I hear you, honey. I have hurt you and I understand you may not be able to forgive me. I am so sorry."

I cried as the overwhelming emotion turned on the tears in my eyes. There was a long pause. I thought maybe it was over and I had some deep thinking to do, to reconsider what I had done, try to come back to reality and find a way to heal the hurt my dreaming caused. I was just about to tell her my thoughts when she threw one last disagreement yelling behind clinched teeth trying to muffle her rage "I did not say forgive. I did not say I could not forgive you! I said heal the hurt, I cannot heal the hurt you have caused me!" She turned her icy shoulder to me, made a cynical face and stomped away. It was all too much for me to process and I had work to do so I apologized profusely loud enough she could hear as I walked back to my office with a lump in my throat, doing my best to shove it down. I knew it was not fair for me to carry this into sessions so I meditated and somehow amidst the squall, found my peace to share with clients.

I continued trying to call John at night with no luck. It had been four days now. I worried because he does not come to the phone and the other prisoners try to explain something to me in Spanish. I got a message from his sister to call a new number at nine in the evening instead of seven. It was almost nine so I hurriedly made the call. To my relief he answered telling me I must refer to him as Chico now. He was attacked by two men with knives and there was a hit out to kill him. He assured me he was okay and only had a cut on his foot from kicking the knife away!

John continued to try and minimize the incident by telling me the lawyer I hired had already filed a Habeas Corpus to get him moved to another prison. He said they were hiding his identity and that was why I had to ask for Chico. He was now in a cell he could not leave with two guards watching to keep him safe. I did my best to comfort him even though I was emotionally spent. He had cried all day missing his family. I encouraged him to write. I told him write everything, what you see, how you feel, it will give you something to do, keep you busy and help you process these emotions. We talked about him documenting it all so maybe one day he can tell his story in a book. He said "thank you Julita." I hung up thinking "I cannot do this anymore, not even as a friend." My heart hurt tremendously.

At work, Ruth and I avoided each other the rest of the week. I wrote out countless times the pros and cons and meditated repeatedly. I truly despised going into work now. Not because of my clients, I loved them, but the tension between Ruth and I had made me ill. The weekend could not come quick enough. I spent it at home meditating and doing yoga. I made more lists trying to decide what to do. I tried to look at it all through Ruth's eyes. I felt horribly guilty for putting her in the middle of my confusion, my mid-life crisis, my whatever the fuck this unsure craziness was.

Then on Saturday, I finally found some peace. I was in a deep morning meditation when it became clear to me, I was in fact being controlled. I mean what if this was a mid-life crisis? Shouldn't my counselor friend know and compassionately give me the time I need to come out of it? Instead it felt like she was forcing me to make choices I was not ready for. Again I saw the beach and the sand dollars as I was reminded how good it felt that day to open my eyes. Life was on my side and it would work itself out. I made the decision to not explain anymore. Not waste another drop of my energy defending or convincing because I have a passion to fulfill. I knew what I had to do and at that point realized knowing what I wanted was not explainable nor did it require explanation. Now it was just a question of timing. My dreams were begging to be heard. I needed to have enough faith in my voice to not have to prove it to another. It in no way makes another's path wrong, just maybe wrong for me. So what if it was a crazy mid-life crisis. It is crazy! But new life, new ideas, new paths require a bit of crazy. And in one swift move I put on my clothes, headed to the hardware store, purchased a "for sale" sign, stuck it in my yard and hammered it down saying "I will not be controlled anymore."

Not thirty minutes later, my second ex-husband appeared at my door. He agreed I should go and be happy. He told me if I was going to sell, now was the time to do it. He always loved to boast his financial knowledge and like I said before he is a financial genius. He loved to talk business and lit up with knowledge saying "if you sell the practice you should get at least two times your salary. But, it is a practice and impossible for someone to take over who does not have your credentials. So, you should consider taking one year's salary and you keep your equipment." I laughed, not having even considered money. I did not have a clue it would be worth that much. I told him I was not even sure I would do this but wanted to see if I get any offers on the house first. He agreed saying "yes you do not have to accept anything and it won't hurt to just see."

He told me why he came by. He was concerned about his brother. He described to me his alcoholism, how his wife feels he may be cheating, and the rages he snapped into being mean to her kids when he drinks. I could not help but smile inside and wonder where the camera was because he was describing our relationship and did not even know it. It was a spot-on description of us and I was either in the twilight zone or this was candid camera. He has no understanding that was why we divorced. I felt so sad for him and gave him my support not saying a word about the comparison. As he left, I thanked the universe for that interaction because it put in perspective how things look from the outside, how confused we can be, naive of our flaws. If he did not want this for his brother, how could he want this for himself? He did not. He is just not aware. I said a prayer that he would find his way and his peace.

There was finally some good news with John. He was moved to a less harsh prison, if that is possible. He said the prisoners left him alone now because he just came from Hell. That is what they call the capital city prison, Hell. He was in a smaller prison but his depiction did not give me much comfort. He described the same situation with overcrowding and how he had to start over getting necessities from the boss. He used cigarettes to buy things like a bed, phone time, and a banana. They eat mainly rice and beans. He was sick of it but still stays so positive and even still laughs. He said he is lucky coming from Hell because no one harassed him. He has witnessed others get dressed like girls and beat with wood sticks. One guy was put in a thong and made to parade around as everyone laughed and hit him. He said he did not laugh at first but then something took over and he laughed too.

John explained how hard it was on the days he did not talk to anyone but sometimes it was even harder to get the calls. Like talking to his daughter and missing her confirmation, she cried not knowing why he was not there or where he was at all. He too cried all day. He said his original old lawyer/girlfriend came to see him and he did not like what she said. It could take another thirty days. A fight broke out while we talked and I could hear the screams of the victim amongst the cheers raging it on. He said he was okay over and over then laughed as the fight died down. Another fight broke out at the end of our conversation.

I dreaded going back to work to fight my own battle. It was so sad feeling at war when I just wanted to give peace to others. The week was heavy as Ruth avoided me; even her family who used to come in loving on me walked in coldly past my office, not even looking my way. I wondered how the story went in her home. Was I really such an awful person? I did not know what to do. Should I shut the voice up in my gut and just stay? Maybe it would go away if I waited it out. But Ruth wanted an answer. She was living her life in limbo she said and so was her family. Here I was living in guilt for doing this to them. It would be so much easier if I was wrong and my perception just snapped back into place. I could relieve everyone of this pain I created. Everyone but me.

The last day of the work week, I stepped out of my office to go home and found a letter taped to my door. It was a stern request to buy me out for a low ball offer and the last line said something like "your partnership with the company will end on December 31st." That was just a few weeks away! I could not believe she had done this. It looked like she got her lawyer to write it but I was not sure; she was very legal in her everything. I felt so cheated. This was supposed to be my friend who loved me, is a counselor and understands people's struggles, yet my attempts to tell her I was lost have left her pushing me out the door. I wondered if I should wait for her to finish with her last client so I could talk to her but I decided I could not bear another conversation. I took the letter and my disbelief and walked out the door so very frustrated, heartbroken, and crying.

I cried all weekend long. I talked to my parents and my son. No one could believe my friend had done this. Everyone told me I was being bullied but I was so confused. Maybe I was making her feel abandoned and maybe it was not fair for me to even think of leaving the practice. It is our human nature to see and portray only our best yet we so easily condemn others for our unhappiness. Maybe this is what I was doing.

I went back and forth beating myself up and crying. I cried buckets. But in my gut I felt this was just another attempt to control me, get me to see things her way and shake me enough to stop my confusion. Part of me wishes it would have worked. I mean it would be so much easier to just stay. I have everything going in my favor. My practice is booming to the point I can work pretty much when I want. I can travel as much as I want. My house, my car, my clothes are all the best. I have my hair done by the best stylist in town and I visit the spa weekly.

I consider all options. I know I want to write so I tell myself, "Write! Do it now, why do you have to up and move and disrupt everything?" Despite my countless hours of meditation, and I mean hours, I have done every form I know; chanting, guided, primordial sound, walking meditation, sleep meditations and vibrational alignment. The answer is no answer at all. It is just a feeling, just a feeling I cannot explain. All I can say is it is a beautiful feeling and when I feel it, I know. It is a knowing I must follow this feeling because everything is happening as it should. No it is not the way I would have liked. I would have liked for there to be more time to make a plan and I would like to know Ruth was happy with the plan.

I decided to call Ruth before the work week began and try to talk this out. We met for lunch and I explained to her the tension in the air, how even her family shunned me and I had no plan to move quickly nor even a plan at all. I told her I have simply tried to be open with her and I was now very hurt. I saw it as a sign to go. She had already talked to other people about taking my place so we discussed money. I explained the offer is not fair at all because I invested not only in the building but also in all the furniture, the assessments, computers and the equipment. She told me it was worth nothing. Still I tried to stand for myself. She did not want to pay me anything close to my suggestion nor did she want to give me my half of the equipment. She was stern in her rebuttal. I wished I could be more like that. I could not stand the way I felt in that moment. My heart was pounding and my mind spun as she controlled the entire conversation. I just wanted out. I could not imagine things ever going back to the way they were as she briefly mentioned me not going. I envisioned staying for a split second and it smothered me. I would have to go back to being the silent partner.

I knew she did not want me to go and I knew she never intended for the letter to push me even further out the door. But it did. It made me see my confusion was too much; it was not fair to her and it was not fair to my clients. So despite me having nothing considered, I must go. This is how I have always been. My first husband showed me he did not love me and it did not matter that I stayed ten more years; I was not in the marriage after that. No matter what he said, it was over for me. My second husband did the same telling me he did not want to be married to begin with and he did not love me. I filed for divorce. It was not just the note, it was the order it occurred. I felt sorry for Ruth because had my past not been my past, we probably could have resolved this but history was dictating my future, and I was done. Push me out the door, no hell all you have to do is gently nudge me, and I go.

I felt like the biggest loser. I was losing my practice and I was allowing it, just as I did my marriages. I felt cheated, so very cheated. I wanted to throw every fucking fairytale that had been shoved down my throat up. Marriage did not work for me though I truly believed I was as good a wife as one can be. My A plus education, successful practice, religion, pleading prayers, and damning confessions did not fulfill me despite my being damn good at it all. I was tired of religion, politics, education, Ruth and my exes pushing their opinions in my mouth under the falsehood of my best interest. I could not even fathom another religious fling to attempt exoneration. I am now fully aware that all of these churches I attended have an agenda of control under the guise of holy men, not much unlike those that have claimed to be my friend.

They are all sleepwalking under the spell of Controligion, not saving my soul at all but keeping it small. I am exhausted by the

American government's regulations pushing things like prescription medications, dietary recommendations, vaccinations and even sunscreen in the attempt to make us think they care, touting their bought research. Then years later we are finding out more often than not, they are wrong. I had fatigued from feebly swallowing the thick, toxic slime. I was done.

It is bullshit, and Ruth not wanting to give me any of my equipment was ridiculous given it was my idea to use it in the first place. I was not even sure I cared anymore. I wanted out now more than ever. I was making money that was nothing more than fuel for war and politics I could not stand. I was creating dependence rather than abundance. I was serving others only as a vehicle to my own advancement. All the while, I was working with someone who was trying to keep me silent even more. I was sick of tiptoeing about my ideas for of fear of hearing her lectures.

That week we agreed on a number and only one piece of my equipment. I settled for nothing more than what would get me out. Nothing for the furniture, nothing for the furnishings, the website I built, the logo I designed, the business I generated, or clients I referred. Nothing because Ruth said it was worth nothing and I was all out of energy to argue with her anymore. She said she would call her lawyer to draw up the paperwork. Keep in mind, my house had not sold; I still had all of my belongings weighing me down and I would be out of a job in two weeks. It was not enough money for me to go debt free; I still had more than the offer in college loans and credit cards. But plenty for me to get by long enough to finish a book, which I speculated may take a year. This is a humongous risk but if I am going to take a risk who better to take it on than me?

I kept reminding myself of the peace in meditation. I continued to meditate as often as I could for comfort during the day and hold on to that feeling of knowing. One of my biggest fears I had to face now was to tell my clients. I worried they would react as Ruth had. In my office meditating between clients thinking of the strife at work and how to tell these remarkable beings I was leaving, something miraculous happened. In my meditation I told myself I had always strived hard to see the best in others. Even when I felt I had been treated unfairly I focused on learning all the lessons I could to squeeze the gunk out of me so as to one day view myself on the pedestal I can so easily place others. I thought about the conflict and how I may very well be wrong because there is darkness in me as in everyone. That is when it happened. I heard my soul and for the first time I could tell the difference between the programmed thoughts and my unconditioned soul. It rebutted the thought of me thinking I have darkness in me by saying "more importantly there is a light. The light is true self whereas the darkness is history, programming, and conditioning. The goal is to separate the light from the dark to get back to soul. Everybody sees the light when they die; see it while you are still alive." Then as if to send confirmation, an angel tapped on my door bringing me out of the meditation.

It was my very first client ever who I began to see back in grad school. I had not seen him in years. He walked in my door unannounced asking to sit with me briefly. He had been to my office enough to know I only had a few moments. "All I need is the five minutes you have between clients" he said as he entered to take his seat. He was a young handsome man in his late twenties, with a story that would rip your heart. He wore cute little studious glasses and a long black coat, looking very "city of angels." He did not come for my advice, but instead, had a message for me. He talked of discovering society's norms did not equate to happiness with all the consumerism, etc. and love comes from within. I told him I was moving for those reasons to escape this society and to finally love myself enough to listen to me and my dreams of being a writer. I explained my fear of telling clients and he was the first client I told. He asked if I was going alone. I confirmed I was and that I was scared to death. He said, "You are doing the right thing; don't be afraid of the dark. It is the moments of darkness that shed light on the soul." Yes, he said darkness and he said light just as I had envisioned moments ago. I began to cry as he hugged me goodbye. I had chills as he walked away and once again I knew momentarily where God lived.

That encounter was the courage I needed to put my faith in me and in the little voice that had remained silent all these years. One by one, I began telling my clients my plan that was no plan at all. Many of them I had known for years, and many of them probably know me better than I know myself. I swear it was magic as these beautiful people not only accepted my decision but celebrated it with me. Not one of them felt betrayed by me as Ruth had but instead expressed admiration in my choice to follow my voice. Rather than be sad or think of themselves and what they would do, I watched them sit in silence for a moment then look up, sucking air as if for the first time and say "go, how motivational" or my favorite response was upon breathing air of acceptance, "thank you for always being true to you and inspiring me to do the same." Every fear I had dissolved with each continued step in the direction of my heart. They felt inspired and in turn I felt for once in all my confusion, understood. I am so grateful for them and that feeling they gave me. I wish for each of them to know how much influence they had in my life and rather than me helping them on that day, they made me feel okay. To make another feel okay is in my book the greatest gift we can give. I only hope they all understand they too are okay. You are better than okay. You are perfect. I want you each to know that. You are perfect and you always have been. The next few weeks unfolded with many tears and hugs as we said goodbye.

On the last day before I left for the holidays, Ruth walked in with the paperwork. She told me the person taking over my spot would be coming in after the holidays even though I said I would be back to tie up loose ends and see any clients still needing closure and a referral. I looked over the paperwork. Nowhere in the legal jargon did it say I got any equipment. There were clients in the lobby and my office door was open so I whispered "what about the equipment?" I suppose my questioning was the last straw. A loss of control ensued that confirmed my choice to move even more.

She exploded—so abruptly I was not even sure exactly what was said because it left my body shaking as I felt my sense of hearing turn inward. Inside of me there was peace amongst the ferocity. I sat in my chair as she stood over me yelling. I turned my attention within where there was the most beautiful quiet. The temper tantrum continued and momentarily I heard her words screaming "You left me! You left me!" The lecture from her intensified while I contemplated what this could mean. I now fully understood things were most certainly happening with purpose. In a split second, it hit me that her not wanting to give me the equipment may very well be another blessing because if I was honest with myself, I had been contemplating the equipment's necessity anyway.

It is supposed to provide a sense of focused relaxation and I am not so sure it is not just an attempt by science to make money off what eastern religions have known for years. Focused relaxation can change the brain for the better, yes, it is called meditation. I mean here I am hooking people to electrodes to induce a sense of relaxation I am learning can be achieved on your own. The research, if you must have it, is proving immense brain changes through meditation as well.

I looked up at the storm that was still brewing. I tried to calmly end it, pointing to the lobby to remind her there were people close enough to hear. The clarity I now had and the deep breath I took to try and get her to breathe as well, generated a small smile on my face. I swear it was not an intentional smile to cause her any more pain. I was hoping to spread the ease. It did the opposite, appearing insensitive making her feel worse. She grabbed the paperwork out of my hand, slammed it on my desk and roughly scribbled "equipment and whatever else you want" in the legal terms. She smirked back at me mocking my calm and threw the pen down. In an effort to guilt me down one more time, she told me her kids were hurting from her stress and physically her menopause symptoms were back because of me. I said "I am sorry I had no answer, I was lost." She screamed "you were in a business!" then turned and stomped out yelling "You left me!"

I sat there stunned, looking at my now shaking hands but this time I did not cry. Instead I thought of all the signs that had come my way so far; the sand dollar tattoo, the ayurvedic spray, the sand dollars emerging all around me and my visit from an angel. I simply breathed. In Ruth's defense, she did come back to my office later to apologize. I don't think she understood the situation or the torment going on in my head over many months. She cried. I was empathetic but confused by the tears that did not seem real. It sometimes appeared she was consumed with me. It was too much to feel responsible for another person's happy. "Maybe I am wrong," I thought to myself as I always do, "But what if I am right?" silently seeped into my mind. Ruth sobbed hard, telling me she loved me over and over through her tears but all I could say was "I do not know what to do with that kind of love." I hugged her apologizing profusely as I dried her tears and told her goodbye.

Job(less)

Still so full of questions, I left my profession on a search for my soul. I had no idea how I would sell my house and belongings in such a short time frame. With it being the holidays, we planned to spend that time on vacation. I put it all aside trusting in life while I left for what would be my new home to celebrate with my son, dad and step-mom. As soon as I arrived the warm tropical sun melted my troubles. Everyone was so welcoming. It was good to get back to living each day unscripted. The outdoor spaces fulfilled this nagging need I found to connect with nature; a need that could not be filled with consumerism, things or people.

A visit to the organic market the first day would test the living without a script life I wanted when Allon asked if we should try to visit John in prison. Taking a moment to ponder the fear that welled up at the thought, I asked myself if I were feeling no fear at all, would I go? I would go to comfort and I would go to experience giving comfort without payment, without return, without reward. To live without a script means walking through not around fiery fear. I told Allon, "Yes, this will be a great adventure."

At my next scheduled call, I told John we were coming. He was very excited and explained the process. He said to arrive early because there would be a long line of families waiting to get in and only a limited amount of time for visits. He asked us to bring food in plastic containers, our passports and nothing else. I did not sleep the night before, worried about how I would handle a prison. Not just any prison but a prison in a third world country. I have never been to a jail or prison in my life. I worried how he would look and had visions of a thin, dirty beat down man in an orange jump suit, cuffed and shackled. I knew he had been in fights and it scared me to think how he might be hurt. I was not fearful for my own safety. My concern was for him and if I would be strong enough to disguise my own discomfort. I wanted to be strong to prevent causing him more pain. Then there was the worry of driving. I hate to drive and the roads are bad. Plus I have just relearned to drive a stick shift. My friend Allon cannot drive. Many of the locals do not drive, there is no need to. So I knew it was up to me to get us to the prison safely.

We left early in the morning to make the two hour drive and be there by eight. I was not entirely sure of the way so I relied on Allon. Not thirty minutes into the drive, I missed the turn and veered off the thin road to turn around; huge mistake! Do not get off the paved road in Paradise; the thick brush on the side of the road prevents you from seeing what is really there. The right front tire sunk deep as the back end of the car raised up high in the air. I had hit a huge hole and the car was now teetering on the edge with the tire hanging off. Allon jumped out and stood on the back bumper to try to push it back down. It was no use. A man walked over speaking Spanish, shaking his head and I interpreted it to mean it was not fixable.

I tried to lighten the mood by reminding Allon with a huge smile of this being part of our great adventure. He continued to stand on the bumper high above me saying "Julia, I did not expect this kind of adventure." We laughed and turned to see a man with a truck pulling in behind us. Well it had a bed but not anything like the giant trucks back home. It was a tiny little thing but he assured me he could pull me out as he grabbed a rope. The man and his toy truck somehow accomplished the task. He introduced himself as the town Doctor. I thanked him and told him I was moving to his village. "Welcome to your new life" he yelled out as he waved goodbye and drove off. Ha! "Yes, a life teetering on the edge," filled my head.

We continued on. In town we stopped for food that we placed in the plastic containers as instructed. We had a little trouble finding the prison but eventually ended up on a bumpy dirt road that grew longer and longer as my anxiety grew. Allon admitted he was scared too but reassured me we were doing the right thing. We pulled into a now overcrowded dusty parking lot. There were vendors selling various food items but I only looked at what the other people were wearing to make sure I was appropriate.

We approached a small worn concrete building with probably one hundred people or more trying to get to the check-in window. Everyone had food items with them making this daunting task seem somewhat norm. Not much unlike the gifting of food items presented when someone dies.   One look at their emotion engraved expressions and I could tell who had done this before from the people who were new like me. There was pain, fear, and tears on many faces. People crammed to get to the window and shelter from the heat under the tiny roof extending off the building. I grabbed Allon's hand and he tried to inch us to the window. We were unsure what to do. After about thirty minutes of waiting in our sweat drenched bodies, we got to the line where the guard asked for the name of the prisoner. I said "John" but the confused guard then asked for another name. I stared blankly, as Allon said all of John's supposed last names he could think of.

Luckily he got one right. The guard took our passports and handed us what was supposed to be a number. But it was not a number. It was a letter neither of us knew what to do with. So we waited. We waited and we sweated realizing they are not calling numbers at all but periodically letting people in another line to the gate. We continued to wait in the disordered makeshift line. It seemed one line only lead to permission to enter another line. After an hour or so, we decided to walk forward through the crowd to the gated entrance and see if the second guard could help us. I whispered "perdon" to everyone fearful to be cutting the chaotic assembly. I shimmied forward with Allon's hand in mine. Everyone appeared lost and distraught so no one questioned us. The confusion in my head had reached its peak. I turned to tell Allon thank you for coming with me, and in that instant the guard pushed me through the gate but put his arm up to block Allon. I turned to try my best in Spanglish to say "es mi amigo" and "please let him through." But the crowd pushed me on in the line where other guards were sternly waiting to inspect food items. They grabbed the food, opened it, took a dirty knife and began to stab the lasagna. I didn't even care. I simply did not want to be alone in here.

The guard handed it back to my trembling hands and firmly pushed me to the next guard. Now I stood in what looked like the entrance to a bathroom. I tried to explain that I wanted to wait for my friend, that I did not want to go alone but the guard was unsympathetic and in Spanish forcefully told me I must go as he took my arm and pushed me toward the door. I was overwhelmed with fear and confusion. I started to cry as I entered the tiny wooden room where another guard firmly stood with a security scanner. Although stern, I was thankful she was female. She did her best to calm me whispering "tranquila" over and over while she scanned my trembling body and patted me down. She mumbled more Spanish, opened the door, and pointed me on my way. I followed the others that had gone through security before me down a side walk surrounded with crumbling concrete buildings and harsh barbed wire. I found a tiny bench to sit, dry my tears, gather myself and hopefully wait for Allon.

A moment later a man stood over me dangling a tissue. I looked up to see the callous guard who had pushed me into the security room soften with compassion. He asked who I was there to see. I mumbled "John" with my shaken words, a few of his last names I am sure of and all the others I am not. I told the guard, whom I knew could not understand me "I don't even know his last name. How stupid can one be?" He said "vamos" taking my hand gently now. He walked me past the gated entrance, where I could see the jail cells. Crumbling concrete block rooms maybe ten foot by ten foot were crammed with life trying to free body parts or simply grasp a touch of sun. Hardened hearts decorated the barbaric bars in the tall windows. Men, many men, I mean they are stacked against each other, stood in the windows hanging out of the bars, yelling as people passed. Two long buildings on either side of the sidewalk each composed of five or six of these small rooms held human pasts captive. I tried to maintain my composure, not looking too hard at the inhumanity. Past the men hanging out of the bars in one room, I caught a glimpse of the ratty bunk beds stacked in threes with little room between the bunks. The guard pointed me into a concrete building and I realized I was going into the actual cells.

There was another large gate entering the concrete courtyard in the middle of the cells where families sat on the floor with their incarcerated love. The guard yelled "John." I was thankful to have on sunglasses, because there was no stopping the tears dripping with my heart beat. And then I saw him. I can only say how serene he looked; walking slowly, with a smile of peace. He had on jeans and a white t-shirt with his mala beads wrapped around his wrist. He grabbed and hugged me! Astonished he was allowed to touch me, I pulled away quickly out of fear. He took my hand and lead me around the corner passed the people sitting on the floor to another concrete room with concrete tables. He explained he had to pay to have the table but most people took visitors on the floor in the room we just left.

He looked good. The white t-shirt he wore, stuck in my mind. I marveled at how white it was, how regal he looked and how clean he smelled. He smiled often as I explained what happened to Allon. He eased me saying he would be here shortly. It was a strange feeling to be in a situation where I should be comforting another, it was the reason I came, but the tables have turned and my concern for him was killing me. He reassured me over and over that he was fine. He explained how he had been teaching the other prisoners English and yoga in an attempt to aptly describe what life he still had.

Allon arrived and we enjoyed each other's company over our guard stabbed lunch. Periodically, John leaned over to lay his head on my shoulder. It reminded me of a little boy who needed comfort desperately. I understood how good it must feel to regain human contact, so I let him despite my unease. I let him touch me and every now and then he hugged me while my heart gushed open with each touch. I looked around to make sure we were not breaking a rule, to see others doing the same. In what seemed like mere seconds, we were told to go. We all hugged as he reassured us this would be over soon. Allon took my arm and walked me through the cell lined sidewalk where men hung out like untamed animals trying to communicate in the wild. I did my best to hold it together but hearing the men chant to send free their voice, the only thing they have left, broke me. I leaned into Allon and cried, doing my best to continue walking to leave the inhumanity behind. We drove the two hours back home.

I sat outside alone that evening easing my suffering burned eyes with cool tears. The stars above brightened the night sky and attempted to lighten the shadow in my mind. But the appalling scene of humans crammed in filthy tiny rooms, seared in my brain knowing many of them had been there for years, would be there for years, maybe decades, maybe life. I laid down to allow the earth to hold me. I thought about love; how those prisoners just need love not that concrete cold. I thought of John's beautiful positive disposition. It stuck in my mind like the smell still swirling my senses akin to the spin cycle on a washing machine of his clean, crisp white shirt. There was pride in that garment. I just wanted to breathe it in.

I had a brief thought about his eyes, there was darkness in his eyes but an ease came off him like the gentle ocean pushing the breeze my way with each wave. His laugh and invigorating presence was intoxicating. I just kept thinking of the way he snuggled his head into my shoulder like a little neglected child. I somehow identify with that feeling as a child and even now. I wonder; was I neglected? No. Is there a lack of attention as an adult? No. Then why do I so desperately need to be filled from the outside? The answer will be the answer. That is why I am here. That is why I am leaving my scripts behind and why I will stay until I feel whole.

I thought about how easy it is for me to see love in everyone. What if we all learned to see love in even the darkest of souls? It's easy to see it in an openly philanthropic person but can you see it in a homeless, a drunk, prisoner? I can! I am humbled that I can as I whisper to myself thank you for that precious gift. And one more time I tell myself no matter what John's story, I am in this until the end as his support, as his comfort, as his friend.

We celebrated Christmas and New Years in paradise. Not in the traditional American way but in an unscripted way on the beach, sunning, fishing, playing, dancing, and laughing. There were no feelings of anxiety or stress that accompany the "normal" holidays I had become accustomed to. We did not worry if there would be enough; enough food, enough stuff, enough money to buy the stuff, stuff that may not be good enough. We did not shop for presents, we did not cook a holiday meal, and we did not stress one ounce as we had in the past decorating, spending tons of money only then to worry if everyone had a present, if they would like it, frantically wrapping last minute gifts, cleaning, cooking and following the holiday rules like the mechanical human doing that last year and the year before and the decade before that only to end up financially strapped from the "Joy" of the season. It was so nice to let go of past traditions and be in the moment with each other. We gave not material gifts but we gave our time, our love. For once I had spent a repetitive ritual without a script, treating each situation as new with no formula and no recipe and it felt fresh, it felt novel, I felt alive.

I absorbed it all knowing this would be my new life as soon as I went back to tie up loose ends. If you can call loose ends "selling your everything." No more clinging to knowing. No more will I fight unwilling to let go no matter how miserable I am. No more scripts of trying to be and stay married, doing wifely duties to keep another happy only to fight like hell, drink pain away, work until broken down, achieve, achieve, overachieve. Get up by X time, do A B C D then rush to work in my android driven machine watching the gloom on the faces of every human I pass following the exact same routine. How magical is that? The voice may be screaming "go take a new path". But how many people actually go? It is scary as hell. Yes. Because I do not know! People turn back on their path simply because they do not know. I have prayed and patiently waited for answers my whole life. Waiting for answers left me rotting in my present repeating patterns so my past became my future. There is no answer in waiting, only regret. The answer can only be found by taking action on an unknown path.

Sure, I questioned what on earth I was doing. I could not explain it to myself. How could I explain to someone else? It was not easy. It was more difficult than staying. Staying would have been easy. The journey is going to be scary but rather than despise it, I want to love the fear, making it my new friend. I begin to tell myself "your heart pounds because you have no script, no guidelines." The fear is simply freedom to cut a new path, write a new script. I wanted to experience stories different from the ones I'd been brainwashed to believe.

I went back home still unsure of how this would unfold. I got an offer on my house so I put my house hold items and car online and had a garage sale. Within two weeks everything was gone. People walked past me handing me cash while carrying my belongings out my door. It happened so fast, I had no time to think. That was a blessing. Thoughts talk us out of our dreams. I sat on my empty living room floor and the space was so very freeing. I slept the last week on an air mattress and got rides from friends because I sold my luxury vehicle in the garage sale! I said my goodbyes to friends and family, packed one suitcase of things I thought I could not live without and left boxes with friends and family of other things I thought I could not part with.

I booked a one-way ticket and by the end of January, I was back in Paradise living on a prayer. The only stress I had in the move was trying to get my little dog over. It took a trip to the vet to get a letter that had to be mailed to the US department of agriculture and then they in turn mailed me a certificate so she could enter the country. The time frame was the biggest issue as I sat in my empty house waiting the night before our flight for the documents to arrive and just like the magic occurring all around me they showed up at ten at night and we headed off to bed ready for a life of adventure.

Risky rebellion hovered over me entering the airport. I knew I would board the plane a programmed patriot and exit an expat. Expatriate, yet another label placed on my person but one I do not mind as it is often used to describe those of us that retire from society—a symbolic flee from the marching orders of the mound and worker ant way of living. I knew it would not be easy to liberate myself from conventional conduct, there is guilt for that and patterns of perpetual thought, there's depression for that. In the airport walking to my final flight, I tried to ease the negative ridicule seeping in. I could hear Ruth's voice the last conversation we had where she threw her final dagger to leave me with a punctured heart, saying "I will never come see you." My body tensed to the negativity but I tried to force thoughts of all the positive signs that pushed me in this direction. Then I looked up to literally see a sign that read "follow your heart – don't let dogma swallow your dreams – don't let others opinions drown your own voice"~ Steve Jobs[4].

---

[4] I wrote this Steve Jobs quote I saw on an airport advertisement verbatim in my travel journal while waiting for my plane.

Miracles are everywhere if we can just allow our eyes to see. It's not easy. It takes valor to be so optimistic. While having the courage to follow your own voice is terrifying. It is terrifying because there is no way to know how it turns out. I have never put more faith in anything in my life; not religion, not my parents, friends, family, husbands or any person of authority. If you are going to go all in, why the hell not be in for yourself? All my faith is in me! "Scary shit," I think as I board the plane with my one true love. My poor little dog is stuffed in her bag and just as anxious as me. Anxious, anxiety, fear, worry: all products of our programmed mind and its connections to our body raising heart rate, skin temperature and more negative thoughts. It's a vicious cycle. One negative thought starts it. Your brain releases chemicals with the negative thought that act on the rest of the body and then you feel crappy. Now in turn that crappy feeling produces more negative thoughts to stir more negative feelings.

That brilliant brain I worked with for years, that I know is at its core simply a survival mechanism often renders us helpless. It does not mean to be so cruel, but it is. It stores negative experiences and it repeats. It reminds us over and over again simply to keep us alive. It is why our ancestors survived. The brain kept them constantly worrying about food, shelter, and predators. If they stayed alert, prepared for disaster, they stayed alive. We are not living in a cave anymore. We do not need so many warnings. The brain does not distinguish if it is real or not. It only knows if something made you feel bad. Then it registers environmental cues as a warning. That is why you can be alone and imagine someone is looking in the window at you and all of a sudden your body begins to produce the symptoms for fear. It does not have to be a frightening event it can be as simple as words. If they make you feel bad, they get stored. The brain does not understand it was a onetime experience, will never happen again, or it is not even true. So that if someone told you, let's say for example, "you are only going to escape responsibility" and it made you feel bad, then that thought gets stored in the warning system and will repeat over and over growing and changing its form to keep you guessing and thinking it is real. So "escape responsibility" turns into; irresponsible, lazy, reckless, thoughtless, uncaring, and a million other ugly obstructions. This is why people have anxiety and fear. The most difficult part of overcoming it is to walk through it. Because if you let it stop you, if you let it succeed, it grows. Then the next time you try to fight it, it is bigger and stronger. Until one day it is larger than you and your dreams. So now you believe dreams are irrelevant, impossible, foolish, noncompliant hindrances.

Wow! See that is my lecture mode I so often spit on others. If you think you did not like the rambling, just imagine what it is like to have that in your head. Here I am sitting on a plane with my dog and my thoughts I want to shed. I beam at the possibilities before me, as my soul tells my primitive brain, my programmed past, Controligion and society "you did not win. You will not win!" I want to write. Do I know any of this will be worth it? Published? Matter? Of course not. Outcomes are never known. That is what makes this so scary, so brave. Bravery can only arise from fear. I cannot steer the same course my entire life and call myself brave. The path before me was once thatched with thorns. Someone scared to death braved the uncut trail not knowing what was on the other side. I am going to see what it is on the other side.

Proverbs

The first order of "business" upon my arrival was to set up my office for my new job of writer. The job my soul wants me to do and has been begging me my entire life to do. I prepared my writing station near the back window so I could look out over the pool and lush greenery outside. I can even open the wall of doors so the entire back of the house sits on the edge of nature basically putting me outside. The first days of writing I could only come up with reasons to advocate my move. I thought of things people had told me. Like Ruth saying I was running away. She was absolutely right. I am running, I feel like I have escaped but maybe not running away but running into. Into life, the life my soul craves. Into whom I am, who I've always been. Escaping my conditioning and the mask I wear like a heavy coat covering and smothering my voice. The more I wrote the more I felt alive, energized and free. I began to see what I had created was space. New ideas need space. The energy here is inspiring helping me fill that space creatively.

Every day I woke up to connect with nature by either riding my bike to the beach for sunrise to meditate or hiking the mountain near my house leading to another extraordinary beach. My dog ran circles around me as she too delighted in the freedom. My soul felt connected to the land while the terrain challenged my body enough to renew my spirit. I could not turn back nor complain for this was the wondrous path I chose. Then I headed home and I wrote, getting lost for hours almost unconscious to the lettering. Something was being born and there was no stopping it. The miracles continued to unfold in the form of unreal signs in nature, mystical people, visions and more sand dollars. At times my analytical mind wanted to call it coincidence but as I began to let Controligion go, the magic grew too big for the human brain to deny. I am in heaven and I did not have to die to get there. How great thou art.

There are days I feel totally immersed in my soul. I am unlearning who I was conditioned to be in order to become who I am. It is a transition that at times is difficult. Even living in paradise, I find myself struggling with the change. The biggest problem is we get used to things and would rather stay in an unpleasant job, relationship, town, or role simply out of knowing. It is difficult for friends to understand back home and I become frustrated with people asking about men and boyfriends. So many people find it hard to believe a woman would go alone. Hell, I find it hard to believe. I heard rumors I left for a man and it infuriated me because that is who I used to be and is who I was trying to break free of. It is unbelievable to so many that a woman can be happy on her own and honestly it is still unbelievable to me. I even had a friend message me about a picture she saw saying "you look very happy, I am glad you have fallen in love. What is his name?" I am trying to fall in love with me, my spirit and the voice in me that has gained enough strength to finally be heard. I left for the love of me!

It is one thing to say it but another to believe it. I keep wishing to wake up one day and there it be; a feeling of total complete bliss in knowing I am enough. I believe it will happen, that it is happening but it is not an all at once knowing of oh, I love my self and need no one else. No, it comes in waves. Life is fabulous, but I still feel lonely often. There are days I feel happy, proud and fulfilled and there are days I cry. There are days I make it through only to watch the light disappear into night. That is when I leave my friends on the dance floor, walk my bike along the beach and cry. I cry for the beauty I see before me and the frustration I feel because I just can't shake the feeling I want someone to share it with. Not only have I been programmed to believe I am not whole alone, I can't perceive the beauty before me properly without a man to see it with me. I tell myself as I would my clients, it is ok to feel sad. We are not supposed to be happy all the time because happiness is an extreme emotion just like sadness. So I let myself be sad and try to focus on the lonely making it not my enemy but my companion, my friend. It is simply space now that I so needed. Just space, space that rather than mindlessly fill with others to make me whole, I am learning to fill with the creativity of my soul.

As I settled in to my new life, past patterns of behavior came forth—housewife, the cleaning, laundry, cooking. I poured my heart into those dishes that so often were left waiting for a man to maybe not show up until the dish had gone as cold as the ache in my heart. It is not the way to a man's heart. Who the hell came up with that? It is another colloquial construct keeping us under the thumb of a man-driven culture. The education and all the references, the repetitive knowledge obscuring any idea of my own forcing me into a number designating my ability as pass or fail. My reality only existed in a box that could be measured scientifically. I now ignored all things modern; research, news, television and even books I love so I can absorb myself in seeking answers from nobody but me. I purposefully refused work despite my unease. I have no income, hoping faith in my dream brings an abundant outcome. It took great courage to walk away from money and security. Never again would I settle for doing things simply because it was done that way in the past. To add more rebel to my rebellion, I go full force into doing things my mind does not want me to do. It was comfortable thinking others thoughts and being told what to do. From now on, if it makes me uneasy, then all the more reason to do it. I spent my entire life trying to do it correctly only to fail. I want to welcome mistakes now. Fall on my face if I must because for me it is the only way to step outside the box. Everything in my being wants to control it all except my soul, my soul wants to flow. Thus I denounced my formal knowledge in a quest to gain wisdom and evolve. We were meant to evolve.

I go to the beach often and get in the waves to symbolize washing it all away. I want to submerge in the unknown, like a huge wave sucking me under not knowing which way is up; emerging with a renewed respect for breath. I baptize away the conditions of my past hoping to resurrect my virgin soul, the one who loved, who loved every day waking up excited to the possibilities finding love in nature, playing outside with no respect for time. The little girl who secretly placed money outside the home of what she viewed as a poor man's trailer while she herself lived humbly in a not so dissimilar rickety wheeled house. The one who wrote stories, poetry and lyrics to songs she belted out happily without any care how it might sound. No one had yet told her different. Others' words had not yet molded her perception of herself, her talents, her soul's sauntering. No care in the world of what others thought, that was living free, and that is who I seek to be.

The ocean is healing and as each wave pushes me against the norm, I consider the idea of changing my name to symbolize a rebirth when I can finally say I have unfrozen my soul. The soul knowing love sending it one way with no expectation of return; the soul loving before rejection and pain, with no limits because there was no reason to have any. I think of sitting on the stand of my second divorce hearing as I told the judge I would like to change my name, and he shocked me with "and what would you like your name to be my dear?" I simply said my maiden name, but confusion at his question set in because all of a sudden it appeared I had a choice. Had I known I had an option I might have chosen something with meaning for me. "Someday do that" I tell myself as I step out of the baptism whispering to the sand and the sea "I love you unconditionally, for you have never given me a reason to doubt my ability."

The adjustment of learning to live in a foreign country has been by far my greatest adventure. I love the people and the way they do things on a whim. I was used to planning activities for some time in advance, but here they happen spontaneously. Mondays are now my favorite days. I have had more last-minute adventures occur on a day I used to dread. From waking up with a message from friends to meet at one of our glorious beaches for playing Frisbee, paddle boarding, a beach bonfire or simply dinner that we celebrate like a holiday. Many times we head off to Nicaragua for a day or two and end up staying the entire week. We don't make plans. We live based on how we feel in the moment no matter what day of the week.

I take great joy in the fact I relearned to ride a bike on nature-paved bumpy roads. David had to push me like a small child as he hooted and hollered when I finally remembered how to ride. I can even go with one hand now which is quite a feat but often necessary as laundry and/or recycling need to be carried in to town. I can fill my bike basket with a weeks' worth of groceries, clip my yoga mat on the back bumper, carry a sack of laundry in one hand and strap my purse over my shoulder. Adjusting to local time has been quite the learning experience. Life moves slowly here. When you accept it, you let go of the ticking barrier society created to keep us moving in a timely direction of their goal. I arrived here with a list of to do's, yet months later still trying to cross off, realizing I came with so many American ways that will drive you crazy if you can't let go. One being calling myself "American" like Central and Southern Americans do not exist or I own some right to have that label over them.

I am back in nature, loving the smell of dirt and rain. I am surrounded by animals, ocean, and sand. I am learning or unlearning all over again to not care about my hair, dripping sweat, my filthy feet or the dirt in my teeth. It is exactly as I once lived as a child, appreciating nature so, I spent my days engulfed in it. I recognize my irrelevance at the mercy of Mother Nature, yet I am larger than life knowing I am part of her glory more now than ever. The mile and half dirt road to my home in the pitch dark taught me appreciation of the moon and stars. Some nights I cannot even see my own hand but on rare instances the clouds break way and the sky illuminates my path so bright, I often stop wondering how I missed its beauty before.

The people here are like fairytale fantasy friends. It is unreal to me how kind they are. I have never felt freer from judgment to say and do and be me. They are teaching me what it means to live differently, to live a life exploring without fear. There is a group of women here that like me are fed up with society and sick of the way Controligion's men have treated us in its myth of matrimony. It is as if we know there is so much more we could not find in our homeland. It is incredible we all ended up here and something in me says there is a reason we are yet to see.

At one of the daily sunset gatherings, I met Jez[5], the free spirited gypsy and her sidekick Elisabeth. We became instant friends. Jez is a native and the most affectionate woman I have ever encountered; while Elisa is a spectacular demonstration of self-love in an earthy wondrous soul. Elisa can make a spiritual ceremony out of a normal day. The two of them have been best friends since Elisa first came to Paradise years ago. Both of them are in their late-twenties but wise beyond their years. We spent countless days on the beach just lying in the surf letting the waves crash over us or sitting outside my pool under the stars listening to soul stirring music with every candle we could find lit. They both can cook a meal and present it like it is Christmas. Elisa taught me how to date myself and Jez taught me how to find touch which I so adore in non-romantic ways. These beautiful women taught me to love myself and to step outside my comfort zone by celebrating life, every day like a holiday.

One of my fondest memories with Elisa is the night we acquired the inspiration to paint my dining room walls with wine. We had been sitting outside with candles burning, under a star lit night sky smoking my new found delightful pot, listening to soft spiritual sounds when we had the inspiration to cover the peach walls in my home because I often complain of the color. She spilled her glass of wine and the way it looked on the cement made me think the chaotic mistake would make a great reminder on my walls to appreciate the spills of life. So we painted my walls with red wine. After hours of experimenting we came up with a formula that made the most immaculate wall cover. We laughed and danced, rolled and splattered the secret wine formula on the walls like children discovering paint

[5] The biblical name Jezebel may have been tarnished because the beautiful exotic woman, proud of her looks wore makeup and had power. She was the Queen of Persia. As with all female suppression, control and jealousies altered perceptions.

for the first time. Those walls will forever be my reminder of the way it feels to be so creative and free to make mistakes that turn out beautifully.

Jez is just as free and loving. I have always teased my friends I am like a cat and just want to be petted, not rubbing you but rubbing myself on you. Jez takes petting to a new level. I remember the first night she stayed at my house. I felt uncomfortable at first because she often held my hand, kissed my cheek and then plopped down in my bed beside me to snuggle up. It took time for me to get used to this type of loving touch that was nothing more than that. She taught me to travel like a gypsy staying in hostels and hopping buses like hobo travelers. The first time she took me to the city on the bus; she curled up in the seat and laid her head in my lap. By this time I was pretty used to her loving ways, but it caught the other travelers off guard I suppose as they often looked our way.

When I finally decided to just let her love me was when my heart opened up more to the possibility that female friends can fulfill our need for touch in many ways. I grew up in a family where hugs were limited to special occasions. This lady hugs and kisses on a daily basis. She says I love you more than I have ever been told by one person and holds my hand the way two little girls would as they skip off to play. Jez's birthday party was another day that shook my script open as so many people gathered on her special day for breakfast that turned into a trip to the beach with a bonfire and then dinner and dancing. It was a spectacular day that only a woman with so much love could bring so many amazing souls together to celebrate.

Miriam is the least self-serving person I have ever known. She saw me sitting alone for lunch that first time I traveled on my own and came up to make me feel at home. From that moment I knew I could lean on her for anything and now she is a huge part of my life. She is originally from Columbia. I love her spicy attitude that she portrays jokingly to divert her kind heart. She loves unconditionally; making everyone feel important. She is an amazing mother, woman and friend. I confide in her often and can count on her wise advice. It is no coincidence her name is the same as the great biblical female who heroically led all women fleeing their homeland. Miriam has made us all feel at home in our fleeing. When I was struggling to make the move to Paradise she often sent me inspiring words reminding me to relax. These beautiful women would teach me that letting go of worry is the beginning of wisdom, not the fear of God as the traditional biblical Proverbs wanted us to believe.

Amos

With such amazing friends my time became wrapped up in all the fun we were having. But being the dedicated person I was programmed to be, I made time to call John almost daily. I was committed to see this through, and somehow felt obligated to him. He was still so upbeat when I called. I worried that I may be the only consistent peace in his life. Some of my friends knew the story and believed he was lying. They told me to be careful, I was too nice and gullible. I did not care. I had seen the conditions he was in. He is human, he is suffering and I do not think he or any human, any living creature deserves such conditions. The only thing he can tell me is any day now he could be released. The anxiety when I called was not as bad but I still felt an urgency to have it all together to make the ten minutes count. It was very daunting when I did not speak to him for days, knowing there was a fight almost every day and people were killed. The phone was often pulled out of the wall in those fights so then I had no contact, leaving the worry to grow.

I am not sure if it was my worry over John or the going out to party, staying in to party, oh who am I kidding, it was the partying; nevertheless at some point I found myself unable to write. Although the book was in my head, almost haunting me, I could not get it out on paper. It began to have a life of its own, keeping me up at night saying things like "I have to have room to breathe." It was begging me to let it live but I could not force myself to write even though I was being flooded with ideas and wisdom I was unaware I possessed. I would try to sit at my computer but there began to be interruptions daily from phone calls, friends popping in, messages, and adventures to be had. There was no time for my words. It is a process that requires an entire day and once you start, interruptions make it nearly impossible to get back in the flow. So I put my words on hold. It is no wonder it began waking me up at night annoying me with words just looking for home.

A few months passed in which I lost my words and myself completely to the party life as I began trying to fit into something outside myself again. I had not been with anyone since John even though I had resolved to just be his friend. Funny how even a man behind bars can keep me prisoner. I was not sure why I was feeling down but I quit writing to focus on editing, and the desolate days started to blend into one big meshed lonesome on the verge of depression. It was the perfect setting to meet a frog, right? And there he was. Cute, charming, well-traveled but of course he is, I mean come on you are meeting him in a tourist town. I had seen him around town every so often. He was always alone. A couple of nights he sat with me and my friends during sunset drinks. Every time I spoke with him, I became more interested.

On my friend Jez's birthday, we started the day with breakfast. I was delighted to see he was joining us. Something about him made me want to be closer to him. I wanted to know more about him, but more than that I just wanted to be near him as I patted the chair for him to have a seat beside me, then scolded myself for being so obvious. We talked for what seemed like hours only periodically engaging our other friends present. The breakfast party moved to my house where he charmed me playing my guitar. The seduction (and I do not use that word in a sexual way, it is never about sex for me, but a yearning for a soul connection) continued as we all loaded up for the beach, musical instruments and all. On the drive, he smoothly coached me on how to drive my stick shift down the wobbly roads. He was so patient, and it was in that moment I thought "wow he could be the one." Oh, I do hate I thought that now, but it is what happened and so I lower myself to honestly portray what a sap I am.

The day on the beach ended in a fabulous beach fire while the sun set. He continued to play my guitar and sat near me at every chance. We went to dinner back in town and continued to talk about all of our similarities; travel, nature, adventure, music. He took my keys and drove me home. Huge! I have met many men, both locals and travelers that do not drive so a man that can has become a turn on. We sat by the pool, this time alone for the first time in twelve hours. We appeared to have so much in common. He said he wanted to change his travel plans because he was leaving the next morning. He said he would go but then come back in a week. He wanted to get to know me better. I believed him and the kissing began. My mind raced with how remarkable it might be if this was him. He seemed so in to me. I was convinced having so much in common there was no way this was simply another frog. He was adventurous, handsome, and a very good kisser. I debated with making him leave but it just felt so right and I did not want the night to end even though I had to be up for yoga and he was leaving. I mean come on, he is changing his travel plans to come back and spend more time with me.

He was extremely passionate and since it was recently added to my list of commandments, I am going with it. "Afraid of passion," pft, move over Italian Stallion. And so I let the knight undress my soul as I tried to feel free hearing my girlfriends' voices tell me "you need more sex, it is natural and you should not feel guilt, you are a single woman." I was still so insecure and simply glad it was dark so my body would not show. Still it was fabulous. I will spare you the details and just say I think more men need to be interested in making sure the woman is satisfied first and foremost. You are going to enjoy it, that is a given. You should not be allowed to take pleasure until you are sure your woman is pleased. Okay, so I was pleased. Thank you very much. Passion achieved.

He left early morning. Exhausted from no sleep, I pulled myself up for yoga and rather than nap spent the entire day checking in with my facial expression just knowing I was grinning from ear to ear. I was feeling ecstatic despite the exhaustion. I did not hear from him until late in the night but just the short message he sent continued to fuel my desire to spend more time with him, to hope it was him, seeing it as a sign he was thinking the same. My girlfriends were all ears as I explained how sweet he was and how much I really liked him. I gushed to the point I had to catch myself knowing I was probably going overboard way to soon. The next day the brief texts continued and I braved it up enough to send a Happy Valentine's message to him only to feel depleted at no response... hmm why did it all stop?

Later that day, I met friends to watch the gorgeous sunset. Even though I had not heard from him I was still grinning from ear to ear over my lovely love experience. A mutual friend came up to the bench where Elisa and I sat. He approached Elisa saying "do you remember Amos?" Elisa shook her head yes trying her best not to look my way. "Well, this morning he was dead set on coming back here in a week but then last minute he decided to go to Alaska, because do you remember Lois? She was here a few weeks ago?" Elisa said "yes." I remembered her too but said nothing as my stomach began to turn. "Well he chose Lois over this" as he swept his arm to show off the sunset. It took all I had to keep my eyes on the stunning sun liquefying into the sea. I reminded myself to just breathe.

"Look at the beautiful sky, the birds" I told myself as the fire in my heart began to melt my eyes. I silently cursed my heart thinking "it is now I hate you. I hate you for being open; for even thinking there is a chance. I hate you for the feeling you cheaply handed me that night, putting a grin on my face all day and then so suddenly ripping it away replacing it with foolish pain." I was stunned by the amount of pain rushing over me but even more surprised I was not breaking down in a freak of tears given the intensity. It was a soft sadness, one slowly sucking the grin from my face as it drowned the dream in my head not just for what we might have been but for the fool it seems I always am. My mind tortured me with "see they are all asses." And "why in the Hell would you not ask if he was single?" The heat in my chest and the heaviness in my heart felt like I was bearing my pain for all to see. I smiled at Elisa who knew all too well what was going on inside me. Neither of us said a word. We just fakely smiled.

I gathered my wrecked soul and walked my busted spirit home along the beach. I tried desperately to stop the ache in my heart, the throbbing in my mind, to no avail. I questioned whether or not to message him but knew all too well he was not wasting an ounce of thought on me. So I fought the urge until late into the night as an early attempt at sleep left me tossing and turning hating my heart and wanting to cry. I decided to stop being such a dishrag about midnight and sent a message. "I did not know you had a thing with someone else and had I known I would have never let you stay." Then of course I beat myself up that it was in no way Zen. I have got to try and be more open to love without receipt, I thought. A true soulful person would wish happiness despite the pain they were feeling. So the softy in me gained enough strength to emerge and say "I am not judging you, just stating my stance. I wish you love."

The messages did no good for my heart as the days that followed hurt. That small speckle of sweet tore a hole in my heart. I am always amazed at how emotional pain physically hurts. It is why some people cut, and/or go without food. Hunger pain, cutting pain briefly distracts us from the heart pain. It in many ways feels better. I get it. I want to cut, I want to starve, I want to drink and stay drunk. Numb the pain, my mind begs me. But I do not. I cannot be a hypocrite after all these years telling my clients "feel it to heal it". And so I do. The heat rose in my chest around my heart and sent a knot to my throat every time I thought of him. Knowing even for a brief moment love can feel so nice makes me fear and crave it all at the same time. I wish I could stop my ruminating mind from yearning for more. No, maybe it was not true love and maybe I am wrong to be so open, to be so accepting, trusting, and forgiving. But maybe I am right and maybe one day it will pay off. I am smart enough to know it is simply the feeling I want. Maybe another man can do the same. But for now my wild heart starves for more like it has been malnourished and will consume anything.

He was in my thoughts all day as the sleepless night drained my eyes. Not only was my heart physically hurting keeping me awake, but my sweet dog was sick most of the night. Animals have a difficult time adjusting to the climate here. There are many risks from tick fever to poisoning from frogs and a hundred other dangers. I held her fatigued body in my exhausted hands as we made our way to the hole in the wall vet clinic. I was so heart sick thinking my one and only true love has been ill now for four days. I felt guilt that I was off partying and wasting time on a man who drilled a hole in my heart while the one that really loves me could be dying. I had thought it was just something she ate, but now "what if I am too late? " I berated my broken spirit even more.

The makeshift clinic was so hot, muggy, and smelly. But it is the best a village this size can do. I held her tight as I helped the vet administer the IV this time in the left leg because the right veins all collapsed. She dug her sweet head hard in my chest as we administered the meds. The vet had to leave because she was needed in another village for an emergency. She showed me the rickety cage we could put her in for several hours until she could get back to look at the blood work. I was not about to put her feeble body in that uncomfortable cage nor did I want to leave her. I had ignored her symptoms too long to selfishly fulfill my needs. The kind veterinarian had just met me, but I suppose she could see my pain as she volunteered me the keys to the clinic so I could stay and hold my one true friend while the meds dripped in her veins. Six hours later we headed home sweaty from the heat, filthy from the dirt, energy gone while my heartache raged on. Despite being grateful my dog was going to live, the pain was still so strong. I know it is just a nagging in my chest for me to change something, for me to wise up, for me to learn. I have yet to find someone who can be authentic with me. Maybe it is I who is lacking.

I sat outside for the next few nights trying to ease my suffering. I knew my lack of control over my negative thoughts was to blame. I am normally a very positive person but when I allow a man in and it turns to muck I beat myself up for moving too fast, for my body, for expecting love in return. *Fuck! I don't know. I always do this. Turn it in on me and try to dig deep to be a better person. Is it me? Is it my actions? Is it my body?* I always hide it best I can. I hate the scars. I try my best to focus and soak in the energy from the mystical night stars while the thought "not a place on my body without scars" destroys my attempt at peace. Is it some cruel joke? Then as if the starry night was twinkling words of wisdom, I tell myself, "No. It is a lesson. It is a lesson on loving self from within." And my heart released the pain momentarily as I considered, "Maybe those of us who need self-love most get inflicted with outer flaws to force us to look and see the beauty in." And once again I knew the message was for me to work on loving me.

The bit of relief I felt from listening to my soul gave me hope this pain was going to end. But when I was just about to get him out of my mind an apology message came in. Telling me in response to the Zen message I had sent, "such kind words from someone I hurt. It takes a big person to do that. Thank you, I am truly sorry." For a moment I felt it was sincere as tears began to flow at the relief there may really be love out there, while I still was slightly hoping it was him. Moments later my beautiful friend Elisa messaged me that she told him I was hurt. Boom! There it is. Not a sincere authentic *I know I am an ass* apology from him, but an, Oh no! Someone else thinks I am an ass so let me smooth my own fucking path, not yours. Amos may be an ass, but life goes on and so I say "NEXT" and alter the list with "plays music," "knows how to pleasure a woman" and beside honest I added "to a fault." I was still so furious and just wanted someone to for once in their life be brave enough to tell it like it is, not how you want it to appear.

The Commandments

~~Higher education at least a master's degree and~~ interested in continuing to learn

Financially stable ~~in a professional career~~ doing what he loves

Family oriented – maybe already with a child since I am not having more

~~Crazy about me~~

Reads

Writes – journals, ~~poetry~~, love letters, etc.

Honest to a fault

Display affection daily, kindness and respect

Romantic

Loves to travel

Athletic

Handsome and HOT

~~Tall~~

~~Hairy Chest~~

~~No Tattoos~~

Loves to dance

Loves music

~~Crazy about me~~

Loves animals

Loves even my flaws

Loves to touch me ~~because he is crazy about me!!!!!!~~

Respectful of others

Listens to me

Proud of me

Confident

Loves good food and wine

Sensual

Bilingual

Single

Enjoys conversation

Able to remain in the moment

189

Over past relationships
Spiritual
Zen
Adventurous
Practices yoga and meditation
Free
Passionate
Plays music
Knows how to pleasure a woman

1 Corinthians

The daunting pain woke me up. It is amazing how when we are not experiencing emotional pain, we forget how badly it hurts. When it hits, man it is almost unbearable. I bore it though. I wore it bravely knowing stuffing it away would only bring it my way again and again. I talked with my girlfriends about it and I put a plan in motion to work on me doing whatever it took to heal. I realized it was not about Amos at all. I am the one who holds on to such constricting beliefs of commitment feeling half a woman without a man. I could run all I wanted from status quo and even live in a land where he is not allowed but the problem was he haunted me in my head. It was time to snuff him out.

I attended a moving meditation with spiritual Elisa. It was one of the bravest things I have ever done. I sat in the outdoor temple in silence as we had been instructed on a huge pillow placed on the floor. The view of the sun setting over the ocean was spectacular and had I kept my eye on that scene my nerves would have eased. I was unsure as to what was about to occur as I watched eclectic groups of people step barefoot on the dance floor, slowly chanting and twirling about like kids uninhibited by societal rules. Music began. We were instructed to stand in our own space on the floor and allow our body to move as it pleased. Some people began swaying and swinging their arms about, others did yoga. I watched then began to sheepishly move as the rhythm of the music picked me up slowly. Before long people were stomping and screaming in tribal like fashion. It was so moving to see others be as free as I have always struggled to be. No judgments, just moving as much as the body pleased.

I am not sure when it happened but I turned my attention inward and no one or nothing mattered. It was the most freeing activity I have ever done as I stomped and swayed and even sat smack down in the middle of the floor when my body said to while others twirled all around me. The sweat dripped from my every last body part. It was over two hours of dancing like indigenous tribesman.   I have never felt more in love with my body and the way it moved that day. To let your body do what it wants to do is a form of self-love giving permission to just be. It was something I would have never done in the past. It was one of those uncomfortable things that did not fit any form of Controligion I had been preached and that is why I did it and will do it again. I want to dance like my ancestors full of joy for the earth. I want to dance free in honor of them, for the little girl inside who used to dance the same and for the ones Controligion shunned and labeled all their rituals sin. Yes, I want to sin, not fit in.

It would be the beginning of me delving into more extreme rituals. Not long after we attended a chanting concert by a famous musician who sings and chants mantras to music. Elisa and I sat in meditation as the songs put us in a trance. Spiritual growth begins when we let go of stories from our past and let the universe write a new script. It's the tool I'm beginning to see will finally break the spell cast over me.

Still, it was time for more work on me in a drastic way because I had all but quit writing. I still felt this nagging that I am not enough on my own and my idea to write was a silly dream. I began researching more ways for me to stretch my understanding of meditation. I looked into India and Peru online. As if life could not hand me more

192

signs, my girlfriend Jez told me a few days later she had a plane ticket she wanted to use for Peru before it expired. We began making plans to go. We asked Elisa to join us. Everything once again began to unfold perfectly from Jez getting her visa to travel to Peru just in time to one of my mentors from past psychology conferences writing an article on who to contact for spiritual retreats in Peru.

Within a few weeks we had the first part of the trip planned leaving the last few weeks open for adventure. We flew into Lima with our backpacks in tow. It was the first time I had traveled so light and it was liberating. I wanted to totally absorb myself in another culture to try and undo my ego's programming. After all I am beginning to understand more and more as I step out of my heritage how we are born a pure beautiful soul slowly tarnished by one sided beliefs depending on the culture, political structure, religion we are exposed. I often wonder who I would be if I had been born into another world. Would I feel the need to adhere to that script as well? I want to douse my brain with ideas from afar to jostle it free of the rigid beliefs of my past. Open it up and unshackle my own ideas, my own voice. I want to eliminate my patterns of chasing men for love and learn a new way all together.

I only slightly researched the place I was going; just enough to know there would be exposure to ancient traditions but not enough to allow my analytical mind to begin the process of condemning it. All I knew was there was a wonderful woman waiting to meet me who had studied with Shamans and I set up an appointment with her for an Ancient Andean healing. Lima was a nice city but it was just that, a structured city. I was glad we were only staying one night. The next morning our flight to Cusco was a bit scary. The plane took off and moments later turned around as the captain announced we were heading back to Lima. My first thought of fear was quickly replaced with "damn, I am going to miss the healing." They herded us onto a new plane and we were off at least an hour behind.

Paz Y Luz[6] is where we were heading which translates to peace and light, exactly what I need. The center had arranged a taxi to Pisac. The mountains and green blue of the foliage were beyond beauty as we traversed the windy roads to the little village. I tried to curb my frustration all the way that we were running late and there may not be enough time for the Andean healing with Diane that I felt I so needed. We arrived just a few minutes before my appointment. *Such a crisp place* was my first thought. I could feel the energy of this sacred peaceful healing zone. I had no clue what I was in for with the healing and frightened at what might come up.

My heart was still carrying the societal opinion that maybe I was damaged due to my parents' divorce or something I might have suppressed. Check in took longer than expected so by the time the peaceful host took us to meet Diane, I was shameful we were late. She graciously does this healing thing for donation. Meeting her changed my mind as her calm hug eased me. It was however too late for her to visit with all three of us as she explained she could meet with only one. Again the disappointment that things were not as I had planned crept in but Elisa and Jez quickly pushed I go ahead. Feeling guilty, I half-heartedly entered her house.

She took me upstairs where a yoga mat was placed on the floor. I could feel my heart begin to flutter at the unknown I was about to experience. She was very calming as she asked me a bit about myself. I revealed to her I had just moved to Paradise after selling my practice because I wanted to try and follow what I believe to be my passion,

---

[6] Paz Y Luz though magical, is a real place. It is located in Pisac Peru. www.pazyluzperu.com

writing. I did not tell her how hard that move was and only briefly told her I was anxious because I only had a year or so of income to make it on. She smiled a wise smile and asked me to lie down and close my eyes. For the first moments my mind was focused on the pounding in my heart. She told me to relax and just notice the images I saw then let them go. She said to breathe and imagine a white light out of the top of my head while expelling my negative feelings to Mother Earth. She said some name I was unfamiliar with in reference to Mother Earth but I went with it. With my eyes closed, I had no clue what she was doing but could tell she was standing over me. My heart still throbbing, I felt drops of liquid mist hit my body. It appeared she had spit on me. I quickly tried to calm myself saying "go with it, you do not understand everything nor do you need to."

There was soft chanting music in the background as I began to feel the wind off what might be a fan waving over me, but later I realized it was a feather. I began to have trouble breathing. But then there was calm as something burned in the background a relaxing smell. I inhaled as if for the first time while bell sounds and maraca like instruments shook over my body. Diane placed cold sacred river rocks on my eyes, mouth, forehead, chest, belly, hands and legs. The ritual continued with more waving of items, leaves I think and then more bell sounds. I began to calm and that is when the sadness hit. I saw my life with my first husband which made no sense to me as I was sure I was over him. I mean that was over ten years ago. I tried to push it out of my mind but it just kept popping back in consuming my experience which irritated me. I wanted to fix my life now not that thing I was so sure I had healed. I felt sad all over again as if I was right back struggling with the decisions to either stay or go in a relationship that was not serving me.

I saw the first time I met him as a child at the ball park which shocked me to recall because our son played that sport. I had forgotten where I met his father at about the age of seven. He was so kind and I remember thinking someday I might want to marry someone like him. I saw us playing football in the street by his house, being in the junior high social club together and working a St. Patrick's Day dance. We were great friends enjoying tons of laughs at the antics of my silly cousin and his younger brother who too were best friends. The images remained in childhood and only briefly touched on our meeting again in college and my expectation I was marrying my best friend. How could it go so wrong? We grew up together, laughed together, and my first thought upon meeting him was that someday I might like to marry someone like him. I felt Diane place her hands on me. It was as if her hands went inside my body. There was warmth that soothed my aching heart as her hands went deep inside my chest. She then went to my stomach and again I felt a deep comfort as her hands appeared to enter my body and soothe the tension. I felt tears begin to enter my eyes. I flashed forward to my current life in Paradise and the choices I had made to move. There was fear and confusion over my decision that began to subside as she pushed into my abdomen.

As the ritual ended, I lay there wondering what had just happened and why I was still crying. I sat up and she told me her impressions. She said I had a blockage in my gut chakra and that related to past traumas and issues with my identity. We discussed the visions of my son's dad and I cried even harder telling her I thought I was over my first ex. She said but it is old past trauma as far back as childhood or even further. I was perplexed with the "childhood or even further remark" but quickly realized I had not told her I met him in childhood. Tears flowed from my eyes as I told her he was my childhood friend and I thought he was my best friend. I couldn't even talk to him now without an argument. I so wanted us to be a family and be together in raising our amazing son whether we were married or not.

I told her about my move, giving up my practice and my worry over finances and finishing my book. She said the most powerful amazing thing I had ever heard; "You will not run out of money, you will not run out of time, and you will not have to go back to doing what you were doing." She told me to focus on myself, work on self-love, and to stop the worry because it was blocking my creative energy. She said to not even think of finances again so my creative energy would unlock and stop editing my book and just flow. (Now how in the hell she knew I had been editing for the last three months instead of completing was beyond me) Diane told me I had always felt like no one was there to support me. She said it will have mental, spiritual, and physical effects to have a chakra blocked. I ask if that's why my lower back always hurt and she answered "yes, it is due to lack of support." I cried now out of relief. She knew so much more about me than the brief introduction. She inquired about my son and if he supported me. I said "yes, he is probably the only one who really understands me." She said "then he is the only one who matters," I cried even more knowing she was spot on.

I called him all the time to check in with how he felt and time after time he said the most remarkable supportive things to me. From "you do you, Mom," to my concern over not going home for Easter and his answer being, "Mom how many times have you spent Easter with the family?" Knowing full well my answer would be every time and his response being "then you know how it goes. So why don't you for once, do you." I felt a renewed since of freedom but also a bit of worry at crying so hard over my ex and that childhood story. I wondered if there was something else in childhood I was still suppressing because the tears were so heavy.

We got up early the next morning to go meditate at the ashram in town. We had simply seen a sign posted on the Paz y Luz reception window about free meditations. When we arrived, a man stepping out the door, said they were going up the mountain to meditate on top. A tall man with a funny furry hat then exited and said we were welcome to join. He hugged me long and lovingly whispering in my ear "our teacher is here." He pulled away looking deep in my eyes as if sending a signal that I should know who he was talking about. I thought to myself how odd as I contemplated if he was referring to God being everywhere. People began to come out of the Ashram to join us out in the cool morning air. I have never seen so many people emerge out of a building as I did that day. Most of them were younger in their twenties maybe early thirties. I can only think to describe them as a diverse hippie group. It was grand luck to be invited to join such an eclectic bunch. I reminded myself how adventurous life is when I go with the flow.

The hike was amazing up the Pisac ruins. All the way up there were questions from the group as to who we were and how we found out about this meditation. It became clear we were joining in on a ritual they had planned for some time and even paid to attend. One girl pointed up ahead in the line to an older gentleman explaining to us he was the leader, the "teacher." She said he was a famous Romanian meditation guru. They were all in attendance for this man, and many of them follow him around the world. "How amazing" she exclaimed. She could not believe the luck we had for simply dropping in on this occasion. We sat for one hour inside an ancient ruin overlooking a spectacular view of the sacred valley and meditated. It was a remarkable end to my Andean healing and wonderful beginning to what would come next. We exited the group laughing at how miraculous it was that we stumbled upon such an event.

That eve the three of us met with a local Shaman who made an offering to Mother Earth. We put our intentions on coca leaves to be placed in the offering packet to be burned. I asked for love, creativity, and freedom. I was not sure why I asked for freedom I thought as I placed my hands over the sacred offering. The Shaman told me I was in a good place to find love and said he would heal my blocked chakra. Elisa had suspected this chakra block was also blocking my sexual energy. I had confided in her several times my frustration, insecurities, and feelings of guilt over sex. The Shaman ritual lasted three hours. We ate an amazing dinner and went to bed early exhausted from all our healing.

The morning was crisp and clean with excitement at what the rest of this spirit journey might bring. We did yoga in the gorgeous glassed in yoga room with breathtaking views of the sacred mountains. We had a wonderful breakfast and then I went into town while Jez met with Diane for her healing and Elisa with another magical healer named Meredith. Both had amazing insights. It was so nice to have my wonderful friends there to share our experiences. I was reluctant to leave my new found sacred home but we already had tickets to Machu Pichu so we headed to the town of Ollantaytambo that afternoon by taxi and stayed at a hostel I had found online through reviews. Jez my gypsy amiga had warned me we would need to travel her way and stay in hostels to save money so I obliged her by choosing hostels with the best reviews, but hostels no less. At least the name said hostel but when we arrived it was clear this place was not your average hostel. It was so gorgeous Miss Jez kept saying "this is no hostel mama," which just made me smile. We ate a great dinner then off to sleep for our early morning train to the ruins.

The hike up to the highest part of the ruins was unreal beauty. At the top of Huayanu Picchu I sat in awe of past brilliance, grateful for my experience and my new sense of self. It was a paradoxical event to be atop the highest peak I have ever physically reached because normally my heart pounds with fear in high places. Yet I have never felt such peaceful serenity as my feet dangled off the top of the peak to the condor shaped Machu Pichu sight miles below. We each found our own serene spots and meditated. Then we explored the city below. The sights and sounds are one thing but to close your eyes and feel the energy, you just know something spectacular beyond human comprehension exists. It is unreal thinking humans alone built this.

We went back to the "not so hostel" hostel that was more of a gorgeous hotel for one more night, had a great meal and then did yoga in the cool green grass outside our room, playing like children turning flips, hand stands and all. We decided to stay and explore Ollantaytambo one more day even though the hostel had no vacancy. I told Jez from now on we could travel her way so we set out in search of another hostel. The second hostel we looked at this young Peruvian man showed us the room. He leaned into me on the balcony to show me the Inca face in the mountain above. There was a heat that came over me. I felt like I might pass out. As we left, I looked back at him and the feeling again overwhelmed me and I tripped going out the door. We continued to look for more hostels and even though I secretly wanted to go back to that feeling, I did not say a word. I wanted for the first time in my life to let life live me. After several other visits, we let Jez decide which one and to my delight she chose hot guy hostel.

On our return, I was disappointed because it appeared the receptionist was his girlfriend. I told myself "oh well, maybe it was just that the Shamans have managed to unblock my chakra and I am simply feeling what everyone feels." We unloaded then headed off to shop and find a bar. We sat outside on the tiny bar balcony drinking, dancing and smoking herb. We went back to the hostel drunk and ready for more fun. We were delighted to see drums in the office and asked to take them to the loft where hot man gave me the hot flash. To our surprise they let us take the drums and when we got too loud, they came up not to reprimand us, but to join us. Soon two more fellow travelers joined in and we drank, sang, smoked, played flutes, drums and just lived. Elisa and Jez went to bed and although I was sleepy, I decided to stay because hot man was sending me signals driving my nervous system over the edge.

He would touch me when he passed me a drink or the pipe and linger in the touch longer than anyone with a girlfriend should. He handed me bent bottle caps as if a sign to secretly say he liked me. It became apparent he was not single when his wonderfully sweet beautiful girlfriend opened up to me they were indeed a couple. She told me how they met and my heart sunk as I realized I was the fool once again. Elisa had already told me he hugged her all sexy too pushing his groin into her, so there it was slapped in my face again that my attraction is somehow flawed. I went to bed finally talking myself into the idea that the energy I felt off him was not real.

My sleep was all over the place and I floated in and out of my dreams. I had a silly dream that I had met my soul mate. We spent a couple days together getting to know each other in my dream and he was perfect. It was not until the second day or so that I noticed as he played my guitar that he did not have a hand and when I finally got the guts to say something, he laughed and coolly raised his pants leg to say "yep, and I do not have a leg either" The next morning, I laughed telling the girls about it. Jez asked what I thought it meant and all I could say was "no one is perfect." We all laughed.

I loved that we had left the last half of our trip open with no plans. It is one thing to be open to everything that occurs while traveling with an itinerary, but even more Zen to go no plans at all. That is floating in the boat downstream. Yep just letting the boat float is my new way of thinking. We chose to go back to Pisac because we wanted to do an even more in-depth healing ceremony. I had heard many people discuss the ceremonies offered for spiritual healing requiring you to drink a substance from the jungle. Medicine is what they call it. I had considered it when we first arrived but I was not sure and or ready for the potent medicines of Mother Earth they describe. By this time, however, I had already had such amazing experiences letting go and taking in all Peru had to offer. I wanted to be brave and try this ancient thing called Ayahuasca. After all, I am trying to live my life with no rules just my own intuition, and my gut was saying "do it."

We got back to our peaceful Paz y Luz, where this time we felt even more welcomed and at home. We had another wonderful dinner and discussed our fears of the ceremony to come. I worried I had some child hood trauma I could not recall that might come up. That is what I was hearing from others experiences and since Diane referred to past trauma being the cause of my blocked chakra, I was concerned for what I might learn. We went back to our room and hit the sack early to be fresh for the next adventure.

The night was restless. I worried what this "medicine" might reveal for me. According to Controligion, this medicinal plant may very well be the forbidden fruit the Bible speaks of in the book of Genesis as the serpent vine. I have learned so much about this sacred land. Controligion stormed in forcefully shunning many aspects of the culture by proclaiming everything not of Christian faith to be the work of the devil. I refuse to live in fear any longer or believe attempts to use intimidation to convert followers. I knew by now I had to do the medicine in order to find some way to break the patterns of my past—relationships that end with me begging for someone to get me, understand me, to beg me back, see my love, see who I am, a deep feeling of lonely that just won't ease and the fears that stop me from truly being me. Fear accompanied my every decision because my life was programmed by Controligion—a sugar coated form of terrorism.

I spent the morning alone exploring Pisac on my own and buying the amethyst I was told would keep others' energy from affecting me in the ceremony (keep in mind I was schooled in scientific ways not allowing for such nonsense as rocks, so this whole time I am working hard to ignore these thoughts). Beautiful Jez had prepared a light lunch upon my return and we sat outside under the warmth of the sun on a blanket for our last meal of the day because no food is allowed after lunch.

At seven in the evening, we headed to the Shamanic medicine healing ceremony. Hungry and tired but more fearful than anything of what I might discover about myself or of what I might feel having never done hard drugs before; I ignore rational thought to follow my gut. From the small amount of research I did, I am fascinated and terrified by the powerful "medicine." Healing by Shaman is still very common in Peru. One of the things that drew me to this country was the connection to nature and the spirit world.

We arrived in the round temple where cushions lie on the floor circling against the sacred walls. There are nooks reminiscent of Machu Pichu's spaces holding sacred relics, pictures of Gandhi, the Dali Lama, Buddha, Jesus statues and Inca relics all sitting in harmony. A bald handsome man wearing a poncho sat at an altar on the floor with candles, musical instruments, a bottle of what looked like brown ground wood pulp and an old stone cup. It was very cold so we grabbed blankets as the others had done. We sat together in silence until the bald man spoke up and said "no need to be silent."

We nervously laughed and then began to introduce ourselves. I noticed others had buckets beside them so we stepped outside the temple to find our bucket. For me this was the worst part. I hate throwing up in general—I mean who doesn't—but I hate even more for someone to see me. It is me at my weakest. It is not just that I feel weak but I feel the pain of the other watching and want to console them into believing I am okay when really I am not. One of my patterns—pretend I am fine when clearly I am puking my guts up. I have been told vomiting is part of the healing and actually welcomed. Still, I silently prayed to the new God I now know to go by many names and genders, Pachamama, that I would not need the bucket. We sat back down and then began to bond with those in the room out of fear of the unknown and looking for answers. Some people had done this several times, while others had never either. I asked the lady beside me who had boasted this was her third time, what her experience had been. She simply said "beautiful." We introduced ourselves and then we were shown the bathroom and told to look for the candle because it would be completely dark.

About nine that night, we began the Shamanic ritual. Each of us went to the altar and knelt on a pillow. We were asked to give our intentions to the Pachamama and then say a toast, "casak," I think I hear him say as I silently practice repeating the unidentified word. There are about twenty people in the room lounged against the circular walls preparing for this medicinal spiritual journey. The room is lit with only one candle and it is difficult for me to see. My heart started to pound as my turn got closer. Judgments clouded my mind; did I research it enough? Certainly not, I was trying to learn to be okay with the unknown, remember? I scolded myself for even asking and then scolded myself again for not researching enough. As I walked to the altar, I felt my chest pounding hard. I had in my head the three things I am going to ask for. I rehearsed vehemently my desires as I waited for the others to take their turn, telling myself to take my time and know I deserved this moment too.

I watched the Shaman fill my cup to the top and thought "oh shit" knowing full well the dose is based on what he believes your body needs. I wanted to ask him to not give me so much, tell him I have never done drugs before, but instead I slapped my controlling consciousness and told her to just shut the hell up for once because this is "medicine" not a recreational drug. I took the cup and closed my eyes holding it to my heart. Silently I asked for love, for creativity, and for healing of my past. I said it again in my head just to make sure I got it correct and then I guzzled the thick bitter pulp hard knowing if I stopped I wouldn't start again.

I witnessed the others sit down, grab their buckets and spit wondering why, but the thick bitterness on my tongue answered my question. The dry burn in the back of my throat lumped like cud. I headed back to my seat trying to hold it down while I sent a message with my eyes to Elisa and Jez, who were next, that I was okay. I was not. The Shaman said the effects can take up to fifteen minutes so I tried to make a mental note of time, calculating how long it took for each person before me and how long it would be before I felt something. I estimated by the time the last person goes, I should feel something. I spit the lingering bitter off my tongue into the dreaded bucket and rinsed my mouth out. I convinced myself this will just be a deep meditative state and assumed my meditative position. The shaman blew out the candle after the last person drank. I am surprised by the darkness. Worrying I might not be able to see to the bathroom, I reached for my bucket to make sure it was near.

Beautiful music began to play as the Shaman and his squad serenaded us softly. Off and on I consoled myself saying "you are okay" and "you are not going to get sick," while one by one I heard people throwing up. Throwing up their insides out, some even grunting loud painful sounds and all I could do was pray to be spared. This was no place to worry about social etiquette. I mean one poor man was so sick it sounded like a demon was exiting his person with each uncontainable heave. I tried to stay calm in my meditation. I felt my senses enhance and at times it felt like people were in my face screaming as their guts excreted. At other times I was all alone. My skin tingled uncomfortably and I gave myself a mental lashing like no other for doing this shit. I told myself what in the world were you thinking? You are smarter than this. I was so scared at this point, losing control taunted me.

I felt emotional pain that can only be described as torture. It was not physical but hurt so badly, every cell on my body ached emotionally. I tried to rationalize what was going on in my brain. I heard myself describing how the synapses were being flooded causing an oversensitivity. Part of me wanted me to shut up and feel it, while part was begging to get it out of my being. The emotional pain intensified and a heaviness smothered me, pushing me down, smashing me to the core. I felt so very alone and scared. I heard myself say this is the weight of the world. This is what suffering feels like and you my dear are experiencing every ounce of pain and suffering felt the world over. It now smelled rancid even though I could barely breathe. Although I was physically in pain, I still describe it in my mind as emotional. It hurt so badly in my heart and I begged for it to stop as I broke down in an emotional lump of sorrow. In that instant, an image appeared to me. I identified it as the PachaMama, but it has not human form. It was energy—peaceful, beautiful, pulsating light energy. It comforted me and I know it is God. It called me baby girl and took my hand saying "You are okay. I am here for you."

I calmed and the pain eased. It asked if I was ready now and said "I have to leave you again, you have to experience this on your own. But know I will be back." In the next instant, I was in a room. I felt so very alone and terrified. There was a fear like I had never felt nor do I ever want to feel it again. I had a moment of clarity and told myself, "You will never do this again, do you hear me!"

I am hiding, crouching down and my heart is pounding so loud that I try to silence it so as to not get caught. I do not know what I am hiding from or what could catch me, but I know it is not good. In fact I know it is horrific. In the next instance I am caught but rather than feel more intense fear, I feel relief. I can tell I had been hiding for some time. The exhaustion from hiding and the fear has made me somehow glad to be caught. PachaMama returns and comforts me. It is now I realize this is coming in waves and that whatever I experience will have an end with her coming back to console me each time. She eased my suffering enough to let me catch my breath and then I voluntarily went back to the vision.

Now I am standing in a line. I see soldiers and I see myself begging, pleading with every ounce of my soul to one soldier in particular. I explain who I am. I was someone but now I have nothing. My entire family is gone and I have lost my credentials but I am someone important. I tell the soldier if he knew who I was, he would stop this. I tell him I love him and beg him to see me. "See who I am because when you do you will stop this." I pleaded so intently my body shook the tears from my face to moisten the dry dirt. In the next occurrence it all began to make sense. Hunger overtook me and I strangely welcome it. The hunger pains are actually soothing for my soul and feel better than the pain in my heart and so what little food I have, I give away. Giving it away comforts my pain. I now know where I am. I am in a concentration camp. There is physical pain but the suffering that causes me the most discomfort is the thirst. I try to focus on the hunger, continuing to give my rations away to give myself some relief from the thirst and emotional pain. Hunger feels so much better. I beg another soldier but quickly realize this one is harsh and not budging from his orders. It kills my heart that he is so inhumane but I still tell him I love him because I can see under his controlling uniform, he too is in pain.

Again I find myself in a line. This time the soldier I see, I do not verbally beg, I have exhausted that option, but I beg with my eyes. I plead for him to know me, to see me, looking deep into his eyes I try to get him to see the love and I silently say I love you as he herds me into the gas chamber. We are crammed in, smashed so painfully close it begins to feel comforting. I wrap my arms around every woman near me, feeling an incredible bond. I do not cry, I am all out of tears. For an instant I want to hold my breath and kill myself so as to not die at the hands of another but then I have a feeling of connection knowing I am the soldiers and they are me thus I will die at the hands of us all. I have an overwhelming experience realizing if I breathe, I die, if I don't breathe, I die. It is all the same. We are all the same and in that thought, I felt love. The pain in my chest subsides as I let go of all fear and simply focus on breath to gently, peacefully, breathe my death.

The wave ended and I grabbed my bucket. I turned away from Elisa and Jez not wanting them to see my pain, knowing full well I had to battle this on my own. I puked what felt like buckets and buckets of suffering. I feared I would fill the bucket to the top. Every sensation came out of me in the form of vomit. The sounds, the smells, the fear, the physical and emotional pain all got expelled. Elisa placed her hand on my leg to comfort me and although I could barely move, I placed my hand on top of hers patting her and silently saying "I am okay." I was not.

I heard myself moan from the pain, feeling it might never end. Then just like that, it ended. I sat back placing my hand over my eyes, hearing PachaMama say "now cry baby girl". I wept so intensely for myself and for the pain of the world. I felt the connection to all things, rivers, trees, rocks, people, all of our suffering, all of our pain. Oh the pain. I told myself this is suffering, and I said it again Oh my THIS is suffering, holding my eyes and rocking myself for comfort. I began to feel peace as the tears poured down my face. The wailing weeping had all but stopped but the tears continued to run like a rushing river, literally pouring from my eyes like a waterfall. It was the heaviest tears I had ever cried. I could only think about the suffering and I oddly begin to describe it as beautiful, thinking to myself over and over that was some beautiful, beautiful suffering.

In an instant I knew that whatever we feel is living. This is life. I knew rather than beg outside myself for relief, I needed to find solace inside. In the moment when I began to breathe despite the gas filled chamber, I knew it was not the end but a new fascinating start. I just let go and breathed a new beginning. I had just begun to feel that it was over when my current life began to take on the sorrow and connections. I saw myself as a child and the heaviness I carried not being of this life but a past life my soul carried. I realized there was something about my childhood exasperating the alone but I was not sure what, maybe it occurred during infancy because as far as I could recall, I had good parents and pretty good experiences. Nothing was wrong with me due to their divorce and nothing was wrong with me due to my divorces.

PachaMama came to me one last time to tell me I have to let go of that energy. I have carried it into every relationship and she left me to see how each one had been a repetition of the past energy. My first husband, I begged just as I had the first soldier. That soldier was compassionate so I begged the hardest, staying with him the longest because I could see he might break free of the faction imprisoning him. I could see his potential and if I could just show him my love, he too would love me back and we would be free. It all made sense because the words I told that soldier were the exact words I told my ex each time I felt he was betraying me. I knew I had to forgive him as I had the soldier.

The second soldier I begged was my second husband, very harsh and unyielding. I would beg him to stop drinking, to stop yelling and despite my words of love he was not going to budge. His rigid program was engraved in stone like commandments of control. The third soldier I begged with my eyes was my business partner and just as I had been exhausted by the begging, I was exhausted trying to explain myself to her and so I stopped, simply begging with my eyes and sending love. The coldness she displayed while I tried to explain my attempts to breathe hurt just as much as it did in that line on the way to gas chamber. My credentials being gone and me giving up everything as I did leaving my practice; every pattern and choice I made began to line up.

The energy in my heart was not of this world. It was suffering and pain of the past. My fears were that same energy. My fear of not having water by my side. I take it with me everywhere. I almost panic if I know water is running low. My brief stint of not eating when my first husband left because the hunger overshadowed the pain in my heart was how I reacted in the concentration camp. My feeling of always needing to be saved and the begging I do in the beginning of any conflict trying to share my view and then quickly feeling helpless and not saying a word. The deep-seeded feeling I always need to escape something. How I am smothering in relationships, putting their needs above my own. The feeling I always need to defend myself and even fabricate my story a bit in order to make it spectacular enough to move another to see me. Giving away all my possessions and credentials and then desperately seeking for someone to save me. My desire to always be perfect so as to avoid any conflict and even my confusion with religion made sense now. As did my disgust with politics and my yearning to move to a country that has no army was perfectly clear, as was the reason I asked the Shaman at the ritual earlier in the week for freedom. I was simply feeling something from a past I could not fathom.

Then I was blessed with the most soothing feeling of love when I finally let go and breathed new life. I felt love like never before. I felt my parents love, my son's love, and my friends'. Everything I had asked for I realized I already have. I am creative, that is why I want to write. I am loved and I am free from my past. I understand everyone simply follows orders, orders of their upbringing, their religions, society's script, the orders from others that eventually cloud their own mind telling them who they are. What we believe to be true is the script we so desperately try to portray. If we falter from that, then who might we be? Our very struggle is about identity and maintaining self. If we lose our self then we feel we lose. But this is not true. We are all connected. The lines I was herded into my past life and the opportunities to beg were really me begging my life to be spared, but for what? For yours? I am asking others to give up themselves for me rather than accepting them fully for who they are. No one needs to see me, I need to see me. As I came out of it, I ask if I was hallucinating and then I cried hard knowing I was not. I was really there. I was in that camp and I suffocated.

I took a breath that filled my soul so completely I knew I would never again need anything other than breath. It has never felt more fulfilling than in that moment. The air felt like new life, new beginnings. There was an emptiness that felt full; full of comfort. It was me free from the weight of the world. The contrast of the suffering I had felt in relation to my present life was overwhelming. I was overcome with joy with the wisdom I was OKAY and always had been, always would be. I knew then and there I would no longer follow orders and that my own desires would be placed above all others. I know that in doing so I would be better for the entire world. We are all connected and what I see in others is simply a mirror of myself. I was the one with the issue of never hearing my own voice, never seeing my own beauty, never seeing me! It is no wonder I attracted people who I had to defend myself to. I never presented myself in a relationship as the full, authentic, confident, complete person I was.

I was living a lie, never fully allowing my voice or opinions to be heard in fear they would leave me alone to what I viewed as a pitiful self so I made relationships where there was none. Trying to love people there was no real connection to because I carried so much guilt for my choices I constantly tried to cover me up, so much so I lost my identity just as I did in the concentration camp. Alone and lost, desperately seeking for someone to see me—to tell me what they see. Tell me who to be. They could not see me either they were merely reflecting a lost soul carrying around a heavy lonely to be rescued. No one can rescue you from your past. It is work only to be done alone. Life kept trying to force me on my own and I fought it tooth and nail. I was unavailable and the mirror I received was unavailable men. Never fully listening to myself, I was never heard. Abandon yourself and you will get abandoned.

I came out of it feeling so very connected. Amid the tortuous chaos of my vision and discovering there was no rescue from outside, I reveled in the insight of serenity coming from finding peace inside. It was perfectly clear to me that suffering, much like natural disasters though horrific and destructive, is part of the natural process of evolution. Evolving us all eventually to a better place. Elisa was holding me when I gained awareness enough to be back in the room.

I whispered to her that I had to get out of there soon. I needed to be alone and I needed to process everything. We walked back to Paz Y Luz in the dark as the morning was breaking the night. It was after four in the morning. I had been out of it more than seven hours. I did not feel exhausted as one might imagine but exhilarated. It was such an overwhelming experience.

I felt good, but I said for several weeks after I would never do it again. I continued to process things for days and still continue to see patterns of my life lining up as if everything was happening in order to teach me lessons about life, about love. I never really understood the idea of past lives and I was not sure if I believed it, but I can say for sure that I do now. I believe we continue and we come back over and over healing and gaining knowledge evolving little by little. I believe the energy we come in with is the energy we went out with and why I continued in this life to attract similar energies. I went out an abandoned victim and came in that way. I still do not understand how my childhood plays into this. I believe it was good. But as I began to have relationships with men I attracted dishonesty and insecurity in souls so lost I was bound to never be found.

I understand I have never fully showed up; I have never been authentic. It is why I have gone back in writing this time and time again to make sure what I am saying is really how things occurred. Over and over I have discovered that even I had convinced myself at times of lies because I did not want to face the truth. I covered my past to be something I am not to fit the status quo. I covered my voice because it did not fit with the beliefs of my family, church, government, men. It is not an all knowing but it is further understanding. I have discovered this evolution will take time and more work, more meditation, more travel to learn more about

Mother Earth and our connection to all things. Awakening happens slowly like a tree growing. Which makes me want to worship Mother Earth more to nurture our connection. I am simply a lone tree on her soil, needing her as she needs me. My roots run deep wherever I roam. I need her nutrients, her water, her sun, her air. I will grow and change and someday die but today I am alive. Breathing in her fresh air and ever so grateful for the way it feels.

On our last day, we went back to Cusco for a night. I walked around the city chained with churches on every corner feeling the control of religion like never before. Knowing an overwhelming knowing in my heart that the Bible had to have been created for governmental control. In the past when I traveled I would go into churches and linger, wondering why I felt so disconnected, hoping for insight. On this day I knew as I walked in only to turn back quickly at the sight of the bloody Jesus and the smell of suffering overwhelmed me. I escaped the heaviness through the enormous old doors and stood outside trying to catch my breath. Here I am standing at what was once an Incan temple for these beautiful people so connected to nature now covered with Christian judgmental stones trying to demonize every belief different from Controligion.

I looked up at the heavens simply asking why? Why would people fall for such an institution that focuses on suffering, judgment, fear, pain? Why would women especially when we are born nurturers, simply wanting to spread love? I continued to calm myself with my breath as the answers floated down from the sky. "To keep us small," I thought. "It is failing now. It is the beginning of the end of Controligion because women are evolving past their suppression, as in all history where powerful people have been suppressed out of fear they will rule." I walked away from the church thinking, "We do not want to rule. We are too smart for that. We want to honor Mother Earth not demonize her nature. We want harmony, peace, love and freedom."

Whether or not you believe I lived a past life. I believed it as soon as I left the ceremony and the days that followed I knew it was real. My analytical mind came into play and of course questioned it but the information I have gathered since continues to push me in the direction of past lives and energy being carried. When I meditate I know it is true. I also feel love and wisdom during those times like no other. It is only when I am outside myself living that I question it but also why I am dedicated to meditation more now than ever. Rather than meditate only during crisis, I do it daily sometimes three times a day. As far as the specific energy Pachamama told me I was carrying, I know it is something real because I have felt it all my life.

I am reminded of the work on water and fueling it with intentions through words, video and music that either evoked positive or negative emotions and then freezing it. Positive emotional energy like love formed beautiful crystals where negative energy words changed the shape to be most unpleasant. Our body is mostly water so it makes sense every thought we have or someone else has can alter our state. It is why I became overwhelmed with my work, with my coworkers attitude towards me and to many people back home that are living a life searching for happiness outside themselves in material things. It is why I had to escape. I already had too much negative energy running in my veins. It was an inner battle daily.

When I first moved to Paradise, it was as if there was a pressure valve on me I could only contain for so long and at week's end, I had to let it out. There were nights I would leave my friends at the bar, all smiles, laughing and sending every ounce of love I had but then I would feel it. Heaviness would come over me and I would have to escape knowing it was about to pour. I could not even muster the energy to ride my bike so I would walk it along the beach and cry, not even sure why. But thinking it was because I needed a man because Controligion's coupledom always seeped in. I now know I am okay, I am a survivor. The work for me to do now is continue to clean that negative energy; my default so to speak. I could raise myself to a higher frequency momentarily but it was hard to maintain leaving me attracting similar frequencies.

This is all very interesting to me. I worked in energy medicine doing biofeedback of several forms and understood how one's emotional state can change someone else's. This is why we can feel tension when we walk into a room where people are upset yet we have no clue they just fought. If in fact I was in the holocaust then it makes perfect sense the loneliness I have felt since childhood was energy being brought into this world. It was as if my default was fear, shame and guilt which are the lowest of frequencies. Simply put, the way you feel is purely energy. It is what level or frequency you are running on. It is why depressed people cannot get out of bed. They have no energy. This was my norm and although I could lift my energy enough to be great for others, I quickly drained and had to escape myself. In relationships I depended on someone else for feeling and often blamed them for my own lacking. I was the victim just wanting to be saved by someone who had no clue what I needed because I had no clue.

In Peru, Diane knew I had an energy block and told me it was the sacral chakra. I had limited knowledge of chakras at the time but have since studied up and it all adds up to correspond with the concentration camp discovery. A block in the sacral chakra is often linked to past trauma and this is what Diane had said and why I worried maybe I had blocked some abuse. It was not, it was my past—my past life. I discovered that chakra is tied to survival issues. It rules creativity, intuition on a gut level, fertility, relationships with others, and sensuality—all my issues.

I began meditations to heal and although I have not been with a man since my healing I do feel more sensual. I feel tremendously creative, free to love and to listen to my gut, my goddess. I look in the mirror now and my body actually looks beautiful to me. I feel secure in being alone—the loneliness has lifted. I truly believe my next relationship will be the best yet because I am okay with myself, I am not looking for someone to save me and I will never again use another as a means of escape; escape from myself by marrying, by absorbing myself in my son, by absorbing myself in school or in work. Best thing I could have ever done was leave it all to force me to sit in my lonely and discover my truths. In doing so I found me. I found God. She is beautiful. She lives inside. See me.

Ephesians

The book of Ephesians was apparently written in prison. I am beginning to see the prisoner in many cases has been me. Trapped in a system I could not be free and constantly trying to break out with honesty. Oh honesty. I have gone back to the beginning of this book a hundred times adding things I did not say, altering things I convinced myself were true but only now realizing were not. Some things I told myself "just put on paper now and you can delete it later." Because it was so difficult for me to face, I had to trick myself into writing it down. But still when it comes to men, I have yet to have someone in a romantic relationship be honest with me. I now understand it was because I could not be honest with myself. Going back and adding the gunk to my story and telling it just as it is has started to open me up to loving myself. It is very liberating to write the difficult things I myself did not want to believe.

I did not at first put down on paper I had slept with someone before my divorce was final in my first marriage or that my second husband was verbally abusive when he was drunk. I did not talk about the sex with the men I dated and how awkward I always felt or many times I faked orgasm. I did not go into detail on all my insecurities until after my trip to Peru. At this point I had not even added the abortions because I did not find the inspiration to be that true until a trip you will read about later. What I was hiding from myself kept me in the dark. We select and edit the memories to construct the story we want to believe, we want others to believe. It is the most horrible prison of all to be trapped in the worry of what others think. I could not learn from my mistakes as long as I was hiding them. Now that I am accepting my past, I feel free.

The most difficult part I am working on since Peru is authenticity with men. I was expecting men to fall in love with who I was pretending to be. Trying to be everything society wanted: smart, sexy, and virginal all at the same time. I am not. I am insecure; I can be the biggest dumb ass and we all know now I have sex. But the biggest lie of all was that I lied to myself over who I was underneath, and still only now is it becoming clear.

I had the opportunity to go to another prison of sorts again to see John. This time I was excited to go. He wanted to hear all about Peru. Given my new found freedom in the truth, I committed to tell him all the men I had been with. I had briefly mentioned to him during our phone conversations but I did not want to cause him any pain if he was expecting us to be a couple. I have learned pain is inevitable and not my place to shelter someone else's by presenting falsehood. All I can do is be honest, present the facts and give him the freedom to choose. It is the bravest thing we can do, be authentic and true. In not loving my authentic self, I always got exactly that, others who did not love me authentically.

Allon and I made plans to visit the prison together again. It was different, there was no fear. I felt so good about going. It was not even the least bit disheartening when we again got separated at the prison entrance. This time I walked in proud by myself, looking at each guard and prisoner sending love to all with my eyes, just as I had in my Ayahuasca experience. When I saw John gallantly enter the prison courtyard, I screeched to see him and hugged him long. I had made a promise to stay in the hug longer, to not pat him away as I had in the past, unconsciously patting the back to signal the hug should end because it had begun to overwhelm me. I wanted to share the love I am learning to give without receipt. I would not even think about it as I began patting away people as if the little love I shared was enough. I don't want to hug like that anymore. I want to consciously hug, tight and long sending love from my heart to theirs.

It was a good hug. The connection to someone who has been deprived so long was obvious in my heart. I could feel his heart beat next to mine and either my heart filled his up or his mine. The exchange of energy was real and energizing. He has been in prison for seven months now and I just wanted to take his mind, his consciousness to another place if only for a moment to give him an emotional break. We remained in the courtyard. I suppose I should clarify. It is not a courtyard like you might imagine with plants. But an enclosed space with concrete floors, walls and ceiling in the center of the prison cells. The only life is human life, heavy from the jail. We sat on an old mattress John had covered in a tattered blanket. It was hot but neither of us seemed to care as we ignored our bodies agitated sweat to engage in conversation. I began by telling him I had been dating and he said he knew. He said you have told me this many times and I understand we are friends. With a big gentle smile, He said "you are living your life Julita." It felt so comforting and non-judgmental.

We only briefly discussed his situation. He felt even the original lawyer turned on him. He said it is all about money and she sold him out. He said he never told any of his family because he was the pillar of strength. He pointed to the concrete pillar supporting the strict concrete walls to give me a visual. I could see his discomfort discussing the situation so when he ask me to tell him about Peru I

221

did not push any further and obliged him with my story. He understood the medicine and said the state can also be achieved with deep meditation.

He said "what you describe is Samadhi. Now you know you are in this world, but not of it." I felt so much peace from him. But still if I am honest, there is darkness in his eyes, a mysterious dark like pools of black water. Calm on the surface but because you are unsure of what is below you dare not dip your toe.

I sat there in this fear evoking place, looking deep in eyes that underneath might very well hold frightening facts, realizing how my experience in the real or imagined concentration camp had taught me to find comfort within. I have never felt so much tranquility inside myself. I told John how I felt now and that it was very much like difficult yoga poses when outside is uncomfortable yet you are able to breathe in peace. He said "yes, and with time your perception of the difficult poses changes as you let go and they too become resting poses. It is just like you experiencing death in the concentration camp, letting go and discovering it was not an end at all."

We touched and hugged and talked and talked. Allon finally joined us and we sat on the old dirty mattress enjoying a picnic lunch. This time rather than anxiously grab some mass produced food at a last minute stop, I took my time planning the meal. We had a new vegetarian restaurant in my little village. John is a vegetarian so I wanted to get him something I knew he would love to contrast the rice and beans he had been living on. My friends at the restaurant prepared the best empanadas, hummus and assorted fresh vegetables that not only looked amazing with colors I knew his eyes were missing, but tasted so good I saw tears well up in his eyes. I have never enjoyed a meal like that with so much appreciation for the minutest details of the texture, color, crunch, flavor of everything we shared.

John slowly ate, holding the small pieces in his mouth longer than usual like he was trying to extract the sensations. He described to us how with the right perception, the prison could be seen as a palace. He laughed and smiled saying yes, if it was just me, I could live here, in my palace. We looked around in wonder of how this man can be so positive. But soon his face dropped the smile as he added, "The hard part is the people it hurts on the outside torturing the mind turning this palace back into a prison."

Before we left, I gave him a book about a horrific experience in a concentration camp. The author survived by focusing on hope and finding meaning in his life despite the suffering. It reminded me of John, all the times I have called and his spirit is simply uplifting. I wrote this letter in the book.

My Dear John,

I know you already understand survival more than one book can teach. I hope you find some peace in these words and feel a connection knowing you are not alone. You have lived through tremendous suffering but that too can be beautiful when viewed with an open heart. I look forward to the star-filled nights when we can lay side by side and share our stories. I am in awe of your strength but I am here to hold you, comfort your soul and cradle your heart. There is so much remarkable life left for us to live. This is just one street we must cross. Know that I hold your hand. Much love — Juls ♥

I can say sitting in that prison with John and Allon was the most immaculate experience since my Ayahuasca healing. Palace or prison it was peaceful and pleasurable from where I sat that day. The laughter we shared was so genuine. I hugged like I have never before feeling my heart open to whatever was in store. To smile and touch and love those two wondrous friends felt so amazing. I looked around the prison at everyone sharing with their loved ones and could feel the love softening the harsh prison walls. There was so much warm, gracious life on that cold concrete floor. I did not want to leave. I wrote John an online message as I often do when I feel like sharing even though I know he does not get it. It said –

The peace I felt today by your side was so beautiful. What a wonderful life it is to sit between two friends enjoying a great meal, laughing, hugging and simply breathing the same air. You would have thought we were in Paris, not a prison.
All my love,
Juls ♥

I did not alter the list. I have not had any romance since Amos. But I am beginning to feel immense compassion towards others including the frogs I bashed. Every one of us is trying to find freedom from a prison; actual or imagined. It is just one street we must cross. Know that I hold your hand.

Peter

Given my new-found freedom with honesty, I find it unusual that the ring I wore signifying my quest to face the truth went missing in Peru. A silver ring with the Tibetan double dorge symbol, I had purchased it at the meditation conference in California. The lady who sold it to me explained its many meanings. "Enlightenment and authenticity" she said and I grabbed it up declaring "I want that." I bought it to represent honesty with myself about what my inner voice was trying to tell me but over time it had become so much more. A symbol of being real, saying without fear of ridicule and for having faith. Faith that all I have experienced, whether I am proud of it or not, has been part of my life's lesson and other than turn people away from me will bring them closer.

I was heartbroken when I got home from Peru and discovered the ring was nowhere to be found in my backpack. I recalled dropping it the last day off the bathroom counter in a rush to leave. It looked as if it had fallen in my backpack and since it was not on the floor. I assumed it was deep down inside my pack as I cinched it up to leave. I have looked everywhere for it but since I am also trying to not be attached to things anymore; I have done my best to let it go. I told myself maybe I no longer need to wear a reminder since I am living my truth.

There is an odd emptiness inside me since my trip to Peru. It was uncomfortable at first but I tried to see it in a positive way knowing a lot of gunk was recently cleared. I finally had room to grow. Like my roots had been broken apart, shaken loose from their confined path free to explore vast spaces. I also felt as if there are alternative forces within me. Like two women at battle over who I am. One woman wants to be free and have these moments at her hand to rendezvous with whom she pleases, never tied to just one man but free to live moments of love, always new, always building and ending just as fast as it begins. Then there is the prude, the one who wants to be taken care of, loved unconditionally, routine day in and out over and over never having to think what tomorrow brings, and she wants marriage. Writing that out made me think on a whole, "how f'n boring." I like the first girl. Besides, second girl, you had your chance. Move over Prudie, Goddess wants out.

Well as luck would have it I met a man who would challenge my new free thinking spirit. I was at dinner with one of my many fabulous girlfriends. A live band was playing and people were dancing as always in this party beach town. My friend pointed him out saying, "how handsome is that man?" I looked up to see only the profile of a man with a camera blocking his face, and dark hair lapping over the camera base. He was a photographer in town but I had never noticed anything but this big camera it seemed he always hid behind. He had thick dark wavy hair, deep mysterious eyes and a scruffy beard. Oh the scruffy beard, facial hair just seems so masculine to me especially when it is scruffy. He was dressed in shorts and a crisp polo long sleeve with the sleeves rolled up, looking very European, yet quite hippie. I continued to watch him taking pictures of the band and dancers throughout our dinner wondering who he was.

Later that evening I went dancing. I was about to leave for my beach walk home when a drunk local grabbed me up and began dancing raunchily. I turned away to try and escape. There he was smiling, knowing his timing was perfect to rescue me from drunk man who was now getting way to close to my back side. I nodded my head towards the beach to signal I was on my way out. He grabbed my hand and pulled me gently off the dance floor. He followed me out to escape the loud music, where he introduced himself. Even though my mind was dead set on telling him "mucho gusto, see you around," the conversation continued as he amazed me with things he already knew about me.

He mentioned my writing and the yellow dress I wore one night. He said "I took that picture of you." I knew the picture. It was one of my favorites that had been posted on the restaurant's web site. The fact he would even remember something I wore months ago was fascinating. I had just noticed him a few hours ago. He became more and more interesting to me as we discussed, well me. The only thing I got out of him was that he was European. We talked for almost an hour stopping often to sit in silence to look at the waves, the stars, each other. He asked to walk me home. I was more impressed when he did not buckle when Miss Prude gave him hell with orders not to expect anything.

At the end of the beach, we stopped to look at the moon. He turned to me and I knew he was about to kiss me. Miss Prude stiffened, preparing to stop him. But he did not swarm in like all the men before. Instead he took a slow breath and placed his hand on my cheek. He stood in silence looking at me and looking at the moon. We took breaths together for what seemed like miraculous minutes as the heat between us built and our mouths were mere inches apart. In that space is where Miss Prude lost her ground. I was overwhelmed with a feeling the space created. It made me yearn for more space. It briefly got Miss Prude to shut her ass too because she was running in my mind telling me "remember your spiritual journey and you have been happy and alone since Peru. You don't need anyone, remember?" But none of that mattered as he moved in even slower, continuing to breathe my air.

It was the sweetest softest kiss. There was heat and energy that unbound my soul as the sound of the waves beat the shore. I just wanted to believe it was real, that this was it and every time he pulled away creating space and slowly moving in again my heart unzipped a tad bit more. I was so taken in, I can't remember how it stopped but I am pretty sure Prude put an end to it because she emerged again as we continued the walk to my house saying "you cannot go to my house." The mile and a half home slowly broke her down as I began to be more and more interested in him.

He was a traveler, with many stories to fit that hippie image I had first labeled him. It went from you cannot go to my house, to okay you can have one drink, to you can sleep in the guest room, but I am not making you breakfast. I do not cook! To me going into the room to make him comfy and not only sleeping with him in that room but moving on to my room to continue the madness. I did not let Miss Prude analyze, as I normally do. She can chill a pepper's spice. I just allowed with no fear for what this might be, what tomorrow might bring or the pain in my heart that could follow, that has always followed. I melted and it felt so free although I still hid my body.

The next morning I drove him home, not sure if I would see him again or if I even wanted to as he asked for my phone number. I just wanted to appreciate the moment for the beauty it was and not expect a thing in return. I went to yoga and then home to write. I had not been home long when my heart stopped to the sound of my phone ringing. An unknown number came up and I knew it was him. "He called me," I thought as I briefly considered letting it ring to not seem so desperate. But now that would not be honest would it?

So I grabbed it up to hear the most fn' cute hot accent say "do you want to stay together?" Prude had no chance, as the goddess in me said "yes" and that was all it took. We met for a beer and then headed back to my house to order pizza. We lay outside in the hammocks or should I say hammock as he snuggled in next to me to share a smoke and I told him a bit about my past. I told him everything about my trip to Peru, the Ayahuasca ceremony and how I begged soldiers to see me as I had begged my husbands to see me and the love in me. He listened so intently. I felt heard.

Hours passed, the sun set, as we continued to visit while his music played opening my mind to sounds I had never even fathomed; so Latin and sexy from Portuguese to Italian and Spanish lullabying me in my hammock. As if the night could not get better Mr. Porcupine who often traverses my back fence not more than five feet from the hammock climbed down from the tree to sit and let us know we were in his space. He moves so slow it is unreal watching him take his time like he owns the place. Well, isn't that living perfectly in nature, I thought because yes, he does. He owns the place as I mentally thank him for letting me share his space. Peter was also tuned to the nature sharing in the appreciation with me. It briefly began to sprinkle and the smell of fresh dirt lifted around us. I felt paradise flood all my senses as we continued to swing silently side by side. The rain stopped and soon the night stars emerged twinkling perfectly to the worldly sounds of his music while we fell asleep.

As I had the day before, I drove him home again on my way to yoga and later he texted to continue our rendezvous. He came back out that night to again listen to music and make out. By Tuesday we are just melting in the moments. I said screw it to yoga to stay in bed with him. Going through the motions again to send him home only to hear from him hours later that his photo shoot was cancelled and he was on his way out. There is this odd split second in my imagination when he texts where Miss Prude wants to grab the phone to text him "no" because he has been very honest telling me about his past lovers and there are many. But goddess grabs the phone first texting "come on over" every time.

We hiked to the rocky beach that lies beneath the mountain cliffs. The rain came perfectly just after floating and smoking in the pools left behind by low tide. We sat in silence back on the beach before getting up to escape the rain only to find ourselves stopping, not saying a word just stopping in the rain and standing side by side. We stood for what seemed like an hour in silence just soaking up a soulful of raindrops as the sun set. The thunder and lightning intensified appropriately matching the intensity in my heart growing fonder and fonder of not just him but the moments created in his presence. We did not run back home to escape the boisterous thunder and lightning show around but walked gently breathing in every ounce. It was perfect but Prude began to gain some ground noticing he pulled away from me when others showed up on the beach. She did not hesitate in pointing that out and added fuel to the fire saying "oh and he has not complimented you one time, it is obvious he is not that in to you nor wants to commit to you." I started on a whole to question it all but convinced myself Prude was Controligion programming and just as I had walked out of society's door, I wanted to slam the door in the face of virgin Prude.

Back in my pool, the rain continued to pour. We drank rum and wine and whatever else we could find stashed in my kitchen. We not just watched but saw the rain on the water like never before. The observations by him add such depth to my perception of things. What I normally see gently turns to match his poetic detailed descriptions. As in the moment he observed the rain drops hitting the pool water. On his knees in the shallow end, gently leaning against the pool wall, I watched this rain drenched man describe water on water making an effortless event appear extraordinary in his description. "I love how it goes up before it goes down," he proclaimed sipping the last of his wine. I sat beside him in wonder surrounded by warm pool water seeing what he saw as the drops danced on the surface of the water going up before descending into one with the pool water.

I battled discussing too much of myself out of fear for someone liking me for what I do/did accomplished versus just me. It is the mask I always wore trying to prove I have some sort of societal credentials. I don't want that anymore. But at some point the wine got to me and or Prude making me feel insecure so I boasted about my education, my practice, the brain, my past work, that I had created web sites in the past and even had one for photos. I asked if he had one to sell his photography. He was overwhelmed I could tell by the idea. I wanted to kick myself for bringing up business and ruining the monumental mood. I knew he was a struggling artist and searching for a way to make money doing what he is passionate about. Why did I have to feel the need to help him? Why can't I ever just let life unfold? He dove to the deep end of the pool staying under longer than I was comfortable with and I knew the symbolism of the deep end and his being in deep thought.

When he came back up he pulled me aside and said "this is too good to be true." He said he did not want to take advantage of me as others had. He said we will need to separate and ask "can you separate this so we can work together?" Then he began to discuss just being friends so as to not have me helping him. We discussed dualism and even though I respected him more than ever for recognizing my fault in giving and not being reciprocated it was silently killing me that the fairytale was ending.

I said something about going to yoga in the morning with me to change the subject and he said we should not be seen together. UGH! He was pulling away from me and fast. He tried to explain his opinions on life and said he did not want a relationship. I knew, he had said this before. He told me that is why he was no longer seeing the last girl. I just listened as I tried to calm my heart. He asked what I wanted and I could not believe by this time my heart had sunk so low, if I spoke I felt I might cry. Prude scolded me saying "see I told you he was too good to be true." I pushed the welling emotion down as I told him I did not know with a half crack in my voice. I could not believe I was holding back tears. "I mean its five freak'n days with a person and your heart is already gone," rampaged through my mind. When will I ever learn? He could feel the tension when he went in to kiss me to ease my heart but he knew the space had changed and he pulled back.

He said "you are cold now" and then he tried to lighten the mood. I knew I had to say my feelings if I was going to let go of this pain in my chest but I patiently waited to gain enough composure to say it with little emotion attached. I internally consoled myself until I could find the courage. I said "I want love, I want one person." I tried to turn it on him and that he was right, he is younger, needs to play and party and then one day he needs a family. I was telling him but truly I was merely talking out loud consoling and rationalizing to myself. Prude kept trying to tell me this is it, get out, get him out, but I wanted to be different and stay in the moment. I mean why should the verbalization of facts ruin the perfectness of the moment? Whether the reality is faced or not it is still the reality and at some point I am going to have to learn to accept life as it is. I did very well getting back to a place of calm fairly quickly, as we went in to dry off. Never in my life had I been able to gather my composure so rapidly as the pain in my heart began to soften. I was very surprised because in the past pain stuck with me for days, months, Hell, years. But it quickly changed back to that empty space I was learning to accept as my new normal.

The phone rang with an invite for dinner from my girlfriend Jez. I whispered to her that he was with me and she said, "It is okay, bring him." At this point Peter had been so honest with me. He told me he dated Jez before me and he was also with another one of her friends. He even fessed up he slept with another girl the night before he slept with me. I was gorged and awed all at the same time. I finally had a man that can be honest. "Honest to a fault" is how I added it to the list and now that I have it, I better appreciate it. The facts burned but I am surprised at how quickly it all heals. Be honest, I am reminded, it may cause initial pain but the respect it forges is so much more powerful. I am choosing this based on reality and the only difference from the other men I have been with is this one is not lying to me. He is giving me the freedom to choose what I want to do.

I reminded myself of all the lessons I had learned, how strong I am now and how I do not want to throw away what has been so beautiful just yet. Maybe there is something more for me to learn from this Latin Lover open sex stuff. I mean I have read about it. There are countries where people do not marry and they report they are happy just being in the moment loving who they share each moment with. I sat on the edge of the bed trying to open my heart. Peter came out of the shower and announced "we are going to the party." He just told me he thought we should not be seen in public together, that he does not want a relationship yet he wants to go with me to a party where at least two of his previous lovers will be? I do not say out loud any of this or question it further. I want to be with him and that is that. It is my choice.

It is a small gathering of about ten people, all of which I know well. I wondered how I would react to being in the room with his lovers. Jez dated him and she knows the other girls he has slept with in the room but only because I told her. But they do not know I know and I wonder how he will react, how they will, how we all will. Everyone mingles and I am surprised how I handle seeing him visit with the two women he slept with. In the past I would have felt so much insecurity, but I do not. Hell in the past I would not have even gone to the party. I would have sulked all night gorging my emotions with alcohol, food or both. But instead I am out in public enjoying myself, the conversations and the people around me.

I only periodically watch what he is doing, not to catch him as in my past but this time feeling my comfort, analyzing it and being overwhelmed the jealousy my exes always blamed me for feeling appears to have lifted. I feel so much confidence in me and in us and in the wonderful moments we have spent. It feels good to be able to stay in the moment with others and share conversations without my mind raging, blood boiling, while plans of action get designed in my annoying mind. I think back to Peru and wonder what else has changed in me. I say a gentle thank you for that experience, for this experience.

We continued the night following friends to a bar and then on to a house party. By the time we got to the house party, Peter was drunk and kept coming up to me despite his opinion we should not be seen in public. He even gave me a kiss in front of others. Confused but not at all disheveled by it, I continue to focus on how good it feels to be in the moment. Relaxed and free from the worry of trying to calculate his next move. It appears I am only playing my side of the board and making moves based on each moment.

He said he would take me home but I had to drive because he was drunk. He was so passionately all over me that Prude had no chance. She already tried to make me agree not to sleep with him again since he obviously did not want a relationship but Goddess won. I stripped off my clothes with little concern for my scars, not even caring how drunk he was. Well maybe it was why I got naked unashamedly knowing he was not conscious enough to see me and it was still dark. We only made out momentarily before he turned away and headed to the bathroom to puke. Now this could have easily turned into me thinking my body made him puke. Issues with body image are evil and love to take coincidental incidences to confirm the mental bashing. But again there is a change in me so my mind separated the facts properly. He was drunk. He was very drunk and although our time together has been consumed with alcohol, this was the first time I had seen it overtake him. I dressed myself to console him.

It is the end of the week. One week together and rather than leave at all, he went to the store so he could cook for me. He told me to sit down and write and do nothing else. He understands the struggle to write because he too writes. But more importantly he understands my personal struggle to keep what I write. I told him since childhood and being criticized for my often twisted, sacrilegious thoughts, I have hidden, destroyed even burned my words for fear I would be ridiculed, judged, discovered. That someone might find my words revealing what I was underneath the virtuous disguise terrified me.

I was joyous to have someone push me to write my thoughts rather than try to change, alter or subdue them. He understands the process, how long it takes to get in the zone and how distractions can render you helpless to get back there until sometimes days later. So to have him say "sit down and write and do nothing else" was the most romantic thing I have heard in ages. I meditate while he is gone to try and discover not what I should write, but what I should do about him. Prude keeps telling me I have to let him go. Something new in me says I need to enjoy the moment, dismiss the fear of falling in love and if I fall, just fall. For goddess sake, I will heal. I have healed so much already. I want to surrender to what is. So I go to my desk to write and I write like never before. Like there is no control over my words.

After Peru I had gone back to my edited chapters adding what I left out so fearful of the shame and disgust I might create by saying what I really feel, how I really was, Hell who I am. I was editing my life in my own mind creating a false world. Editing it to fit society, religion and all the rules we believe we must follow. Now I just write. It has never felt more free and having him there supporting me fuels into reality what was once just a dream.

I wrote all day while he cooked all day. It was one of those meals that takes time and fills the home with so many aromas it becomes more than a meal. It becomes a pot full of love. The way I used to cook before my ex-husbands took the joy out of it by not appreciating my pans of devotion. The meal was amazing and romantic as he lit candles and played his seducing music. We sat outside in the flickering shadows drinking red wine and sharing our souls. He had worked on documentaries traveling the world. He stayed with people in the desert to study them, slept on a shrimp boat to write and take photos. He reads literature that I have only scarcely heard of but know enough to know it is brilliant. He brushed his thick hair back. His light brown eyes tinged in green pierce my soul as I remind myself to let go and enjoy the moment.

We decided to go in and watch a documentary. He had been describing his passion for stories, for film, for writing, for people and for combining it all in documentaries. He chose one he loves in the hopes that I would like it. It is about a psychopath who lies so well he convinces the authorities he is a kidnapped teen and even convinces the family. It was a very odd choice in that I am overcoming my lies and beginning to face the lies others have told me. I told Peter the man in the documentary reminded me of my friend John in prison. There was something about his eyes like dark floating pools disguising secrets. His charm made me think twice. Peter expressed his concern warning me to be careful. I assured him I was different now and truth is now following me. We chose another documentary and I can tell he is as delighted to share his joy with me as I am with him. We snuggled as my dog made herself at home between us. I could see she was happy. I was happy. We all fell asleep on the couch.

We spent two more days together writing in the morning and playing in the evening. Falling asleep beside each other often snuggling, but that was it. We did not have sex again since he said he did not want a relationship. On this night we decided to go to bed early because Peter had arranged for us to go horseback riding at sunrise. He mentioned he was feeling a sore throat come on so I decided to give him his space in bed. I lay on the other side of the bed contemplating his European ways, wondering what it could be teaching me. He was so open and honest. Even though I have this nagging need inside to make him the one, he truly only wanted what is best for me and even tried one evening to fend me off on another man flirting with me.

Peter was sitting beside me. He saw and heard the remarks. He then asked me if I liked him and even said "you should go and sit by him." He was not in any way being sarcastic. It was a genuine, open invitation to go and find happiness. The Prude in me did not like it, she wanted him to sweep me up, see it as a competition and fight for me. The goddess loved it and wanted the freedom as my whole contemplated it all trying to learn to be more open in the entire situation. I continued to lay in wonder thinking maybe this is all this is, a wonderful lesson in moments. At that thought he reached across the big bed to touch me placing his hand on the back of my shoulder. I took a deep breath feeling warm electricity tingle down my spine. I simply lay in love grateful for getting exactly what I want, just simply touch.

I got up early for the horse riding tour he arranged. Prude told me this will have to be it. You have to let him go. Let this be the end to a wonderful rendezvous. Go on the tour and then say your goodbyes. I coach myself into staying in the moment and loving myself enough to enjoy the day. He awoke as scheduled and although he was sick, he said "we have to go, you will love this." It is nice to have someone want to make me happy despite the way they are feeling. While getting ready, I pulled out my shoes I had not worn since Peru. I was going over my grateful list in my mind to remind myself how to cherish these last moments with him. At the very instant I told myself "his honesty although not always appealing is so refreshing," I shook my shoes for scorpions and the ring for authenticity fell to the floor. I grabbed it up knowing it was a sign. I have finally been honest with my past, my issues, myself and maybe this is the lesson he has taught me. We have both been sometimes hurtfully honest and neither of us has rejected the other. On the contrary we have accepted and honored. He knows I want love and is open to let me find it and although I am still accepting this is now just friendship, I have not pushed him away either as Prude would have me do in an attempt to manipulate and test him. I put the ring on and whispered, finally as I headed out the door.

We rode our bikes to a farm not far from my house yet I had never seen. It was beautiful. The horse men are already up despite it being 4:45 AM and they are preparing the horses. They told Peter to saddle up and fetch another horse for me. I had no clue he knew how to ride but he does and he does it well. He looked amazing in his newsboy hat as he rode off into the sunrise to fetch me a horse. I stood in the cattle stall with cows, roosters, chickens, dogs and cats all around me. Stinky mud past my ankles and I didn't even care. It was picture perfect as he rounded back in the stall with my horse. I breathed deep in the moment. It felt so fantastically unreal. We mounted up. It scared me to be atop such a large animal. We headed to the first beach as the sun continued to rise and although I have been to that beach many times, it had never looked like this. Misty rays of sunshine rising up over the ocean warmed my heart. As my horse began to trot, he rode up beside me, pointed to his waist telling me you have to let go and move with the horse. He demonstrated the relaxed rocking motion in his hips. I smiled secretly inside thinking of the chakra opening exercises I read about that said to move the hips freely to release blocked energy, laughing to myself how ironic and quite the metaphor for life. "You have to let go and move with the horse." I thought.

We dismounted at the end of the beach to roll a joint. I was stunned I said "yes" to smoke first thing in the morning. I was feeling so very free. We mounted back up. I hoped the smoke would help relax me. We trotted off a little faster to the second beach, across rivers and rough dirt roads. It is a long trek. More than an hour later we arrived at the whitest sand beach in this area. Again it was breathtaking. We sit under the shade. The guide pulled out his machete to chop us coconuts. I ventured off on my own to experience the beauty alone but also to give Peter his space. I have been told I require too much attention. This is true. I like touch.

I tried to mentally manufacture the love I need while walking the sandy shore before heading back where the next joint was being rolled. I took a seat next to Peter leaning against a tree. I so wanted him to touch me. I do not know what it is I think the touch will bring me. I told myself if you want to touch him, touch him. And so I did. I leaned my body next to his and I could feel the love swelling up in me. I analyzed the feeling then told myself "see, if you want it for you, then go and get it." He does not even have to respond. And he did not. He did not pet me back as I would have liked but all I needed was to feel a human connection and I got it. I cherished it hard knowing I may be making him uncomfortable. I tried to record the feeling it has given me. Record it so I could reproduce it on my own, regardless of another. I want to make it for myself I say as I set a goal to hold it every time I feel it, study it and discover how to make it alone, on my own.

The hours on the horse have made my thighs and ass so very sore but I try to not let the pain interfere with this magical moment as we mount back up for the trek back home. It is a route I have never been and I fall in love with this country once again. The lush green, the flowering vines, the smell of fresh dirt and rain. I forgot the pain as we crossed rivers and lush fields riding for almost another two hours. It was only ten in the morning when we finished so we stopped for breakfast and a cold beer. I reveled in the beauty of the morning and expressed it to Peter. He was cold at times and even more so when I somehow manage to bring up the subject of relationships again. He unemotionally blurted "I do not want a relationship." Prude screeches with delight saying "see." Despite his answer and Prude's mocking, I on a whole feel better than I would in the past telling myself it has been a beautiful rendezvous so let it go.

I was just about to try and tell him good bye when he grabbed his throat telling me how bad it hurt. Yep, you guessed it; I offered to take him home with me. I made him some tea and debated cooking for him. Cooking has always been my show of love but the pain I got from my second husband not showing up or fighting with me if it was not on his time made me say I would never cook again. I reminded myself that I am practicing unconditional love now with no expectations and so I cooked. I chopped every herb and veggie, I know will help illness. I used more garlic than usual, after all, he is Italian and I played my music making a pot of love.

He awakened to the smell. The fear I have that he may not like it subsided with every bite. My heart began to sing when he asked for more. I was reminded how I used to love to cook. How I used to love to hear my family compliment me and my efforts. It is short lived because he says he must go. I debated if I should say that I want him to stay because I do. I want him to stay and I want to start it all over again even if it is just friendship, but I did not say a word. I let him go. I hugged him gently not as I would have had he loved me, but just as I would someone I am trying to let go. I do wish I had held him harder. I wish I would have loved him with my virgin soul and held him like I wanted, long and hard. Not holding back just simply sharing the love I feel because I feel it. This is the lesson I will take with me I think to my now dual personality.

Peter 2

I was startled at how I felt the next day. I was sad but it was not suffocating me. I still wrote and I still had some enjoyable moments. As if life wanted to test me to see if the lesson had been learned, he messaged me not more than twelve hours after I told him goodbye. I did not even have time to alter the list. He found a sand dollar and wanted me to see it so he messaged a picture. See, this is the point I could scream. This man listened to me. I told him the sand dollar story soon after we met and not only does he listen, he remembers. I had even forgotten I told him that story. I suppose having lost my voice all those years has made me gracious to be heard. He asked if I had ever tried Negroni, the best cocktail ever and then said "we should have an aperitivo." I had never heard of it so he explained it was a before dinner drink. I was not sure if he was asking me out? I ran the thoughts through my now annoying thinker. I decided to be straight up and ask if he wanted me to meet him. He gave a sexy "claro" and once again, I was on cloud nine. Prude, however, was not.

I met him at the restaurant bar where he worked for my first Negroni apertivo. We visited off and on as he took pictures. It was more of a friendly vibe so I ended up going off without him to meet friends elsewhere but more importantly to prove to him and myself I can be just as European and move on. Later in the evening I was dancing with his friend Joel when Peter showed up just smiling and watching us dance, not the least bit jealous as I still wished him to be. He visited with me like we were simply old buddies. Later he asked if friends could come to my house for a pool party. I said yes because I still wanted to spend time with him but soon after I worried because I was not sure what friends he was talking about. I did not want to see him with a girl and especially not at my place. Let's face it, I am not that open minded yet. Relieved it was just Peter and two of his male friends, we headed out to my place. The three boys got in my pool naked to my delight. I sat on the side in joy thinking how beautiful they were and how lucky I was. Mentally I told Prude to just calm down because had I listened to her none of this would be taking place right now. I was forty-one years old and I had three gorgeous men in my pool from three different countries. My girlfriends would die to be sitting where I am in this stunning country with this amazing view—three naked men in my pool. In my gratitude, I pointed to the stars and then to the three of them announcing "I get you all to myself." Joel yelled "ladies night" like he often does at the bar he tends. Jokingly, I asked for a dance from them. I pointed to the cement slab beside the pool saying "it's the perfect dance floor." "I dare you to get out of the pool and give me your best sexy dance." Peter and Joel jump out to oblige me while shy Moses danced his best sexy moves in the pool. It was hilarious. Sitting on the other side of the pool taking it all in, they gave me a show. Joel yelled again swinging his stuff all around "Ladies night."

Peter raised his glass to toast "to the girl who did nothing and now does everything." He jumped back in the pool and swam to my legs dangling and dancing in the warm water. Prude reminded me how he merely treated me as a friend tonight. I mentally shushed her and told myself to accept it as it is. At that moment he grabbed me by the waist and I didn't even fight back. I was pleased he pulled me in the water, dress and all. They begged me to join them in their nudity. I was only slightly reluctant, not out of morals anymore, but the light was on in the pool. Oh, it feels so disobedient. "I have a goal to get naked in front of a man," I announced. They laughed and urged here is the moment supersized, not one but three. Prude tried to think of a way to ruin the moment, shame me or something but before she even had a chance, I agreed with the boys and shucked the wet dress. I slowly relaxed staying to my corner of the pool so I was positive nobody really saw me. At least that is the story I wish to believe.

Peter announced in his sexy Italian accent "I do love you Julia" saying it time and time again grabbing at my hand trying to pull me close to his nakedness. Prude reminded me of what he said earlier during our apertivo "that he knew he could love me forever" and just as my heart began to open he added, "in another life." So prude won this time and I kept my naked distance from him. We swam and drank and smoked and sang. Moses hopped out to get my guitar to play. We all got out wrapping our naked bodies in towels to dance. It was glorious fun. Peter grabbed his camera. Joel put on one of my hats and a scarf. He is very eccentric in a New York model sort of way. He took to the cement slab near the pool making it his runway and gave the camera man a show any paparazzi would be proud of. Moments later the sound of my alarm halts the music playing on my phone long enough for me to realize it is my wakeup alarm to meditate at sunrise. We had stayed up all night and drank every bit of wine and alcohol I had. Peter and the boys left. It was clear it was over romantically. He did not even hug me goodbye.

A few days later I saw him out sitting with… well, I would say ex-girlfriend but I'm not sure what you call it if it was not a relationship.

I did my best not to look his way and left shortly thereafter. The next morning he messaged me that he needed to talk. He had a fight with his ex and he wanted to just run away, asking if I wanted to go for a drive. We decided to drive aimlessly and just see where we ended up. It was raining. The winding tree lined road was gorgeous. A few hours into the drive we realized we somehow had taken a wrong turn and rather than driving to get lost, we were heading right back to where we started. I was reminded of how this non-relationship, relationship I was in is ironically quite the same. Me trying to just get lost in love with no expectations and day in and day out circling around to the exact same place I began. Discovering we were heading back symbolically represents that neither of us really cares.

We had scenery, Argentinean music, wine, bread and cheese. Oh and dark chocolate with coffee bean. He smoked his cigarettes and then we both smoked pot. He stopped driving on occasion when he saw a view so we could sit in silence to take it in. From the steam rising off the hot mountains as the rain cooled the day, to the raccoon on the side that most people briefly glimpse as they aimlessly pass, we stopped to capture it all. He pulled over often and we sat in the stillness to observe furry creatures make their way into the lush jungle. He stopped. I loved that he stopped. Every time I was like a little kid excited to know what it is he saw. At one point, he pulled over and I anxiously looked though I saw nothing. He turned down the music and rolled down the window saying "listen; there is nothing to see, just listen." It was the boisterous sounds of frogs, tons of frogs croaking and singing their songs as the night began to fall. I love he is awake enough to catch and share these moments with me. I so wanted to touch him and so as I did the day we rode horses and laid on him solely for myself, I reached over and touched his hand with mine. It felt so good even though he did not touch back. Prude took count of each time I touched and he did not respond rubbing it in that he just wants to be friends. It has once again been one of my favorite moments. I told myself "see if you can just stay here, in the now, you can have this every day."

I looked out my rolled down window smelling the earth and rain and I am aware this is heaven. "This is heaven" I announced and he agreed. He asked me to talk of my dreams. "God" I thought to myself, "I am in love. I am so very in love." For a man to be interested in my dreams, my stories, my writing just makes me want to yell something ridiculous because this feels like love to me. The most glorious release of freedom emerges over me with him, having never in my life had another not smother my voice but instead encourage it. We discussed dreams all the way home. He imagined us traveling the world just as we did today, me writing while he takes pictures and makes documentaries. It felt so awesome to dream with him. So I tried to convince myself I could love him as I do my other male friends and I could let him go and even accept him with other women. I mentally conceived a picture of it to see how I felt. I concluded that it hurts. I sat quietly trying to make sense of the imagined pain. Peter broke my silence with questions about me again and relationships. I said I wanted to be happy and I always thought that meant happy in love but maybe I am just programmed to feel I need a man, a husband. "Maybe I do not," I said, "because I am happy now and I do not have it. Maybe I just needed to focus on loving myself." He responded "yes, do that."

Later, back at home, he asked if it was okay if he stayed. He wanted to stay and wake up, meditate with me, and then write an article he was working on beside me. I was so in love with the idea. I was so in love. We decided to watch a movie in my bed so we could fall asleep. I just wanted to be touched. When he reached out and pulled me close to lie on his chest, I was pleased. I would have made love to him if he had just made a move. Here I was the one who said she never really wanted sex, only to snuggle and now I have what I thought I wanted and what? Oh yes, now I want more! But he only snuggled with me. I cherished it. The sleep was so refreshing, some of the best sleep I have had in a while. Periodically, he reached over to touch me gently with a hand on my back or my arm. He pulled me close at some point in the night and kissed my forehead repeatedly. I want this to be enough. I feel loved and so I leave it as it is. I let him sleep in. I made breakfast knowing full well I had initially told him on the night we met I would NOT make him breakfast ever.

We ate, meditated, and then we both wrote. He cooked dinner again and we repeated the night just lying beside each other snuggling. We did it all again the next day too. Meditate and write, only stopping periodically to eat or when he so thoughtfully brought me green tea. He had his ukulele and after dinner asked if I wanted to play music. Damn! I cannot stand much more. Of course I did. These days have been unbelievable with him. The rain started to pour as we headed inside to sit at my old rustic table where his computer was set up. He sat up a chair beside him and handed me my guitar. He pulled up chords and gave me some instruction. We began to play while he whispered a song. I leaned in to hear his voice and guess what? It was fucking good. I am so fucking screwed! We took turns trying to play the songs he loves, everything from Irish medleys to Arabian jazz. His music is so beautiful. I cannot believe my ears have never experienced this.

I could not stand it anymore so I leaned over to kiss him only briefly touching his lips with mine. I could instantly tell it bothered him. "Why did you kiss me?" I shrugged my shoulders not saying a word but not feeling hurt either. Just feeling good in the moment and at my bravery for doing what I wanted. With each song, he sang a bit louder as his comfort rose. His voice, the rain, the music, the wine; were breathtaking. We continued to play for hours and I periodically put my hand on his back or arm just to feel the heat, wondering if this was appropriate love without conditions or desperation. How could he not feel this? The answer came when he asked if I was ready for bed. "I am" I said bracing for the romance. He said "okay good, because, I am going out!" He could see my face drop, asking if I was okay. I tried to hide it but he wanted me to talk. I went to hug him bye. I tried to hug him hard as I had promised myself to love without expecting anything in return, but how can you do that when there is nothing. He stood cold and stiff. Not even a pat on my back. My mind immediately went to my ex who did the same thing. FUCK! Here I am again begging for love. Begging for affection, begging! Have I learned nothing? He grabbed a chair and said "sit." I am at least comforted he will talk with me. I should have just gone to bed to think about it. I could feel the lump forming and I know all too well when I get overcome with emotion my words suffer. I have never been able to explain myself. I just wanted to take some time to process it.

He would not let me, asking over and over for my feelings. I quickly tried to think of the right words. "I want to spend more time with you" I said. He looked up saying "you do not want me for a boyfriend; I am not a guy for relationships." Unsatisfied but trying to accept it, I said "I wish I could have these moments and let you go as

I do my other guy friends. I suppose it is because we slept together at first. I feel something more." He tried to comfort me saying he loved spending time with me. But I was so frustrated now "I want love" came out fast. "If you are not the one for me it is not fair for you to take up space." I mumbled, "You cannot have your cake and eat it too." He stiffened and looked at me hard. I am not sure if he misunderstood the saying or if I have just royally pissed him off. I tried to explain but just mumbled crap came out now that the tension had risen. He got up to gather his things. I continued to try and make sense of it and to decipher what I meant and what in the hell he thought I meant. "I can't have my cake" he said as he shut the door ignoring my plea for him to wait. I stood in shock.

I went to my bed and cried. Will I ever learn? What is so terribly wrong with me? Is love not in the cards for me? How can I be any kinder? Despite all the answers I have received, I am lost. Peru showed me so much about my life but still I cry myself to sleep feeling lost. Feeling as I did the day I walked across the stage to get my "knowledgeable" graduate diploma. Not with all the answers I had hoped to have but full of more questions, bigger questions, overwhelming unanswerable questions. I woke periodically through the night wishing he would show up begging me back, saying he wanted to try, and he loves me in this life too. It did not happen.

I did not hear from him for two days. He messaged me about some shoes he left at my house. I ignored him for many hours. Trying to soothe the pain that had reemerged, I waited hoping it would go away but it only infested. My heart hurt and I hated the feeling. I told myself to get out and do something but I went back to bed to cry some more. Why are my feelings so untrustworthy? If I am supposed to follow my heart why is it still leading me astray? I tried to meditate but ended up just crying. I got another message from him that he wanted to chat. I ignored it as long as I could and then decided to be honest. I messaged "I do not know what to say to you and frankly I feel like shit." He replied "me too" and then instantly I felt better. How Zen is that? I feel better because he hurts too?

Part of me, that Prude in me wanted me to tell him to f off, but I didn't. I wanted him even more now. I was so confused. I decided to ask him out to my house to try and at least end it better. He told me he too was confused and that I hurt him telling him he was taking up space. I explained that if you are not him, the one, then you are taking up space. He said "but I love spending time with you." I explained how hurt I was at his coldness. Rejecting me exactly the way my ex did. I tried to hold back tears but I had been crying off and on for hours and there was no stopping them. I sat behind him on the stairs so he could not see me. It did not matter. This man can feel. And just as he felt me turn cold the day in the pool, he could feel my heart hurting. He begged me to not be upset. He grabbed my hand and took me inside to dry my tears and then pulled me onto the couch, patting his chest for me to lay down on him. He consoled me so sweetly. Brushing my hair from my face and saying "I do love you." He grabbed his phone and played a song holding it to my ear while my head lie on his stomach. He looked deep in my eyes while he whispered the words. I did not understand but as the song continued to play it became clear.

He is a good man. He was just so confused himself. Maybe he really does love me and he just does not want to hurt me. He does not trust himself. He simply does not feel he is good enough for a relationship. Those are the words I keep getting time and time again. So just like all those before him he said "I am not good enough for you." And then he added "Besides I leave soon to go back to Europe." I continued to cry because in another time, with more time, he would be perfect. My family would love him, my dad especially. But I know I cannot force it. So I just laid there and felt the love between us, trying to appreciate it, knowing it was coming to an end. He said "it is better to suffer a bit now. I know how I am. I can be mean when I drink." I did not understand because we partied a lot together and I never saw that side of him. It began to rain hard.

I laid there in the warmth of his love, my love, someone's love. He stayed until dark and then I paid for him a taxi home. Prude shut the door saying "and you paid emotionally too." I did not want him to leave but I will not beg. I knew he was going out again. He does party so much more than me. I tried to keep up but I honestly just want to be healthy. I stayed in to sulk and go to bed wishing he would return, show up and say he loved me. Again he did not. As much as I did not want to say "NEXT," I forced it but changing now to something Elisa and I heard from a friend describing the loss of his job with ease as if the loss was actually a gain moving him in a higher direction as he said, "NEXT LEVEL." I see I am dating and doing the same. Each end is a beginning to something better. So I altered the list that has strikingly been right on target. I mean my last addition was "honest to a fault." I got it. I added brave to the list because his honesty was so very brave, yet he feared letting down the armor men have been programmed to wear. He was good at living in the moment, connecting with nature and he was so accepting of everything I was, so I added non-judgmental. Lastly I added likes to sit outdoors, visit, dream and driven to reach goals with me. NEXT LEVEL.

The Commandments

~~Higher education at least a master's degree and~~ interested in continuing to learn

Financially stable ~~in a professional career~~ doing what he loves

Family oriented – maybe already with a child since I am not having more

~~Crazy about me~~

Reads

Writes – journals, ~~poetry~~, love letters, etc.

Honest to a fault

Display affection daily, kindness and respect

Romantic

Loves to travel

Athletic

Handsome and HOT

~~Tall~~

~~Hairy Chest~~

~~No Tattoos~~

Loves to dance

Loves music

~~Crazy about me~~

Loves animals

Loves even my flaws

Loves to touch me ~~because he is crazy about me!!!!!!~~

Respectful of others

Listens to me

Proud of me

Confident

Loves good food and wine

Sensual

Bilingual

Single

Enjoys conversation

Able to remain in the moment

253

Over past relationships
Spiritual
Zen
Adventurous
Practices yoga and meditation
Free
Passionate
Plays music
Knows how to pleasure a woman
Cooks
Brave
Lives in the moment – living each day with passion
Connects with nature- Loving the ocean, mountains, stars, snow, rain and sunshine
Non-judgmental
Like to sit outdoors, visit and dream
Driven to reach goals with me

The Acts

I was hurting but it was not going to break me, I vowed. I was so very strong and looking back over all the pain in past relationships helped me to see, I pull through. This did not last long enough to drown me, all though it was the longest time someone has spent with me consistently. That is pretty sad because it only lasted two weeks and just friendship in the end. It was, however, the most soulful. I do not feel the need to bash him as I did all the others. I know I have to look inside, I created this. There is a lesson.

Okay, so if people are drawn to us consistent with our personal belief system, what is it that I believe now? If this man is not available for a relationship then I must not be either. On the positive side, he was the most honest I have ever had and so maybe I am no longer living behind a mask. He was so brilliant and talented. Maybe I now believe that about myself. He was adventurous and spiritual and this I know for sure of myself. So the thing I still need to work on is being open for a relationship if it is what I really want. I also need to hear people and quit trying to hope for what a person says to change. He complimented other girls in front of me, telling me how beautiful they were and that he would like to be with them as if I was simply his best guy friend. He said "no relationship." He meant it. Still I was confused. I began looking into possibly going back to Peru for a workshop on love called Munay-Ki which means "to love" in Quechua.

I tried to move on as the weeks passed. I fluttered my goddess wings even more to the disgust of Prude and went skinny dipping in the ocean with a mutual friend of Jez and mine, named Nathan. We are just friends and we kept our distance but the tide came in and ruined my phone in my clothes pocket that I had nervously sat near the ocean edge. So the whole point of this, other than I am becoming quite good at shucking my clothes, is I had convinced myself I had not heard from Peter because my phone was ruined. I did what any girl would do and placed a status message online that my phone was broken to make sure he knew how to find me. You know, just in case. No word.

I moved rather quickly on to a handsome man who had been showing interest in me for some time. Roman and I often met for lunch. His sense of humor was just what I needed. I thought. It became rather interesting to see his negativity emerge when he was not being funny. But who am I to talk? Everyone thinks I am the most positive, good energy person they have ever met, yet I have written a book up until this point full of negative comments. So I pursued him.

One evening Jez and I invited him out to my house for a small get together. He ventured the mile and half out even though he was not feeling well. He had not been at my house long when he began to get very ill, so I offered him my bed. Jez and Nathan left so I went to lie beside him to watch a movie and nurse him. That is not really even the reason. The reason I let him stay is because I was lonely, plain and simple, lonely. We ended up falling asleep with only a kiss good night. I was not sure I wanted him there because I was still so wrapped up in Peter and that kept me from falling sound asleep. I mean it is obvious where my heart is but I will not wait another night hoping for him to show up. And just like magic, my bedroom door opens and guess who's coming to dinner.

My heart jumped out of my chest, not from fear but from relief. I am relieved he is standing in my door and for a moment I forgot there was another man in my bed. Thankfully Roman was asleep. Peter just stood there and whispered pointing to the lump in my bed "who is that?" He was as calm as someone who'd simply seen a stray dog in my bed. I jumped up and walked Peter outside the room totally prepared to defend myself and the fact I did not have sex. He simply asked again who was in my bed, not the least bit upset. I swear it was as if I had a stain on my shirt and he was just asking me what it was. Still I apologized saying I did not have sex. Either way it appeared he did not care. He tried to hug me, and said "sorry I will leave" when I pushed him away. As crazy as it is, I did not want him to leave and I was pleased when he pointed to the other room saying "I'll just go lie down in there."

Ha! Yes, I fucking have two men in my house, in two separate rooms, one is unaware the other is there while the other does not even care. I could not go back to sleep. So here I am with one man in my bed whom I have not had sex, although he wants me and the other I so passionately want asleep in my guest room. He will not have sex with me because he loves me in another life and feels he is not good enough for me in this one. This is freaking unreal and I love it. I am in love with this crazy life. In the boat riding along, letting the adventures come. It is in moments like this I am very glad to be writing a book because this is the kind of mistake that makes the best story.

I took Roman home when he awoke not saying a word but knowing full well I would tell him soon. I am a confession queen. I came back home to Peter. I let him sleep but curled my exhausted body up snug into his and fell asleep to his heart patting my back. At some point he pulled away from me and it was obvious he did not want me touching him because I reached out to pat his back and he pulled away saying he was ticklish. Now, I know I have to end this. I want it to remain the beautiful rendezvous it was and leave it to those wonderful memories. I do not want one bad memory to cloud my entire recollection. I do not want to dislike this man. I want to love him. Love him, let him go and only have fabulous memories of him. I know I have had bad things to say about every man in my life and I no longer want that. I want to be surrounded by beautiful love. Just like every time I gain the strength to tell him goodbye, he asked to make me breakfast and I experience delight letting go of my rule I mentally made to go with the feeling the moment just gave me.

We ate and then swam. I talked openly to him about Roman. Peter was not in the least bit jealous. I explained that I am confused and maybe I only want what I cannot have. Peter again told me "I am not good enough for you." Oh, it made me angry. This is what countless of these damn "frogs" keep saying. So frustrated, I blurt back "and you think Roman is?" He replied softly "No, neither of us is good enough for you." I sat in silence with my distressing uncertainty. We dried off and I took him home this time knowing it would be the last as Prude rubbed it in my face saying "you should have listened to me long ago" and "you have crossed the line teetering with another man's heart while yours is wrapped up tight."

No, Peter did not want a relationship but the miracle is whether he wanted it or not, it was. It was a brilliant relationship. Much of it is what I want for the rest of my life. I want that same spark, that passion; it was a passion for life. I want the intelligent conversation, the shared interests, the music, the moments, the heat between the touch and the passionate space between the kisses. It was the space between the kiss that took my breath. The anticipation of the next touch was the moment my heart's tempo changed. I am more hopeful than ever there is someone for me only free and ready to love. I can't help but wonder if the last two weeks have been this spectacular with someone who does not want to be in love with me, how spectacular it might be when I find the man that does. The man who wants to touch me just to feel the heat and wants to cherish the space between our kisses. I want to believe he is out there and he is looking for me too. Maybe if I want him to find me, I have to stop looking, maybe if I want to be rescued as in the fairytales, I have to stop searching and let him seek me. Still I am ready for change. I am ready to learn what love really is. I want to go back to Peru for the workshop on love so I began to look into it.

The unusual feeling of emptiness in my heart continued to oddly feel better than I recall ever feeling alone. It made it easy to continue to enjoy the days despite an occasional yearning for more Peter. Sure, I woke each day missing him, but I was in no way floored as in the past when relationships ended. My amazing friends made it easy to move. Our spur of the moment, middle of the week get-togethers that turn into all-out celebrations are the best. It goes from one friend like wonderful Jez saying, "I want to cook you dinner, Mama" to Nathan coming over to help, my neighbors bringing over the wine, Micah trekking over in her beast of a vehicle where she picks up friends walking in the rain saying "come on we are going to dinner." And before you know it we are lounging around drinking wine, listening to music, moving the entire dining room table outside to eat under the stars at the rare instance the rain has cleared. It always ends up the same. But it is a "same" I am happy is part of my new life routine now. We drink wine, we laugh, we smoke, we eat, we dance, and we sing.

One of my new favorite friends Micah has taught me a thing or two about dancing and singing. We may not be the best at either but you would never know it by watching how she engages in both activities like she is a rock star. It is so much fun to be around her. Often times, we do not let the fact that we just had a make shift party stop us from doing something the next day as well. We often load up in Micah's Bestia (her larger than life vehicle) and traverse the rough roads at times nearly tipping over to get to our destination. We have great laughs over how scared we were that the car was stuck in the middle of nowhere, we nearly hit a tree and dumped over or the river was high and the crocs could have been out. It is a life I never imagined could be this spectacular. Micah, her roommate Anna and my neighbor Sarah all moved here on a whim. They are adventurous, fun, beautiful, successful, independent and single. In fact there are many women here like that, like me. Looking for a life free from status quo with adventure that fuels the soul. We are not wanting to live the way you and Controligion are telling us to live anymore! Everyone that lives here has taken a risk to break away for the one who matters—the soul inside us all begging us to love ourselves enough to seek happiness despite society's approval.

All of these adventures with these remarkable people make it easy for a girl to find love in other ways. I spent some more time with Roman and although he is fabulous, my confusion over what I wanted pushed him away romantically but he remains my friend. I still think of Peter but I think of him fondly. I let the thought pass out of my mind simply like a cloud passing by. I heard he was leaving back to Europe soon so I messaged him that I would like to take him to dinner to say goodbye. He responded with "already have another invite." I did not let it get me down nor did I feel the fool for thinking there was something because for me there was. I have just not quite figured it out yet.

The night before he left I saw him at a bar. I was of course drinking and seeing him made my heart jump. I know not to try and numb it with alcohol but I also do not take my own advice, ever! After one too many, I approached him because he was in no way trying to approach me. I told him bye and I would miss him. He said "I miss you already." WTF? I gently hugged him while whispering "I love you" under my drunken breath, not even realizing I had said it then in a split second felt relief he did not hear because he said nothing and the music was blaring. I pulled away feeling successful I had slipped it in unnoticed while I continued a drunken whisper of "one day you will love me too." Fast thoughts swept my brain with how pathetic I was, "Just stop it," Prude reprimanded me. He must have heard me because he said "I do love you." I pretended not to hear it and just walked off tucking my bad decision away in my aching heart.

I headed to the bar for what would be bad decision number two. The huge super moon that night brought even more disorder because I was hit on prior to the Peter incident over and over by what many would call the hottest young man in this area. He is in my book, gorgeous but he is very young. His friends call him "Ari" short for the masculine name Ariel in reference to the biggest bravest cat, the lion. He is macho and manly with muscles in places Prude would never let me see. I am not even sure how old but I speculate twenty something.

As soon as I arrived he hugged me tight and told me he thought I was beautiful. I was very flattered this man would even deem me good looking. My nerves and my prude would not even let me consider flirting with him so I pushed him away. To my surprise he came back a few drinks later and seduced me again. Still early in the eve, I had not yet lost my inhibition to my drink so I pushed him away once again thinking how odd this young man was representing his name well as the nocturnal creature hunting his prey.

He would not listen to my rejections and over the next hours Ari repeatedly returned to find me and try his hand at wooing me. Each time his hugs and words became more and more seductive. I continued to be shocked and flattered while telling him he was too young and pointing him in the direction of the young girls dancing. He probably came back five or more times and the drunker I became the longer I let him seduce me. At one point he had me pinned against the bar and I turned to look away and there was Peter watching.

Had it been the way I wanted Peter would have come and rescued me as he had the night I met him, but he did not. Talking to Peter, telling him bye and walking away with my heart in confused pieces, I am sure was the weak moment that pushed the next events to unfold as they did. Oh and my alcohol doused brain. Yeah maybe that was the real weak point. One of my funny male friends was watching this all go down and gruffly whispered in his hard to contain voice that grows louder with each verbalized thought "Missy, if you take that home, hehehe he is going to last two seconds hehehe and cum all over your stomach," he chuckled his boisterous rough laugh that reminds me of some great comedian. I assured him I was not about to stoop that low and besides I was heading my drunk ass home.

I walked down the street to catch a cab when young Ari approached the taxi at the same time and hopped in the front seat at the exact moment I climbed in the back. He told the driver to go to my house and I gave in when he turned around with his big blue eyes and all of sudden became Zen. I often tease my spiritual neighbor Hawk "if they are Zen, they are in."

So sexy young man twisted my heart with his comments of "life is about experiences baby. I just want to spend time with you. It will be a great moment. I know you are curious. It's all about moments. What if you regret not having this experience? What if when you are eighty you wish you had let yourself enjoy more moments?"

"Fuck," trekked my tattered mind because somehow this young man has spoken words he has no clue how close they are to my own mental coaching. I often consult my eighty-year old self for advice. It is a technique I used with eating disorder clients because it became clear to me dealing with my own body issues that nothing is ever good enough until I look back. I could slap myself for wearing a t-shirt over my swimsuit when I was a young teen. We all did it where I grew up. We were so shamed into believing it was nothing to be seen that we covered beautiful bodies believing they were unsightly. It makes me wonder what I would tell myself in forty more years. So I would have clients imagine their body at eighty in detail—the wrinkles, the spots, aches and pains. Then I would have them imagine the advice their eighty year old self would give them.

I have been doing that as well trying to get over my own body issues and I can tell you myself at eighty is a feisty old lady. She cares nothing of the sort for others flaky opinions or even her own negative thoughts. Although she cares deeply for others, she cares more for me. She wishes I would love myself so much all judgment good or bad would fall fast away leaving me free. She begs me to live this life fully saying yes to things that rock my soul, trying new things, failing and seeing it as my greatest success because failure is where I learn to see. Money lost, she could care less. Material objects she pleads I let go, body image she says "fuck it." Be in your body fully, proudly, it's as good as it gets. Thank it for stepping out of the bed in the morning without the half hour ritual she takes to just feel peace. Love recklessly because broken hearts pass and if you think you might like it try it. It is the only way to know. Eat the damn chocolate and the pizza when you please, you my dear are too damn vain to let it overcome your body. Body flaws, she tells me, you have none; they are precious signs you lived, and risked and gave life. She tells me to indulge and over indulge and she says take this man to su casa!

So even though I hoped for love and knew this would not be it, I went on the counsel of my eighty-year old self, as I told Ari "fine but get down, I don't want anyone to see you." Never mind he is huge and can barely fit in the tiny taxi to begin with, I just pushed his head down to the front floor board to hide. He in the front seat and I in the back, I consoled my soul while my eighty year old being told Prude to "shut the fuck up" when she came out of my mouth telling Ari I did not want to have sex. He agreed. No need to read between the lines here. By now we all know this is my pattern. I want the attention, not the sex but one thing leads to another and another. Because as you can imagine the kissing was amazing, his body was hot and my sexual goddess was begging Miss Prude to just let me have this moment PLEASE! I can only assume he was a bit disappointed I was not the experienced "Mrs. Robinson" temptress I think all younger men are hoping for, because I did not assertively seduce him.

Oh no, Miss Prude would not let me, but the twenty something young man somehow turned very wise as he took me not once but twice over the next hours. My body was pleased but my mind was consumed with guilt over the huge age difference. It did not help that he told me I was the oldest woman he had ever been with. Even his attempt to soften the edge of the statement by adding "hottest old woman" did not curb my guilt. We both agreed he should leave. I laid in bed alone unable to sleep feeling like I just hit rock bottom. Hard body rock bottom, but rock bottom none the less.

The next morning I lied in bed for hours still unable to sleep. I finally pulled my adulteress body to the kitchen to try and nurse my hangover with food. My thoughts battled each other as I decided the only refuge was sleep since I had none. Not a wink. Back in bed I tossed and turned at my life, my choices, and my damn heart. I knew I only did it to try and make myself feel better and to rub it in the face of the one I wanted who would not have me. In the past everyone I slept with, every single one, was hope. Hope he was him. That he was the one. At least that gave me some comfort in believing it was not just one night. But this, this time I knew. I knew better. He was not going to call me in the morning or ask me out on a date. Hell, he probably won't even acknowledge I exist. I knew this and I did it anyway. It was as if my trip to Peru had given me so much insight that to repeat the pattern again, sickened me even more. I had just about beat myself down to the brink of depression when Mother Earth decided to take over and the bed began to shake me out of my guilty conscious. I suppose she had had enough of me bashing myself.

Since I was not going to talk to her, she decided to talk to me. It only lasted moments but it was a big enough quake to make me wake up, literally, wake the hell up and stop berating myself. In the fury of the earthquake, my friends began to message to make sure everyone was okay. The pounding rush of adrenaline Mother Nature can evoke in the human spirit casts so much light in the hollows of the heart that within an instant nothing matters but people. We decided to meet up for "one" drink as we so often say to calm our nerves and celebrate living. It is in those moments you realize you are not in charge and life must be lived fully. I told myself not to tell a soul what I had done but the moment my friends saw my face it could not be contained. Literally, the "cat" was out of the bag. Confession pursued and all I could think about as I told the story was the day the priest berated me for saying "no sin" in confession because as his reprimands reminded me, I was born sin. Now, I just wanted to scream back at him. "I got one now Mother Fucker!"

To my relief, my gorgeous friends were not about to sentence a penance on me, instead they were ecstatic, actually excited for me and told me over and over it was okay. The guilt lifted and I began to laugh with them as I described the details. I cannot believe I live amongst such beautiful non-judgmental people. I opened up even more and freedom began to fill my chest. We laughed hard over some of the funny moments, like him trying to comfort me with "you are the sexiest old woman," my description of how "taut" his skin was and my comedic friend's warning it would "not last long, two seconds and then cum all over your stomach." When they asked me his size, in an effort to not be too blunt I said "Well, I couldn't ride my bike, if that is any indication." The laughter exploded to the point of tears. In between the laughs Micah blurted out, "how did he get home? Did you call his parents?" I have not laughed so hard in days. I have come to cherish that act because just to have his hot body want me was confirmation to my femininity. My only regret is I did not engage in the "act" with more conviction. Prude hates I said that. Feisty eighty lady loves it!

As far as the frogs go, not every frog made the book. There were brief kisses, make out sessions and a few more one night stands that as open as I am trying to be, letting go of guilt, I still hate to admit. There was the hot tall hairy young man back home who pushed and pulled me up and down his emotional roller coaster, the man I could not continue seeing because his kisses included little tongue swirls, the one who needs to come on out of the closet, and oh the one my son chased away, declaring "if you are going to date someone, at least date someone with your level of intelligence. Besides, I just have a bad feeling." The man was simply a young soul but my son was right, as he usually is, finding mug shots online of the man's arrests! So I moved on to the Next Level.

Looking back there was a pattern of people coming into my life and challenging my preconceived idea of love and what I even wanted. Some people left a huge impression and changed my entire perception of what love was and who I thought I was. Dating, being single—it is not easy. Guys say the right things to get you to cave. But isn't that what we all do? We all put our best foot forward. It's not that great men are not out there it's just they are not out there begging for attention. They don't need it. They are already happy. That is why it was so important for me to challenge my own programmed idea of happiness. It is why I still need work and why I am thinking of going back to Peru.

John 3

Oh, Canada day. Living among a plethora of diverse people lends me the opportunity to celebrate holidays, I never even knew. I was so closed minded living in that North American box. Outside the box is a world of people and traditions I am so grateful to be introduced to. I spent the day with my Canadian friends, celebrating Canada. We had tons of pool fun, drinks, smoke, good food, colocho (which is twister in Spanish) and our made up dance move game. As I settled into a hammock to watch the joyous commotions continue, I received a phone call from John's sister. I had to move away from the music to hear her repeat "John is out." "What?" Is what I think I said. The moments began to speed up. We both were in shock and tried to think straight enough to decide how to get to him. It was dark, I had been partying and it is a two hour drive for me. She however, was five hours away from the prison so it was obvious I was better situated to go get him.

Since it was so late and I had been drinking, I called Allon. He sent a taxi for me. John then called me and hurriedly explained he had walked to a taxi and the driver was letting him use his phone. I could tell he did not know what to do either. It was very odd how we all so desperately wanted this moment, but we were in no way prepared. I told him to tell the taxi to head my way and I would get in another taxi and meet him. John said "it is so expensive." "I do not care," I told him, "Tell the taxi I will pay."

I jumped in the cab and felt fear and joy so balanced there was no room for tears. I went through my head again as to how he looked. Would he be skinny, drawn rough sad face, would I hug him, or he me? Would I cry, would he? Should I buy him food, a beer? I had no clue. I hooked my phone to the taxi's radio and just sat in the back seat dark listening to songs John had introduced me to as I told myself to just breathe. I arrived and sat on a bench at the park where we agreed to meet. I tried to calculate how long it would be before he arrived and then I got a call. He told me to look across the street and there he was. I walked his way to meet him in the street. He looked healthy, still with some of his muscle, the only oddity was the paleness of his skin. There was little color in his face. He had not had much sun inside that Hell. It was nine months enclosed in a tiny cage. We hugged but it was not movie quality gushing emotion, only subdued confusion. We paid his taxi and headed to mine. He was obviously shaken. In shock, I assumed as he described his discomfort at how everything seemed so big. He said he had no clue where they were taking him when the guards came to his cell. He grabbed what little he had when the guard ordered him to come. He was worried they were moving him to another prison.

They walked him to the gate, handed him a piece of paper and said "you are free." No one had any clue this was coming and they did not even give him the option to call anyone. It was already dark. He had no money so he just began to walk down the long dark muddy road miles from town. He walked a long time taking it all in before he found the main road and a taxi. He said the taxi guy was scared asking where he was coming from because he obviously knew what was down that road. He told him "the jail" raising the poor man's tension even more. "Still, the man was gracious enough to let me use his phone and that is how I called you," he explained. He could tell the guy was still afraid but agreed to take him to meet me.

John continued to describe the overwhelming feelings he was experiencing. He said everything is huge. I do not know what is happening to me. Julita you know psychology, "what is happening to me?" He felt his mind was on overload as he took in the different feelings. He drew a deep breath patting his chest. I told him it probably is sensory overload. You were in a closed dark space with nothing but concrete walls for nine months and your senses became used to that. Now your brain is on overdrive trying to process all the incoming sensory information; the new sounds, the sights, the moisture on your skin, the air on your tongue and even the smells. He said "Yes! The new smells, I walked out of the prison, down the dirt road and touched a cow just to feel it. I then smelled my hand and I was overwhelmed at the smell." He laughed saying "it smelled like cow shit but I thought it smelled good. Ha, I did not care that it stunk, because it was different. It was a different smell." I sat away from him in the back of the taxi and many times we just sat quietly. I could tell he was trying to come to terms with what just happened. I asked him where he wanted to go and he said "with you. I do not want to see anyone tonight. I need to take a pause. I don't want to talk or tell my story to anyone but you."

"Okay, let's go to my house," I told him and the taxi driver.

We arrived and the oddness remained as we walked through the house absorbing each room and some of his things that were still here. He grabbed my guitar and played a bit. I kept nervously asking him if he was hungry, thirsty, tired? I could tell he needed comfort but I did not know how to do that. Eventually he asked to sit outside. He looked at the stars as if for the first time. I sat in silence wondering how that must look. To go from small congested solid stockade to having so much space around must be overwhelming. We sat in the hammock for a bit as his fingers fumbled to play guitar, trying to recall songs nine months nearly erased. He stopped periodically to say something about the prison—the filth, the inhumane conditions, how you lose humanness, how wrong it is to treat another like they are not even a human, sleeping on hard concrete, sleeping in rancid bathrooms, the fights, the death. Every day was spent working your ass off to pay the boss for necessities, for life. Eventually earning enough respect through unspeakable ways to become the boss, yet not wanting to be the boss. The danger it entailed exceeded the title. The overabundance of drugs created madness amongst already maddened men.

I just let him talk and on occasion he would stop himself, inhale like it was his last and say, "I am here now." He so wanted to believe that but I could tell even this yogi was having so much difficulty being here. I decided to comfort him as I would my clients, reassuring him to talk because you need to process it all. Every time we tell our story it takes away a little of the pain. I told him to tell me. Tell me as often as you need. I do not care if I have heard the story a million times; tell me again and again until you can tell it like it was simply a bad movie you watched. He sighed in relief saying "aha, yes Julita, Thank you." We sat for hours into the black of night with story after story pouring from his pained mind.

I was not sure where he would sleep but I told myself to just do what feels good. It felt good to hold him, to comfort him so I fixed him a glass of water and placed it on the opposite night stand. He said he wanted to shower. I lay down in deep thought and told my mind to stay in the moment. Stay, I scolded. We scoured through my closet for something for him to wear and laughed when he put on my white lingerie store lounge shorts. He said they felt so comfortable and I agreed to let him wear them because he needed just that, comfort.

We lay down and I held him sending love to his heart in hopes it would heal. He said his mind was like a car engine, revving, and racing. We held each other for a very long time before he kissed me ever so gently on my forehead, my cheeks, on each side of my mouth but not on the mouth. It was so very slow and healing in an odd way. My mind was off trying to convince me to stop. Saying things like do not do this out of pity, do not do this at all. I was not sure what I wanted as my mind tried to take me into the future to prove to me why, but I did not let it. I sucked in the air around us and felt peace in my heart knowing my mind had not much power over me anymore. No not much at all. I lay there taking in this beautiful thing as I realized my soul was winning, loving as it was brought to this world to do. The moment continued to grow into the strangest most beautiful thing I have known to this date. Slow and sweet, weird and wonderful so much so it is not humanely possible to put down on paper because it was not sex. No, it was not sex, at least as us humans would know. It was two spirits swaying in a dance to soothe each other's soul.

I fell asleep for what few hours were left of the night. His racing mind must have shunned the sleep, he was up way early. I caught a glimpse of him out the window doing yoga in the sunshine. I smiled at his peace and closed my eyes to fall back into my ease. He left to be with his family and I awoke to all of his things gone except books and books he left of his writing from inside his prison both real and mental. I was overjoyed he would leave his words for me yet afraid to open it. Eventually my curiosity won days later. I sat with one of the four notebooks open. Pages and pages of tiny handwritten words etched like room might run out or time or both. My mind stopped on one painful sentence. I closed the book knowing I was not ready for it as the tears began to fill my eyes. I shut the notebook and sat it on the other three in my lap. As my mind went back to the day I held my own secret journals just before the burn. I took a long deep breath to clear the overwhelming feeling and thought "I hold in my hands pages and pages of pain, pages and pages of beautiful pain," exhaling freedom as I placed the books in my wooden box of heavy words for when the time is right.

I did not hear from him for several days. He came to my birthday a few weeks later but there were so many people there I am sure it was overwhelming to him and he left early. He sent a message that he was moving but it was as if all our deep soulful conversation came to a sudden halt. I convinced myself it was because I was a part of a past he was trying to forget. I thought about how I made time for him almost daily for nine months and now it felt as if I was being rejected but I also held on to the fact I did a good thing and this is love the way it is meant to be.

Over the next few weeks it became obvious things had changed or should I say my perception of him changed when reality began to blow the sacred candle out I had lit for him in my heart. The wonderful social media tool clarified things when a picture was posted of another child of John's he never told me about. Later I got a message from a woman that she and John were together and had always been because they were raising their young son. It is well-known that some of the locals tell stories. They tell females whatever it is they need to hear in order to get them into bed. I have heard countless tales of foreign women falling for their macho ways, tinged with sweet emotion only to find out he is married or has children and/or a live-in girlfriend they never once mentioned.

So there it was and as the reality began to open areas of my brain I had closed to see the best in him, I began to go back and question everything he had told me. Maybe he did or didn't attend law school and then med school for a while. So his mom is not a Doctor and his dad may not be a Neurosurgeon. He has more than one sibling and has more than one child and he may have a wife, girlfriend, or both. He may have never traveled to India and he may not have a Chinese mom which means his last name may not be Le and he may or may not have gone to Germany where he learned to speak German. He may have slept with a girl in my bed! Oh and he may have stolen my money.

Fuck! I refuse to be a victim any longer. I do not ask enough questions. It is as if I am afraid of the truth. But wait just a minute before you judge because until I put it all together in that paragraph you too may have forgotten the so-called truth, just as I did. That is the whole point of perception it is what we want it to be. He was very charming and warmed not only my heart but many hearts where I live. The truth is simply whatever we choose to believe. I grew up in a society that supports lies. It is only in being honest with oneself that truth comes out. Well isn't that an 'aha' moment, because yes I am afraid of the truth. I even lied to myself for years.

Of course I would believe anything I am told. I let people tell me what they may and I stroke their egos for lies that disguise. Was I used by him and by her? How many more kids does he have? Is his story at all true? I do not know but when people leave us with blanks in their story we get to fill it in and we fill it in with the worst case scenario. It is not my concern anymore. I am no longer taking responsibility for another person's misery. I do not regret anything I have done. I have done what I wanted and I have learned. What I need now is more time with me. I still have so much work to do. I must go back to Peru and finish what I started. I do not feel like kissing frogs anymore. The commandment list can wait another day.

I booked the trip that was now last minute because I sat with the decision so long. I was preparing to go to bed and dream of Peru. Thoughts of my last trip there were in my head when I got a message from Peter. It was just a link to a song. He often responded with music. It is like he takes in everything you say and mulls it around in his mind until he comes up with a song that expresses the emotion more appropriately than mere words. It is so sweet and compassionate. A rare quality I have yet to see in any man I have ever dated. I snuggled down in my bed and clicked the link. I watched the video that thoughtfully had the words to translate it. The song mysteriously paralleled everything I told him about my life, my experience in Peru; feeling like I was never seen, begging people to see me.

I felt heard, like my voice, my story, my life mattered. Someone really listened, someone cared enough to see below the mask I wore and to understand the struggle I always bore. The song sent chills with the translated words I saw you. I listened and replayed it feeling it in my soul, rejoicing that maybe my heart is okay and can feel correctly. Maybe I can trust where it sends me and the people it places on my path. Tears fell from my cheeks. I continued to replay the song and lay my head on my wet pillow. I told myself "just love Juls, just love."

What if those two weeks were all I will ever get? What if long love is simply not in the books for me? Can I be happy loving me, my life as it is now? The most difficult part now is letting that beauty go. Respecting it and letting it go. People get stuck in a depressive past reliving over and over the pain, but it is just as unhealthy to stay in a past moment of bliss because it deprives us of the present. There too will be a mourning period. I must let it go. "Go back to Peru, take the Munay-Ki Rites to love and work on spirituality," I whispered to myself as I tried to fall asleep but then awoke feeling the need to add to the list nothing from John or Peter but something just for me. "See me." NEXT LEVEL

The Commandments

~~Higher education at least a master's degree and~~ interested in continuing to learn

Financially stable ~~in a professional career~~ doing what he loves

Family oriented – maybe already with a child since I am not having more

~~Crazy about me~~

Reads

Writes – journals, ~~poetry~~, love letters, etc.

Honest to a fault

Display affection daily, kindness and respect

Romantic

Loves to travel

Athletic

Handsome and HOT

~~Tall~~

~~Hairy Chest~~

~~No Tattoos~~

Loves to dance

Loves music

~~Crazy about me~~

Loves animals
Loves even my flaws
Loves to touch me ~~because he is crazy about me!!!!!!~~
Respectful of others
Listens to me
Proud of me
Confident
Loves good food and wine
Sensual
Bilingual
Single
Enjoys conversation
Able to remain in the moment
Over past relationships
Spiritual
Zen
Adventurous
Practices yoga and meditation
Free
Passionate
Plays music
Knows how to pleasure a woman
Cooks
Brave
Lives in the moment – living each day with passion
Connects with nature- Loving the ocean, mountains, stars, snow, rain and sunshine
Non-judgmental
Like to sit outdoors, visit and dream
Driven to reach goals with me
See me

2 Corinthians

I booked to go alone this time. I wanted dig even deeper into my soul to seek answers and let the past go. Despite my struggle to be happy single, I still secretly yearned for another to love, to love me, to see me. As in my last trip, I did not over analyze any of the rituals I would be partaking in. I did not let myself internet search anything. I simply sent an email to Diane that I wanted to come back and participate in her workshop. Luckily she had room for me so I told her to book me for the first half of the workshop. There were two parts and several days in between the start of the second so I asked her if it was okay for me to decide if I wanted to do the second half after taking the first half. I did not want to commit to anything I may not like. No matter what I was determined to do whatever the first session entailed, put my judgmental mind aside and totally absorb myself in the Andean tradition. I had no other plans. It was nerve racking and freeing all at the same time.

My son was visiting me before I left for Peru; in fact our flights, his back to the USA and mine to Peru, would be leaving the airport on the same day. His being with me was a big part of my decision to go. Despite things in his life all of a sudden taking a huge turn with him considering moving out of the USA as well, to follow his dream, he urged me to go to Peru and do what I needed to do. I nearly backed out of going so I could go with him to the USA and help him move but his exact words which I always find brilliant were: as he circled his finger around pointing at me and then turning it around to point to himself; "How about this, you do you momma, and I'll do me." And so I did. I left to do me. It was the best thing I could have ever done for myself after up and moving to Paradise.

I absolutely love an airport. I love watching the travelers. You can tell who is for pleasure, for business and even who is going way and who is coming home. The changing and adjusting required to stay in the now makes travel a great teacher symbolic of life. I have learned a lot in my travels about baggage. The less you take the easier trip it makes. It's letting go of things that do not serve the soul and learning to stay calm amongst the storm of life; like bumpy flights, delays, changes, and the energy of others often negative moods. You learn patience and creative ways to meditate.

I really appreciate my yoga practice when I try to sleep in the cramped seat. I can put my body in a confined place and find comfort in even the most uncomfortable space. It's a good time to contemplate challenging beliefs. I love the challenge of staying at peace through all the lines, the delays, the often frustrated angry public pushing, rushing, and scowling at their discomfort of change. I try to maintain my energy in that space, keeping my perception positive. I meditate often, in the lines, waiting for my flight and on the plane. I don't full out sit in lotus pose for the entire world to see or even place my hands in the traditional mudra but I meditate, none the less. Being forced out of your comfort zone when you disembark to an airport you have never been is also exhilarating to me, studying the directional multi language signs, the people, and the energy.

I arrived in Cusco and hot hostel man from the last trip had seen I was traveling online and offered to pick me up. I was curious what the feeling was I felt for him so I did what I did and let him. It did not take long for me to realize it was not as I had imagined. It was nothing to do with him it was just not anything close to the soul connection I had already discovered and I had promised myself I would not take anything less. I debated if it was even the right thing for me to have done, to see him since he had just recently broken up with his girlfriend. I love that anytime now I begin to question my choices, I just make a date with my soul. She told me straight up how it is. Morning meditation eased my doubt with the message that bubbled up "You had to know. Learning what you do not want is just as important." It is true. I would have always wondered. So I did not even give it a second thought. Instead I heard her, and more than hearing her, I was now listening to her.

I left Cusco for the Sacred Valley on a bus packed so tight with locals; I could not believe it possible to fit even one, when the bus would stop to pick up more. I kept thinking "okay that's it, no one else can fit as people packed standing back to back in the isles." The bus stops continued and it went from crowding the isles to people stepping in the space between the seats, standing over me in my leg room, to crowding around the bus driver and on the exit stairs. I smiled inside as even in this cramped concoction I felt like I was on an adventure my little girl heart never dreamed or read about in the fake fairytales. She would be so proud to have read a book about this.

The bus ride took longer than expected with its many stops so I was in a rush now as I peeled myself out of my cramped space. The bus had stopped at a Y intersection. I was not sure where I had landed but time was ticking and the workshop would be starting soon so I chose the path to the right, lugging my suitcase down the rocky dirt road. I laughed moments later when the people on the bus began yelling out the windows trying to tell me in Spanish I was heading down the road out of town. It is one of the great discoveries of traveling alone. People are good and they will help even when not asked. The fear of getting lost, which I always harbored, subsides with each journey so much I actually enjoy the feeling of going where my feet take me, information free. Information is heavy, weighing us down with the time it takes to acquire it and then the thoughts of that knowledge mulling around in our brain keeping us from seeing life unfolding while we try to recall the information. I waved a big thank you and turned my feet the opposite way to the path my compact friends now hanging out the bus windows hooted and hollered while applauding with approval.

Across the bridge I found a little tuk-tuk to get me there in the nick of time. I walked up to the gate to ring the bell. I had a profound feeling I was not just pushing a bell to open a door but closing one as well. I released the bell and felt a breeze tingle my spine as I thought "whatever my heart is missing will be found in this sensual space." The moment I saw the metal door open to the lush green valley that Paz y Luz is so perfectly positioned, I knew I was in the right place. I only had moments to spare, but just as life had been unfolded in perfect timing for me, it was all the time necessary.

The first meeting confirmed my choice to come back. From Diane's hug that put so much loving energy in my heart, my eyes filled with relief that the long journey getting here and my worry over leaving my son to fend for himself were irrelevant now. Everything released as soon as she put her arms around me. Then I looked up to see Meredith, a woman I had met last trip to Peru. She is a healer like Diane. To see I would get to spend time with two of the most spiritual women I have ever been blessed to meet was worth the trek.

We received the first rite and then did an exercise that to this day I continue to practice. Diane told us to go outside, find a spot amongst the lush gardens and lay down on Mother Earth. We all made our way out to find our space in her glorious mountain lined valley and lay on our stomachs as instructed. Then you place your hands in a circle and put your mouth in the space as if to whisper a secret. That is exactly what you do. You whisper all your secrets to Mother Earth. Diane explained that telling her all your shit is fertilizer to her, she loves it, she needs it. So I did, I spilled my guts from childhood on. As I began to focus on things I had pushed aside in my mind, I was taken aback at what I recalled. Things I did not want to remember or talk about because I love my parents and I do not want to perceive them in a negative light. No one does. That is why so many people put up with unhealthy things in their adult lives—because we learned to deal with it in childhood, we deal with it as adults. It somehow becomes our normal. It feels like home. I realized there were things that were not healthy.

I had forgotten the feeling of being alone many times as a child and at one point had a very profound memory of standing in the front seat of the car as mom drove. I must have been no more than two or three. It was before seat belt laws, I was small enough to stand up so quite young. I remember kissing my mom repeatedly on the shoulder and her stopping me. It was not mean or stern in any way, but it hurt and is consistent with the rest of my childhood where love was not openly expressed. It was as if it was a bad thing. One time she told me in response to saying I loved her that saying "I love you" should be saved for big moments and not abused on a daily basis. So I stopped saying it to her and we did not say it much. I told Mother Earth about my father's open expression of affection when he was sober. When he was drunk he was not nice. Not nice at all; picking and poking at my mother's, mine or my sister's flaws. It was hard not knowing which man was coming home, if he came home at all. When he did, and he was sober, he was so loving. But then my parents divorced and that little bit of love was taken away from me, too.

I whispered to her how the living conditions in the trailer I grew up in became grotesque over the years. The trailer began to deteriorate and became infested with tics. At one point I had tics on me so bad the teacher found one on my desk in elementary school. I was so embarrassed that when she blamed it on the boy with dark skin who sat there in the class prior, I did not say a word as she moved me to another "cleaner" desk. I poured out the entire gunk from all the men who rejected my love and neglected my needs for safety, for health. I turned my attention to my son and my worry over leaving him to move on his own. Was I neglecting his needs? Tears rolled down my cheeks at everything that came up. It was very powerful laying there with the cool crisp mountain breeze blowing over my shoulders as the sun blanketed me with warmth. When all the crap is out and you can't think of anymore then the next part of the exercise is turn your head and place your ear to the cup your hands have created and listen. Listen for the message Mother Earth or as they call her in Peru, PachaMama has.

She said your mother loves you very much. She had so many other things in the way blocking her show of love as you wanted to see it, but it was there. It was there in more ways than you know. It was there like it is now. She tells you she loves you now and you know it to be true. Your father did everything to be better than his dad and continues to battle the beast of alcoholism his father bestowed on him. He is a good man fighting the battle much better now. Regarding my son; she said you were and still are the greatest mom if you could just see how great. I saw peace signs in my mind's eye and heard her say, if more kids had a mom like you, there would be peace. By now my hands are filled with water from my eyes and the salt is running in my mouth.

The insight continued as she told me you have always put other's happiness before your own. You convinced yourself that was your happy, seeing others happy. The greatest thing you have ever done was following your own happy. Because by following your happiness to Paradise, to Peru, you did not shut the door on your son's happiness, but quite the opposite, you opened it. I knew she was right. My moving had opened a door for him to follow a lifelong dream. He even told me he had learned more from me moving than in all his years of schooling. Now the insight I gained from parenting is not to say in any way I did not have screw ups. My goodness, I was in no way the perfect parent, I am not sure anyone can claim that, but it is by far the only real thing in life that matters to me. I have always said of all my accomplishments that could receive compliments everything pales in comparison to hearing, "you are a good mom."

We went back inside the breathtaking circular glassed conference room to share our experiences. Everyone had their own amazing insights from conversing with PachaMama. I told Diane, "book me for the second half, I am staying." I slept amazingly well that night even though I dreamed of boas!

My sleep was some of the best I have ever had and my dreams were so very vivid. One night I awoke in a panic because I had been shot in the back. In the dream nobody listened to me. They all could see I was shot but they kept reassuring me I was fine despite my pleading to take me to the hospital. I ended up driving myself to the hospital. Diane said I should pay very close attention to what the dream meant. I knew immediately it was my pattern of trying to be perfect, doing everything on my own and then feeling betrayed by society while playing the victim and never feeling I have ever had anyone's support. That day was one of my favorite days as the entire group opened up so much sharing their struggles. The energy in the room was so overwhelming with immense emotions surfacing, we had to take a break. When we gathered our composure Diane led us in one of the most beautiful meditations I have ever experienced. Heavy tears fell from my eyes the entire time, from everyone's eyes.

Each day we received one of the rites in the morning and spent many moments in meditation. Every single day got better as more and more insight was revealed. At one meditation I had my feet in the ice cold water of the sacred river. I was thinking of Peter, how in love I am with his spirit, his intelligence and our dream to travel together. My programmed mind trying to protect me as it always does came in to the conversation telling me once again, "you have to let him go." I began a mental debate saying "maybe I should stop communicating with him, maybe I should continue, no it's not about outside things, you have to let him go in your heart, you should let him go" then like magic my mind stopped and my soul rose up as she often does to say gently "Maybe you should do nothing, maybe you don't need to do anything at all." In that very instant I heard a big splash in the icy water at my feet and opened my eyes amazed from the sign Mother Earth just gave me. I smiled when I realized everyone was leaving the river and Diane had thrown a rock perfectly timed to my soul's answer to rock me from the depth of my meditation.

That evening, although we were softly advised to limit our contact with outside sources, I checked my messages to have a wonderful loving message from my son on how proud he was of me for traveling on my own to follow my soul, and then a message from Peter. It was nothing more than another link to a song. The hair on my skin stood on end as I listened to the song about a river (I had just spent the day at the river thinking of him!) and travel. I went to bed with love in my heart for having such wonderful people on my path.

We did healing sound meditations in the evening, yoga in the mornings and activities in the day that grew in intensity to the point of unbelievable mystic moments. On the last day of this first half of the conference, there is still a second half to go, I sat in a meditation gaining insight that would forever change my view of being a parent. They are just off God's wing and they are here for us rather than us for them. Some souls need more healers than others and some none at all.

I needed my son from the get go and that is why he tried coming to me so soon. "It was him, it was always him," powerfully whispered over and over. "It was always him" came again and again as freeing tears poured the last of the guilt down my face. "The soul enters at the breath, forgive yourself this instant." Relief trickled from my head down my spine as the healing released the years of negative beliefs. He was always ready for me way before I was ready for him. I came out of the meditation knowing I had to go back and rewrite the first chapters where I had left out the part about having abortions. I had to go back and share for me, for all women, for the entire world because our perception from this human perspective is so very limited.

We have to stop judging decisions of our past, our future, our present. We cannot love wearing the cloak of a judge. When we understand we are all loving energy coming and going in various forms, judgment and guilt melt under that knowing. I went to sleep with my son on my mind and the conversation we had when he was four telling me he could see me before he was born, he knew me and that I was going to be his mom when I was ready. I knew it was true and that old soul was here to teach me a thing or two.

We had a break before the second workshop began. Some people left and other people who had taken the first workshop elsewhere were arriving. A beautiful woman named Eve arrived and we immediately hit it off. We discussed our lives like we had known each other forever. She too almost did not come to Peru because of obstacles back home. We both decided it was fate we were here together and even more so when we discovered the first time I came to Peru months ago she was there too. Our paths just did not cross then. We decided during this four day break to try one of the ceremonies offered with medicine. I was not ready to do Ayahuasca again as I was still processing the connections with my past life but I had heard there was another medicine called San Pedro that was supposed to be milder. Since I had discovered some issues with my childhood in Diane's workshop, I wanted to do what I could to heal.

We met with the Shaman the day before to prepare our intentions. I briefly told the Shaman about my Ayahuasca experience in the concentration camp and he asked me to stay after the meeting to visit in private. He said people do the medicine when they are fed up repeating patterns and whatever happened in a past life carries energy, yes, but there has to be something more that occurred in this life. I told him I was divorced twice, that my mom and dad divorced, that I left my practice selling it for less than it was worth, and…. He stopped me from my rambling with a gentle signaling of his hand. I was disappointed that he may not have heard me or understood my struggle, when he calmly whispered "there is a lot of leaving in your life."

My mouth literally fell open like I had never considered that before. It was more truth than I could have ever uncovered in years of therapy. There it was plain and simple. "A lot of leaving." Then his insight continued as he told me to set my intentions for the ceremony tomorrow by writing down in my journal "to be healed from the past unconsciously and consciously of being the victim. To heal the abandonment and to ask in the ceremony what is it in me that has invited these experiences of abandonment by others and then me abandoning myself, my projects?" I left his house feeling like the five minutes with him had summed up my forty two years of existence in one sentence. 'There is a lot of leaving in your life." I thought of all the leaving done to me and by me. I thought of my books, my writing I neglected and or destroyed. No more, I pleaded in my mind. No more.

I went back to my room and etched everything quickly so as to not forget my intentions and then I added one. I mean surely it is okay for me to ask for one extra. So yes I wrote it, "love," I want love of my soul mate. I felt so heavy all night long and fell asleep crying like the meeting with the Shaman had opened up another wound, a wounded reality I had never faced. "A lot of leaving." Then the thoughts—*What if there is no soul mate for me? What if in this life I am meant to do it all on my own? How would I live then? Would I truly quit looking for him? Could I be happier just living for me? Could I wake up every day and do what I want to do simply to gain a feeling of happiness for my own soul? What is love anyway from another? I believe I know very well what it is for me to love. I have done it. I am doing it but from another? I get it from friends and family but from a romantic partner I still do not believe I have. And maybe that is the flaw. Maybe that is what life is trying to teach me.*

I awoke early with the sunrise and did my meditation by candlelight. I could feel the energy off the candle and saw streaks of light shooting from the candle to my heart. It literally felt as if the candle was warming my heart to ease my nerves over the day's ceremony. But more than the nerves was a yearning to be free of my past. Since I was told San Pedro was smoother than Ayahuasca, I felt safe I would not have such an overwhelming experience. I was hoping it would smooth my life out to bring love. We gathered in the outside ashram at nine that cool morning. Yoga mats and blankets were laid out for us. I looked around and was so relieved to see there were not any buckets for puking. Yeah! I won't have to become a basket case in front of everyone. Yes, I will certainly be able to hold it together. Then I learned we would need to drink two cups. Ugh, I barely got the Ayahuasca root down, this medicine is coming in two doses! I was relieved when a young lady I met the first workshop went first and only gagged slightly announcing "Ayahuasca is much worse". I sat waiting my turn and my damn heart began to pound just as it did before Ayahuasca. I tried my best to calm myself with breathing as I made my way to kneel and place my intentions "heal and understand consciously and unconsciously past victimhood and abandonment," and I snuck in "love."

I gulped the green sludge with ease the first cup, but the second cup felt thick in the back of my throat and I had to stop, making it that much more difficult to begin again. I thought of my repetitive "lot of leaving" life while sucking the second cup down hard, symbolically breaking the patterns of strife. I sat back on my mat and patiently waited to feel. About fifteen minutes later I felt drawn to be in the garden with the sun on me.

I found a little twig tree about three feet high with only three leaves that looked like it was struggling. I had to be near it, feeling we shared a similar struggle. I sat my blanket on the dry crackling grass and then meditated near the tree. It was not long before I began to interact with nature, that tiny tree, the sun and the earth below me. I heard a voice say "you will never sell yourself cheap again." I knew it was talking about leaving my marriages, selling myself short, not feeling good about what I got, and leaving my practice the same. I hear "your book will not be sold cheaply and you will never sell yourself cheap again in anything, not even relationships."

I felt sick periodically but nothing would come up. Then it happened. The loneliness I felt as a child became crystal clear as my deceased grandfather, whom I had never even met, came to me and explained why he had to go. He apologized for leaving me with the others' pain. I then understood where the abandonment came from. I saw myself being born to a grieving mother. She was about eight months pregnant with me when her daddy died and I was born amongst the grief. I had the notion it was hard for her to hold me. Everyone around me rather than celebrate a birth were grieving the death of this magnificent man. I just wanted to love yet I came into grieving hearts. It made sense that my strong mother at her painful loss would decide to not love so much to not hurt me should she need to leave me. My dad's smothering love made sense too as he tried to step up and fill the gaps during his sober moments to make up for the guilt of the times the alcohol took him away.

My grandfather then came back and said "all the wonderful stories you hear about me, it is you. I am part of you." He put his hands on my face and made me look up, saying "You chose this. You wanted to come into this life to be the best human possible. You chose this. You chose your mom and a family grieving over my death." He continued saying his energy was in me, part of me and that is why he died right before I was born. "You want to be the best, giving love the way it is meant to be, just giving, without receiving. So you chose the challenge to come into a family grieving." He said "and you keep choosing men unable to give." I cried hard telling him, "but I want love now." He touched my chin trying to raise my eyes to him, to get me to look at him and said "I am part of you. Look at me. What is my name?"

I looked down because for some reason I could not look up, like I did not want to see the truth. He said "You so desperately want love. Look at me," he insisted "I am you." He gently grabbed my face turning me to look up at him saying "What is my name? I am you. What is my name?" I was overwhelmed with the clarity that swept my soul as I looked deep in his eyes and it hit me that his name was Bud Love. L-O-V-E, Love. "Yes," he whispered, "Love."

I knew what he was trying to tell me but it was just like all the rest of the wisdom I think I know. It means nothing until you feel it, really feel it. It is one thing to say it, to say you believe it but to truly feel it, how? I thought. Waves of sickness like I have never known came over me as I tried to neatly stay on my blanket kneeling with my body hunched over like a helpless beggar. I offered my guts to the little tree I could now see had one small bud like my grandfather's name! It was mystical, ironic, enchantment to be interacting with a little tree representing a grandfather I was just now meeting. The ground beneath me began to breathe as I witnessed the cracks in the dry ground inhale and exhale. I had the feeling she was trying to comfort me as her respirations slowed like a great mother trying to calm me with breath. I was overwhelmed with the connection to Mother Earth and the knowledge she is a living, feeling being. I had the immense sense our very own spiritual powers come from communicating and connecting with nature.

Still dry heaving, the snake inside my insides twisted my moral fiber. I heaved and heaved with no relief. It would come and go. I could hear others off in the distance puking liberation, while I suffered. I could not find release. I periodically looked up to see the cat sitting off in the distance with his back to me. He slowly turned his head to slyly tell me "I am Cat and I will do what a cat does. I take care of my own needs. If that involves licking myself in public then that is what I need," as he demonstrated the socially unacceptable behavior.

I understood. This is where I have failed me. I do not take care of my own needs. I put others first, going above and beyond to make you comfortable while I will sit back hungry, cold and unloved. Doing nothing for myself especially if I feel it will cause me embarrassment, from blowing my nose in public, going to the bathroom in a public restroom or what I need now which is to puke my insides out. I give and give just like the most recent giving away of what little money I have to various needy people, continuing victimhood. Cat said, "I will love you, but I will need my space to take care of my needs and you must do the same." I agreed, imagining how nice to love and have my space when needed. Then I imagined him needing space and I felt that damn lonely come over me and my insides twisted. Cat covertly looked over his shoulder again reprimanding "see, it is not fair for you to love, take your space, but not be able to allow another the same." He said "I will come to you when you understand this fully.

Stop trying so hard," he scorned, "in your efforts to seek love, you are actually pushing it away. He is here and he wants to find you just as bad as you want him. Let him find you. Let him find you."

I felt sick again and doubled over in the dry crunchy grass no longer caring if I got dirty. The blanket below me I so neatly placed was now disheveled. My head was covered in the parched grass pieces because I could not hold it up. I felt some comfort smashing it in the earth. I begged for relief. The Shaman came to me. I told him what I was experiencing with my grandfather but not the cat. It was just too weird and I had no time for explanation as I doubled over in pain. The Shaman had been chanting earlier but now he stopped to comfort me. I asked him to continue singing because it was helping me feel like I might throw it up. He laughed saying "Yes, I have a friend that says my singing also makes him sick."

He began to chant at my hunched over helpless body. I felt the knots well up in my stomach. I heard the ingested plant speak to me "We are not letting you go until you accept you are love." I pleaded I did, but my mind quickly countered it and the dry heaving continued. It felt like a boa had swallowed a huge meal and was just wreathing in my gut. The Shaman laid me on my back and rubbed the knots in my stomach asking "Is it possible you carry some of your mother's pain?" I cried, "Yes, all of it." "Let it go," he commanded. "Let others carry their own pain" and instantly I felt some relief. He stood over me for a long time as I wept. He continued singing and shaking some sort of dried plants at my back saying "Let's shake this mother out." All of a sudden I understood by being the victim, I neglected my own needs. So much so I sought others to care for me in impossible ways only love of self can do, that only self-love should do. From not protecting and respecting my body to letting others use me, my time, my finances, my nurturing and my love. I have to start putting my needs above all others. It is not selfish; it is selfless, filling my needs on my own so much, my self requires less from another. To care for me will free my soul to be love, not need love, be love! I think about the cat doing his repulsive act of licking in public to prove his point. Then, perfectly timed, Cat came to my head and meowed, letting me know I was on to something.

I dry heave and feel some relief but I know it is not over. The Shaman told me it may come out the other end. I laughed, "Yes that would be right since I fear using the bathroom in public." He calmly laughed whispering "Yes, control freaks do." I thought of Cat and headed to the bathroom to take care of my disgusting needs. Thus began the unending countless trips to the bathroom because I feared pooping my pants. With each wave of knots I made my way to the bathroom, struggled to find the light and sit to extract the beast while hanging my head over the trash. The wave would end; I would go outside and repeat this process time and time again. After some repeating this ritual, I was convinced I was stuck in something similar to the movie "Groundhog Day."

The Shaman rescued me from the repetitive crazy by bringing me tea and saying "Let's go for a walk." I could barely stand but he urged me to move my heavy legs. We made our way to the front where I knelt to the ground clinging to the earth for support. He tried to get me to drink the tea and look at the mountains. My head felt so heavy, I could barely lift it. I looked up to see the sun was setting realizing this has now gone on for over eight hours. I bowed to the earth crying telling him it will not let me go until I realize something else. He said, "Yes, you are stubborn." I laughed countering with, "Strong! I don't want to be strong anymore." He rubbed my back and gently asked

"So when did you sign up for this Fiercely Independent North American Women's Social Club?" I felt a wave of sickness and laughed at the timing knowing he was so fucking right. "UGH," I huff. "I just want to puke that up," I want out, I want out of the club, I want to puke my membership up." I know I need to let go. That in order to be loved, rescued, I need to quit doing it all myself and I need to accept how worthy of I am of love. I beg him to make it stop saying "It is enough insight for the day." Just like that, he calmly said "Come on then, I am closing the ceremony."

What? I cannot believe it is over when I am still out of my mind. I muster up the strength to walk all of a sudden realizing maybe there was never anything bad in me needing to come out. Maybe it was just in my head. I head back to the outdoor ashram where everyone is sitting looking like they are perfectly fine. The Shaman closes the ceremony while I sit looking at the others wondering how they are okay. My cute little friend Eve must have read my mind because she looked at me and said "I am not okay" and we burst into laughter. Everyone laughed and laughed. It was only the beginning. We all continued to laugh; fuck, it felt good to feel something other than pain. It was freezing dark now but we didn't even care as we moved in closer to each other. Well, I had to crawl to get to the other side and that just made them laugh harder. Someone mustered up the sanity to say "We should go inside to eat the soup the Shaman made."

We helped each other gather up. Inside we sat at the huge table occasionally shifting from one extreme to the next; laughing, silence, laughing, and silence. I still went in and out of sickness as I forced the soup down. We laughed more as the night ended. The Shaman urged me to stay but I wanted my space so I gathered my things to follow the others home. We laughed all the way back to our room because the place seemed odd. This place, this earth, the world, appeared odd and our legs moved strangely. We hugged our goodbyes and smiled our way back to our own rooms.

I tossed and turned, meeting the pit again and again throughout the night. Nothing ever came out. I reminded myself it was because, I was good now. Maybe I was always good. I was glad to finally see daylight rise over the mountain. I sat in my meditation and realized I was never bad, I was never sin. But quite the opposite, I chose a family challenged to love because I am love. I wanted the test to raise my being to a higher place. What better way to prove you are love then to come into a world where it is unavailable? Learning to love the way it is meant; only giving.

I chose men unable to love for the same reason. But asking a starving man to feed me, always left me starving. I made a vow to feed myself as I closed the curtains to turn off the day. I just wanted to sleep now. The part that always shuns me for having needs as petty as sleep must have died last night. I told Cat thank you as I climbed back in bed, curled up like, well a cat, and slept the most healing sleep for more than sixteen hours.

I spent the next two free days walking to town alone, writing and just sitting in the warmth of the sunshine that was the most refreshing contrast to the cool breeze. The advanced workshop began and just put a wonderful cherry on top of all I had learned. I struggle as to what more I should say about the workshop because I want people to have their own experiences if they decide to visit Paz Y Luz. I do not want to spoil the surprises I was so grateful to have. I went into each day not knowing what we would do, without any expectations, and that was part of the healing. I feel it is not my place to take the sacred journey of another and taint it with ideas of how it was for me. So I will just highlight my insights from this point forward.

We worked with Shamans and meditated at sacred sites, rivers, rocks and atop mountains. There were only women this time, six of us from five continents. The more we shared, the more we connected and it became obvious this eclectic group of women were destined to be on this journey together. I began to realize more and more how much of a front I put up throughout my life all in an effort to fit in. Not only did I destroy my words, I even changed my sharp pointy handwriting to match my friend's big curly letters in elementary school. I recalled spending hours practicing each letter over and over until inevitably that part of me changed too. Again as in the first workshop each day topped the last, with field trips to places my imagination could have never even conceived.

One very touching exercise that I believe healed the story my grandfather opened my eyes to in the San Pedro ceremony, was a visualized rebirthing. I truly felt I was born again this time into a world where love reciprocates. Each day I had new insights. I saw my life changing from one of stable ritualistic commitment to one of free spirited love and travel, lots of travel. Not the way I traveled in the past—on cruise ships, first class, luxury hotels. I realized that was not being a traveler at all. That was being an upscale tourist taking my lifestyle, opinions and pessimism with me. But the way I now go, with no itinerary, no plans, and deeply connecting with nature as Diane and the Shamans so eloquently taught. My connection to Mother Earth was strengthened every day as PachaMama continued to speak to me confirming my desire to travel. She so eloquently whispered high atop the mountain that day, "I see you. Now see me."

I continued to worry about money periodically but signs were literally everywhere as in the day driving away from a sacred sight we visited. I sat in the back of the van with my thoughts on money. We stopped for a bathroom break and I stayed in the van alone. I closed my eyes trying to remind myself of Diane telling me to stop worrying about money because it was draining my creativity. I began to focus on what it feels like to have plenty of money, even an abundance and began dreaming about being a successful writer, traveling the world free from the strains of financial burden. I recalled Diane telling me I would not run out of money. The van door opened pulling me from the dream and I looked out the window to see a huge dollar sign painted on a giant boulder that moments before closing my eyes I had been looking at but never even noticed the sign. I sighed knowing it was not only going to be all right, it was going to blow my expectations.

That same afternoon, Eve and I journeyed into town to have our Tarot Cards read. It was such a funny free-spirited thing to do and we laughed that both of us with our "educated" minds, she is a lawyer, would consider anything so unempirical. That is until the reader began to uncover things oddly matching our misshapen lives. She discussed my soul mate, pulling her face down making her eyes bulge as she tried to come up with the word in English. Eve and I laughed hard each time she did it, trying to help her interpret the word. Eve blurted out "what does he have scars, big droopy eyes?" Finally the reader found the word saying "suffering, he is suffering right now." Just as the cat had told me in the San Pedro ceremony, she urged me to stop looking for him because he will find me. She said I would never marry again, which I have to say still saddened me. Then she said your book will publish and you will not need to worry about money. She read Eve's cards and then reached under her makeshift table to pull out two small bottles wrapped in twine. She handed Eve one with dark liquid and what looked like coffee beans floating in it. Mine was clear with specs of herbs and what I thought might be chopped up garlic. She said "drink it." I suppose her interpretations that were fairly accurate must have increased our faith in her because we did not even question. We turned up the concoctions and drank. Mine was awful, bitter and garlicky changing in the back of my throat to a burn like it might have alcohol.

I exclaimed "holy crap" as concern for Eve wiped the smile off my face because she does not drink. It did not take long for me to see she did not care because she was now giggling like a little girl. We walked out of their laughing our asses off that we would drink something not even asking once what it was. We both quickly began to feel drunk. We walked the streets of Pisac, or should I say stumbled, wrapped in each other's arms, proclaiming to all the locals in our stuttered voices "we would not be controlled anymore." Eve added "I am a magistrate in the court of law for god's sake."

On the last day we got up early to meditate at sunrise and it was such a beautiful ending, no let me rephrase, it was such a beautiful beginning to my new life. I sat beside Eve as the sun popped over the mountain. Tears dripped from the beauty as the rays penetrated my soul. Eve whispered to me "listen" as she quietly played me a song softly on her phone. We sat absorbing the energy of the mountains, the sun, the song, and each other. Eve is such a wonderful woman. She thinks I helped her but I only helped her hear her own beautiful soul. It was she who comforted me.

Earlier that morning, there was a bit of disappointment that one of the Shamans was sick and would be unable to give us the final rite.

His wife, however, had decided she could do it. Women were not allowed in the past to be Shamans and were not allowed to give or receive the rites. Thankfully all things change and I found it most appropriate that on this last day receiving the last right in the female Temple of the Priestess on my knees as the female Shaman touched me, I had an image of me marrying. Not my soul mate, not a man, not even another but myself.

I told Diane later that day and she smiled saying she could do the ceremony. I purchased a ring in town as a gift to myself and although I considered doing the ceremony before leaving, in the end I decided to wait. Out of respect for the commitment, I found it best to continue working on my relationship with me, a long engagement. I want to take the time to plan just as in any wedding, so as to give myself the wedding of my dreams.

I stayed at Paz Y Luz as many days after the conference as they could fit me. I never made an extended reservation. I simply awoke each day deciding in that moment where I wanted to be and they obliged my free spirit letting me stay as long as they had room. There is such a healing magic in those mountains, the valley, river and the spiritual traditions that there is no way a former member of the Fiercely Independent North American "Programmed" Social Club could ever make sense of. And so I don't. I just feel it. I did not want to leave but all things end. I had to go see who the new me would be.

Malachi

Malachi, the last book of the Old Testament and hopefully the last book of mine. I am exhausted by the tales of hardship, sin and destruction; repeating patterns and crying in disbelief, blaming everything and everybody for my suffering. To tattle on the world for making life rough was relieving. It was easy just like when I had marriage clients write their spousal complaints, but turning to see my own flaws was the hard part. I hope I now see me, my truth and own my contribution to the ending. I am not one to bitch and moan about my problems. I think many people will be surprised to see I even had any. I choose to be happy especially in the face of others. It is genuine because I love people. I love you. All of these issues only surfaced in mind in my alone time. I do not wish for anyone to have to help me. Whether that is simply a female quality or something learned, it is time I allow humanity to be there for me too. I need others. I need you to pull me out of my writing cave that I adore but like everything can become damning if I stay gone too long. I am an escape artist, accustomed to people leaving me as the shaman in Peru taught me, but I am also drawn to leave.

I arrived back to Paradise on the same day my son returned from the United States and we left the airport together ready to begin an awesome adventure. We both walked away from that landing knowing we were walking into the spectacular unknown. We could never go back to the place that deprived our souls. We had changed.

We had faith; faith in our own soul's ability to know. We set out to chase the dreams our spirits sought by beginning a life on a path uncut.

As in the last time upon my return from Peru, the weeks that followed were full of continued insights and inspirations. I felt a renewed energy to take care of my needs as Cat had shown me. It took time to process what the encounter with Cat during the San Pedro ceremony really meant. For the longest time I did not even want to think about it because in the realistic side of my mind it was crazy to consider, "I am Cat and I will do what a cat does." But as time passed and I got back to my life, because that is what we do; we go right back to doing what we have always done despite new insight, things began to click and I knew what Cat meant. It was about my neglect of my human needs and not letting myself be all it means to be a human being; relaxing into my humanness even the things I was conditioned to believe bad—one being my sexuality. I have never let myself be full on human. I have tried to pretend I was something else, searched my soul for something more, tried to be a spiritual being, a healer not aware she needed healing, a know it all brain expert, a sinner confessing in the hopes my human faults would end and bring back virginal grace but the reality is I am living in a world in which all I have is my imperfect humanness. I am learning to see it differently. Maybe the imperfections are not bad pieces but badges. I don't want to seek anymore, not right now. I want to be my flawed human wearing my badges proudly.

I contemplated hard on what to include and whether or not to say things that would hurt. I came to the conclusion I had to present it as my perspective at the time I perceived it. It is not my job to shield others from the pain of the truth, nor is it yours. Our human error is in only seeing the anguish truth may cause but that pain is what it takes to evolve. Lies keep others in the dark literally stalling their chance to see the light. My perspective has since changed. That may be the greatest lesson of all. Our perspective of the past defines our reality of the present. It does not matter if it is the truth or not. It was my truth at the time, my personal memory but now that truth has changed, thankfully changing even my memories. I now see the divine lessons I needed to learn. It is no different with lies we tell ourselves or others tell us. Whether we continue believing our lie or someone else's, we remain powerless to the perspective chosen for us or by us. All in all, lies lock our perception. There is no growth in the untruth. Lies keep us in the dark and the liar even darker.

Now to reveal the lie I have been telling you from the very beginning. The commandment list was never about your soul mate. I knew this when I created the list in graduate school but I wanted to use it on myself the way I had clients use it; unknowingly. I wanted to believe I could attract a man if I raised the bar setting higher standards for relationships and so I did my best to use it blindly although I knew it was always about me. As women, especially of my generation and the generations before me, we are programmed worshippers of men. Worshipping them as in the Bible, the prince in the fairytale or the authoritative ruler; seeing them as something more than human, we more easily dream big dreams for them.

In graduate school, I was working on a project to help troubled teens develop goals when I had the idea. It was a trick to make them dream their own big dreams. Because we expect someone else to come along and give us the life we long for; I developed the questionnaire originally called "The Best Mate." I gave it out with the instruction to dream huge. To let yourself imagine Prince Charming came to rescue you and write down what that dream looks like; how will they behave, what are their dreams, what activities would you love them to do, volunteer in, their job, education, life, etc. Every person who filled it out did so thinking they were dreaming another's dreams. When they were done dreaming I would have them go back and cross out the underlined "at" in the title that said "The Best M<u>at</u>e" so now it read "The Best Me."

It was some of the best advice I have ever given. Because the "And they lived happily ever after" created an unachievable expectation raising generations of girls believing it was outside of us, in him or in stuff. See for yourself. Go back to your "LOVE COMMAND<u>ME</u>NTS" list and read the title crossing out the letters in the word commandment not underlined. It now reads "LOVE <u>ME</u>." It is how to do just that; how to love you. Then in the instructions if you do the same, the hidden message will now read "A positive relationship with <u>me</u> is the key to happiness." Everything you wrote down was about you. What we want in another to rescue us is what we want for ourselves. These are your wishes; this is your key to happiness. It is our responsibility to be the person of our dreams, not wait for a fantasy that may never be. If these are the qualities you want in your life then put the qualities in your life. Be your own hero. The Commandment list is how you can learn to love you. Make the list and then become the list.

I knew this when I began my own list but I did not know it is more than the wanting, it is the doing. I did not discover this for myself until after Peru. When I came home and had contemplated why I thought I loved all the frogs so. I decided to do the things we did together anyway to show myself I love me and I love my dream. Doing some, if not all of the activities everyday was the key to my own happiness. It is not just in believing this or that is what you want, it is in the doing of what you want. Just as a list of morals means nothing if you do not behave in line with them. It is action. Take the action to be the list. Take the action to feed your soul. Little by little without even realizing The Year of the Frog became the year of me as I became my dream.

Maybe you have heard "make yourself happy" or "be the love of your life." It seems easy enough, but seriously I had to learn to "make" myself happy just as I would make another. I would constantly hover over another "are you okay, can I get you a drink, something to eat, make you comfortable?" I wanted everyone to feel at home, but I had trouble doing the same for me.

In going through this process for myself, I learned who I was. Who I was wanting others to be is who I was underneath. I was so caught up believing the fairytale that every time the frog failed I was disgustingly let down and blaming him for my unhappiness, never realizing what I sought was my own soul. Each frog was a lesson in letting go of who I was not, so who I was could show. It is no wonder my fairytale vision I had in the beginning of this journey was not frogs turning into princes but princes turning into frogs. Every man began as a prince in my eyes full of miraculous potential. But as I began to know them, the spell cast upon me turned my perception to dreadfully judge behaviors I once tolerated. Little by little the prince in my view began turning into a frog bearing only problems, not the princely possibility I had previously conceived. Getting to know them was getting to know me. The frog's reflection mirrored my own toxic wart spell covered soul. But it also reinforced my soul's potential showing me golden pieces I myself had hiding within me wanting out to breathe.

Dating helped me see what I needed to work on in myself to break the spell. It is not easy. It is school, no it is worse; it is boarding school for disciplinary problems. It is a mirror. It is why I so wished for commitment; to stop the madness and stop showing me my f'n problems. There is no way to teach these lessons; it all has to be lived and some lessons feel like torture. But it is never the end. There is no end. There are only beginnings. It became very clear I walked around like I wore a scarlet letter. My friends could see it in my face if I succumbed to my human desire for sexuality. The idea of sin so burned in my brain I could not even enjoy the most pleasurable human act. Is it even the least bit ironic before my encounter with Cat I had an encounter with Ari the human version of a bold feline? Yes, I do believe life places people on our paths to teach but we have to be open to the lesson. I confessed like a child the shame of my secret while my friends looked at me in disbelief that a single woman in her forties could be so disgraced by enjoyment. From now on I declare to enjoy it.

After each frog the list altered with me learning what I wanted and what I did not want; sometimes adding to the list, sometimes taking away. It was not just as easy as writing it or erasing it. The work was then for me to actually do it myself; becoming more like each of the wants and working to remove the want nots. It was all about learning to love myself enough to take the action required for my own happiness. I had to learn to go at it alone, give my happiness to myself on my own. Life presented me with a ton of short love lessons to teach me to let him go and see my happy dream remains even when he leaves. I am as happy if not happier with him gone, with a new lesson learned; I forgive myself and move on. I have to force myself to date because there came a point where I found myself in a place almost overly okay alone. Still, something in my heart misses a love I have yet to know. The fact I miss it makes me believe it exists.

When the opportunity presents itself despite my solitude, I let my human be human braving the love terrain accepting that it may end in pain. I go full on because like travel; everywhere I go, I find pieces of my soul. All connections are sacred. We are discovering our self, letting go of what we are not to remember what we are.

By studying the love I thought I felt with each, I discovered who I am when I am functioning at my best. On the way back from Peru the second time, it occurred to me I was not even searching for him but searching for me in my highest conceivable form. Every man I dated had a way with words I am so passionate about. I believe life was trying to teach me to love my own writing. The entire list— writing, meditating, dancing, loving nature, it is who I am at my best. All I need to do is keep functioning at that level. It was a love for me in the company of my best being. It is who I was as a child stepping outside the box, surrounded by adventure, tadpoles, toads and frogs, then coming in and writing about the love I was feeling.

This is not a list! This is your bliss. It is how your soul wants to express itself. Let it be your guide. Follow your bliss to find happiness by altering it as you learn what you want. Because some of us do not even know what we want and if we do, we often stall because actually doing it is tough. So we look for a savior to do it for us. But magic happens on your path when you step into it on your own. Life will give you all you need to continue living your dream. And for me that dream was to get back to being the girl I used to be.

New Testament

To rise above my past, I had to walk through it realistically to understand the meaning. With all of the journaling and editing, I gave myself the gift of studying my life more intently than any classroom subject. We are all writing books with our lives. The pen is in our head scribbling memories haphazardly like an elementary rough first draft. The beautiful thing is if we are brave enough to go back, we get to edit freely until the story perfects to align with all we've been dreaming. Reality stays reality but perception alters. Pain lessens when you see the lesson. I only hope to keep my life book interesting so I feel inspired to turn the page, take a chance, and make mistakes to construct the most excellent story. I wish to love and show compassion to all so their book is full of smiles and laughter I helped give, and for those I fault, I hope it teaches a lesson we can all, in the end, forgive.

I relied on another to make me feel how I didn't feel alone. Clinging to relationships that did not serve my higher being meant I had no faith in believing there was a better future. Our soul is trying to guide us but we just don't pay attention. Staying in a bad relationship for love is not love. It is in fact harmful to the statute of love because you are advocating disrespect in the name of love. Leave for love. Leave for the love of you; for the love of love to prove to all humankind better waits when we stop clinging to things, resisting change even desiring unhealthy relationships because we know how the day ends. To resist change is to resist evolving.

My ex-husbands were the greatest teachers of the hardest lessons: lying, cheating, insecurity, and over-indulging to numb it all. I came to terms with my first husband's affair only when I realized I was the cheater. I was carrying the energy of a long history of infidelity in my family and I too was battling the urge to seek love outside myself, outside my marriage. I cannot tell you the number of times during our eleven-year marriage men flirted with me and I fought wanting more. I even kissed a few. I imagine if I had the opportunity to have an affair sooner in the marriage, I probably would have done it. Just as most women who devote our lives to being mothers, I was simply denied the opportunity to cheat. I was preoccupied doing mom activities and rarely did any partying while my son was young. Had I been exposed to the life I am now with a party around every corner, I would have been a big ass cheater. More than likely, I would have lied to cover it up, maybe even put my hand on the Bible to prove my lie. Oh most certainly, I would have put my hand on it, I mean come on, I did not even believe it.

What you read about my first ex is all the bad. But if you look back, it fits on less than three pages. Three pages! I was married to this man for eleven years. There was a lifetime of good my mentality would not let me see. This happens when our mind produces more negative thoughts than positive. Even memories get contaminated. This is what depression is. When you look at the world with a stained soul, all you see is stains. The truth is this man was a good man. He has a kind heart and if I was just picking a father for my son, I made a fucking fantastic choice. He loves our son dearly. Everyone is battling their own programming. He did not have the perfect life growing up. He was following his orders as well. He did the best he could marrying a young and lost soul. We got what we needed. We both got a saint out of it, an old saint at that. I call that a pretty damn good deal.

My second husband was a rebound. He was an attempt at fulfilling the rule of financial prosperity society feeds us. We had more than our fair share of luxuries and travel that was exquisite. In the beginning he treated me like a queen. I believed I was giving my son who was now a teen a great opportunity. I was simply seeking change and choosing to love rather than to fall. I hate to write these words because he too is a wonderful man. His family is amazing and I still love them so very much although I had to pull away from them too in order for me to get a better view. He still is a great friend to me. I know if anything ever happened to me or any of my family he would be the first to respond. But it is my truth and I have to honor it now. The day after I wrote that semi-guilt ridden apology, I got a phone call from him. I was walking with one of my best girls, Miriam on the beach. He called to finalize a deal we had verbally made on some property. I did not agree with him. The moment he sucked in that gruff breath, my body began to automatically respond tensing to his rage that always made me cave. My head raced and my heart began to thrust as it had in the past. Damn almost three years later, I had all but forgotten the hold he had on me. Just as many who are exposed to abuse, I forgot how bad it was. I had even convinced myself it was not abuse. It is part of the spell cast on us as women to minimize and soften brutality. I had to be honest and call its name. It was abuse and so I went back and changed the story yet again to include it.

During that phone conversation three years later, I was right back there under his thumb as my body physically began to respond. My old script stated "gently agree with him while he rages," but this time, my peaceful walk with my friend and her silent strength were enough to push me past my heritage. Rather than shrink, I grew saying firmly "No! I will not let you talk to me this way; it is why we are divorced. Think about discussing this with me in a respectful way and you may call me back when you are calm." I could not believe I had lived like that. Still my heart was racing and it took hours for my mind to calm.

I nearly lost my entire being in that relationship. I was forever silencing my voice to soften his abusive passion; then trying desperately to love it out of him in the brief moments of peace with little bits of my soul struggling to breathe. I went home and called him back, firm in my stance. To my surprise, he agreed with me and I made the decision to close that chapter of victimhood for good.

I feel for him. He would not tell the story anywhere near the story I told. It was always clear he did not even recall the rages. He was not his soul during those times, he was a programmed robot. I stayed with him because I knew the battle he was fighting; we are all fighting the energy we inherit. He was simply doing what was done to him. Nighttime drunken rages were part of his childhood. My heart still hurts for him. Because I see him; I know who he is, but he does not. It was my pattern to attract people to lift up because I could see so much good in every one but myself. That is why we worked for a bit. We were both one in the same, unaware of our beauty beneath. I could see him but I could not see me.

Because I did not work internally to fix, no find (I originally wrote "fix" but that is not correct when we find our core we see we are not broken) myself, I wound up with more of just that; my perception of a broken self. I met him online. Had I been completely honest then, I could have saved us both the trouble with the profile title "broken woman seeks broken man". Although I do not want to admit it, no one does, I too inherited a vehicle prone to a drunk driver. When I was not consumed with school or work, I was consumed with wine. It was my relief, my release, my reward. He was my twin, over consuming in work and whiskey. Consuming ourselves to keep from seeing ourselves; neither of us had anything to give. We were two starving souls asking the other to feed us. We both had outer assets full of attractive sparkle distracting our troubled truth. He had stuff, money and power. I had youth; ten years younger, vitality and an eagerness to travel. I now understand it like this; it is one thing to tell someone you love them but to engage in the activity of love is something different. Quite different and for me it was foreign. It is unfair to tell a starving person you will feed them and never present the food. We were merely saying the word "love" while we left each other starving. We were both wrong in that our love was superficial, only on the surface but nothing underneath because underneath, we were empty wells with nothing to offer.

On to Joshua, well what can I say? Desperately trying to earn my love smothering me with attention to mask his uncertainty; the poor man was being the best he could. I want to jokingly say bat shit crazy, but the funny thing is, it is no joke. Maybe he tried so hard because like so many of us, like me, he was trying to overcome past patterns of insecurity. And just like my marriages reflecting me, I must admit bat shit crazy? Um, yes certainly. I was just out of a second marriage. Feeling like a total failure, probably the most insecure in my life and I got a reflection of that. I do not doubt he loved me; he just loved me more than I loved me. And is exactly why it felt uncomfortable and crazy.

Matthew was not much more of an improvement with me still hiding beneath a mask of confusion, it is no wonder this frog would not, no could not, be honest with me. Mark, Luke, Isaiah were mere reflections of my own ambiguity and fear of letting go. Amos was of course another lie but it was so much more. It was me desperately wanting the fairytale, taking an innocent man and force fitting him to my idealistic fantasy. Then I woke up to wonder why the dream was not mine? Seriously, after one night? It is frustrating and ironic that we cannot see our own disease. Still after all these years, I attached to everything to make me feel something I myself was lacking. To fall in love with a story I completely made up in my mind of how it could be the rest of my life with a person I spent one night! The best thing I could have ever done was stay with that broken heart; to sit in my pain and feel it. It was not easy. But it healed and it healed fast. I do not even know the day it happened. I just quit feeling the pain and began living again. No let me rephrase that, I just began living again and the pain quit feeling.

My friends helped. Elisa and I going to moving meditations, the yoga, and chanting concerts pushed me to heal and grow. Working on me helped me deal with the issue now so I would not be dealing with it the rest of my life. It seems silly to look back on that quick fall. Reading my words is embarrassing but it was my awkward truth. A truth that revealed to me I am the one making up the fairytale, I am in love with a figment in my mind; in me. I am in love with a dream I created all on my own. This is what we do. We take a man and place them in the play running on expectations in our head. We feel it, smile thinking of it, fall asleep dreaming of it until we have a life plan that devastates us when the fantasy ends. Heartache set in after one night because I was not in the moment. I spent a lifetime with him in my mind. The pain set in as if it were years. Now, rather than be off on some mental rendezvous, I will let him go and be the dream alone.

The encounters with Roman and Ari boy in "The Acts" were attempts by me to fill the gap from the piece of my dream I thought left with Peter. I still desperately needed to fill space and resorted to my old ways of using people to give me what I had not yet learned to give myself. I did not spend enough time with either of them to see the reflection but I was repeating patterns in some form or fashion. I would consider it to be the same pattern of avoidance with over-indulgence to be the lesson here because it is always my superficial way to escape reality. Had those encounters turned into anything it would have been me again believing I was lowering myself, in an effort to pick someone else up. I hated lifting men up and loved it all at the same time; it kept me busy avoiding my own insecurities.

John may have been committed but so was I—committed to rigid beliefs attempting to control what tomorrow would bring. Because that is what rules are; policies to follow so we can have a sneak peak at the future. All of the lies may have just been life trying to teach me to be okay with the unknown and I can say this was quite the spectacfuckular lesson. When someone leaves you with holes in the story, you get to fill those blanks in. So here is my interpretation of a man who had an awful lot to hide. I can only assume his life was full of tragedy. So much tragedy I will not even try to convince anyone I understand. But I believe he was merely doing what he needed to do, all he knew to do. Beneath his lies was a heart full of honest love trying to escape some awful confinement worse than his imprisonment. We all fear rejection and just want approval. Often the only option is to say what we think others will accept. This is why we hide behind lies because we fear the truth will turn people away.

We only want love. Most lies are simply a desire for love. Think about that. Nobody tells untruth to hurt another, they lie to keep doors from closing, to keep hearts open, to keep love flowing. I think he hid behind spirituality, not wanting to face his truths either and thus why we were a great match for a time. We were one in the same hiding behind spiritual disguises trying to gain approval and love.

We have to consider sometimes when people lie to us it is our very own fault. Perhaps they have seen how we respond to truth. If we can't accept the truth then we can't accept them. Everyone is just trying to fit in.

I learned a great deal from this man most of all to be okay with the unknown. What better way to learn to love the light in someone than to love light unseen. Now, that I do believe is faith; faith in the human spirit and the god that dwells within. I realized another's story has nothing to do with mine and you cannot carry someone else's energy. Nor can you lift your energy to make good things happen for another. Everyone has to be allowed to walk their own path. I can only be responsible for me. I have to let others carry their own pain. And if that means pushing them for the truth then that is what it means. Ask questions. Ask lots of questions. If it makes you uneasy to ask, then all the more reason to ask and if it makes them uneasy for you to ask, then all the more reason to ask.

Never, ever think another is more spiritual than you. Not much unlike the religious fallacy that hovered over the churches I grew up in where nobody questioned godly authority, I had more faith in him than me. I said earlier, "I felt oddly connected to a man I do not know much about, do not even know his truth." Yes, that was me. I did not even know my truth; my identity. I held on to potential as I always did because we all have that. But having potential means we are not there yet.

We are all the spirit evolving from the dust, to uncover our sacred heart. Each at different levels, no one is greater than the other just closer to the core. It is difficult, damn near impossible to understand yourself when you are trying to understand someone else. The few brief moments I spent with John were fun but there was also a lot of doubt in my mind. Doubt over who he really was, doubt over if I really even liked him romantically, and doubt about his stories. That is the truth I often fail to face because I see people in their best light. I am learning my ability to see God in others is a wondrous gift but often, I see what they do not. I cannot bring it out in someone else. I cannot make them see what I see. I cannot love it into them or love flaws out. Everyone has to play their own game. Trying to pull another up out of their darkness hinders their own progress. Strength does not come from someone helping us; it comes from us helping ourselves.

Still I learned some tremendous lessons. During his imprisonment, I learned ten minutes is more than enough time for a meaningful conversation when you are mindful of your words. The limited talks trained me to choose words wisely. I learned peace can be found even in a prison. I am so proud I put fear aside. To think I was a friend to someone who in some eyes may not deserve the love I gave makes my soul shiver with godly grace. Many would deem what I did the most uncomfortable position to be in. But as yogi John said with the right perception even this pose became resting. I rest feeling the risk I took to love someone so blindly, in such horrific conditions, may have been the act of love I am most proud of.

I am certain we are all godly; we are all good and we are all worthy of love. We are all worthy of love! My little girl inside who never wanted to look for God in church but instead sat outside in wonder if butterflies were angels, puppies were saints, the homeless guy were Jesus, and if the lady begging were God, is so very proud of me for getting back to seeing God in everything. Although I do not see or talk to John anymore, some months later I received a message from him. It read in somewhat broken English, that I have only slightly edited:

Julita, I believe life is a cycle, a short one. Every single human we get to know has something for you; to make you smile, challenge or teach you in a bad moment. Nothing is random. Some people have something beautiful to give. Like you. You came to my life in the right moment, the right time. Julita not only the fact you got a lawyer for me, but every single call you made; those 8, 6, 4 minutes you dedicated to me while I was in jail, saved me. There was always something bigger and more powerful behind it. It was more than a single call. Right after every one, I found myself in peace. Your voice helped me get through. Thank you."~ John

The message made me cry because I felt confirmation I did the right thing by putting all doubt aside to just be loving. It reinforced my desire to continue to give more than I receive. That is love. Call me gullible all you want. I will not stop. It is living in faith that whether or not it ever comes back to me in a form measurable for others to see, it reciprocates in ways that give my soul power forever changing me.

As far as how Ruth treated me during my struggle with work, being offended does not make me right. My ego always used the offense to defend my position. In many ways I was wrong. Ruth is not a bad person. In fact she is quite the opposite—a remarkable woman who has had to become tough to withstand the shit she's been dealt. She is strong, she is a survivor. I know her story and that is why it hurts to have caused her additional pain. The note she left on my door to buy me out crosses my mind as the turning point. The pain I felt from it was not merely a loss of friendship but it made me question myself, my yearning, and my soul. I was so hurt, perceiving it to be manipulative as I did the conversation where she wanted an answer telling me her life was on hold, her family in limbo. But then again who is the manipulating one? Well, yes that would be me, throwing all my confusion off on her, forcing her to make a decision for me because I was too weak. When we believe we are powerless, we permit others to choose for us.

I had not yet learned how powerful my intuition is. I needed people to go against me to challenge my very own belief in me. It was pleading with me and causing me distress because I was not hearing my soul clearly. Feeling is the voice of the soul. Learning to hear your soul and follow it is what faith is. The letter on my door may have initially felt like a childish bully's blow but that attempt to control has proven to be the greatest gift. The sleepless nights over it and the ache in my heart were simply my dreams saying "see this is good, we are waiting for you. Follow us; for God's sake follow us." I was trying desperately to explain to her something I could not understand myself. It was as if I had no choice as I began to follow my inner guide and now I know the questions only get answered in the following. And because I did, none of that pain matters anymore.

Lastly Peter, I completely understand I am the list and I thank him for this. We engaged in activities that brought my soul forth. It was not just that he did things for me or with me, it was the common interest in cultivating dreams; my dreams, his dreams, our dreams. He shared my love for writing and deep thoughtful conversation. He was good for my soul because he was the first person to make my passion a priority by saying "write and do nothing else." Giving my voice precedence was something I so lacked because I never had enough faith in my words. I would put off writing until I could take no more; my words would explode on paper with such ferocity it felt dirty. Afterward I would destroy it out of fear it would be found. I would be found.

Many of the items on my list were done during the days with him. I found if I continued to do the things for myself, I can feel just as happy as I thought he made me. Even happier because I recognize it is I generating the joy. I did not fall head over heels in love with him. I fell head over heels in love with me. That is ultimately the key. I was falling in love with me. We are simply in love with the feeling someone or something brings forth that we already are. I was in love with a man in my heart my entire life never realizing it was my heart. Peter just happened to catch me at a time when I was uncovering who I was and he had enough similar qualities. We enjoyed our time allowing our souls to shine. I liked the me I was with him. He was a man of words. Words seduce me because it is my divine calling. I know it is my dharma because when I write my energy thrives. I feel connected to something bigger than me. These teachers in my life are trying to teach me what I love, what my purpose is. Crazy, maybe; I often write like crazy. I am obsessed with writing and when I honor it each day I feel alive; a blog, a poem, a haphazard journal entry or a cheesy lovey message to my friends. I let my soul peak through momentarily and love feels me.

I never had someone be as honest as Peter. Sure, he often told me more than I wanted to hear, but it was so brave and rather than turn me away, it drew me in. No, I did not want to hear who he was sleeping with, but it was what I needed to hear to learn to accept the truth. I had never accepted any truth. Not even my own. I was living the edited version of a life that felt honorable in my mind. I discovered I was forever wanting someone to love me unconditionally but never presenting the true conditions. He told me more than once he did not want a relationship and every time my heart blocked the words with feelings of hope. No matter how many times he said it, I still felt I could be the one to change it. I was doing that with everyone and with everything. No matter what the truth, I always felt I could change it by ignoring it. I was not a full out liar. I was an ignorer of the truth. And worse of all I was ignoring the truth of my soul. Just as Controligion had taught me to never doubt its tales; I stood strong in untruths to demonstrate blind faith in everything but me.

It did not happen instantly; I now understand even when you have an enlightened 'aha' moment, it still takes time to implement that knowledge within your lifestyle, your thought patterns, your behaviors. It was after my second trip to Peru it happened. The crying spells stopped, the heavy lifted and just like Cat took care of his needs there was a shift in the way I cared for me. Little things that may seem invalid began to shake me. For example I am sitting in my hammock with a couple of friends asking if I can get up and get them anything. I look at my empty cup thinking I would love some more green tea but when they say "no thank you" my normal response to tell myself the same is hit with an inner dialogue that commences to convince me to get up. Get up and make myself some tea. Not quickly throw hot water over the bag so to move on caring for my guests, but slowly brew, slice ginger, squeeze some lemon and give myself that spoon of honey to make my tea the finest in the land, like I would if I were serving the king of France.

I began taking myself on longer walks because inside part of me wanted to turn left rather than the normal right to explore. I missed yoga more to stay with myself filling my head with grateful thoughts of how lucky I am; loving my bed, moving all over it like I was having a morning love affair with the bedding. I meditate and cook a fabulous breakfast for myself. I make tea and tell myself "sit and write and do nothing else" making me feel my dream is important to me. I write all day if I want, swim when I want, grab my guitar when I feel the inkling, walk to the beach or just lay and listen to music outside under the stars. I watch the raindrops in my pool go up before they go down. I dream of adventure and travel. I take my breaks in nature to find inspiration. I sit in silence, taking in every detail with not my camera but my photographic eye creating postcards in my mind. With a full heart, I take it all home just as I did as a child and write a book, a blog or poem.

Every relationship or lack thereof was a reflection of the way I felt about myself at the time. Whether it was insecurity or overindulgent deceit, it was all lessons geared to uncover the real me. It is not necessarily that I was attracted to negative qualities but attracted to similar qualities based on false identity beliefs. Who or what was causing me the pain was where I went wrong looking for something to blame. I tried to come up with a million things to fault but instead it was just my own shadow haunting.

Not one person intentionally hurt me; they were fighting their own battles and had I been in touch with my soul, I would have known it did not align and could have left easily. I needed them to rub me raw to show my flawed identity. There was a space in my life when I had to fight. There was a space in my life when I had to lie. It is not the essence of me; it is who I had to be in that space. Evolving and learning this is not who I am, is as important as learning who I am. I left those relationships only when this was learned and accepting I did not like myself with those qualities in my life.

I think true love comes as a reflection of what you yourself are generating. If you are loving yourself and honoring your soul you will attract someone doing the same. That is what creates magic passion, two souls in line with their own. If you can keep the balance and keep honoring your soul it can grow. But when ego of either kicks in, is when you may think you are not even close to being each other's one. Maybe that is it. Maybe we are all soul mates and the ones who bring us joy are simply resonating with us at the level of our soul. While those that bring us pain are pointing us in the direction to uncover soul by making a change.

I am not looking for or chasing anyone anymore. I am focused on being me and feeling my soul with soulful activity. I will not settle for someone who wants to become a passenger on my path but remain conductor of their own simply crossing mine a time or two. If by chance I cross a path of someone who wants a grand adventure, I am open and ready to jump off the end. But keeping my heart open means it must not then close in an attempt to lock you in. My heart will stay just as open to lovingly let you go.

Until then I will continue to resonate at a joyful level on my own. Maybe it will bring someone already on a grand adventure themselves but the work is to stay tuned into the soul practicing soulful tasks and sharing these experiences to raise the frequency to a level unimaginable. It is why my time with Peter felt so good but not devastating to me when we lost connection. We both were tuned to the same station for a moment. When he left, I soon discovered all I needed to do was get back in tune. Love is a dance and rather than crumple to the floor when your partner steps away, stand on your own and dance anyway.

The biggest change is I quit kissing frogs. It was as if I felt the need to give every potential man a chance just in case they turned out to be my soul mate. I realize everyone on my path is a soul mate and everyone was mirroring things I needed to face. People wonder how someone like me could get involved in so many relationships that now obviously seem unhealthy. But it is no different than how we ignore the truth to support any programmed belief. Just as no adults questioned the priests because they wanted to believe and no one questioned if the Bible was really God's word, I was programmed to believe; believe things that seem unreal, believe words, believe spells, believe a frog not pleasant at first with a little love will turn to a prince if you have faith enough to break the curse. I wanted that deep rooted belief so desperately, I could not see reality while the story was still being written. You never know the end until you reach the end.

If we believe something to be true we only see facts to confirm the belief. It is not until escaping it that the tide of the mind begins to turn. Whether it is a prince in a fairytale or the Prince of Peace, it just goes to show we are all looking for a savior.

We forget who we are, who dwells within, what we want, what fuels our passion, year after year the programming continues until we have no clue what we desire, what we love, how to love. Our power is lost leaving us believing we have no power at all. Thus we look for another to fuel us. With no voice I found myself marrying twice to please an unpredictable future and ending it twice to please my depressive past. Kissing frogs I found there was no prince at all only one lost soul attracting another. The initial attraction was the lostness oddly feeling a connection with nothing to connect. It is no wonder the identical reflection over time irritates as it should to pull the poison. It is like asking someone on the moon to give you a kiss. It is not going to happen. I never realized that until now but I was trying to love men on the moon. I loved them; I loved them all but we were so far apart. They loved me too; the signals just never got through.

I have no ill feelings about any of it. I had the best love I have ever known and it had not a thing to do with him. It was me in those moments I was in love with; the adventurer, the musician, the writer, the singer, nature lover, gypsy traveler, a raw and flawed honest to the core soul simply looking to soar. It was merely an act of bravery for me to once and for all honestly let my soul go. I realized I am whole on my own. I can do all of those things on my own. And I can have love without anyone else. Companionship is good, but amor you will only find love inside yourself.

Revelations

The Ayurvedic spray is almost gone. The potion that moved my dharma to line up with my passion of writing and placing me in a life of paradise is drops away from being nothing more than an empty bottle. The transition unfolded with little effort from me until it came to the end. I have never finished a book and I had to fight my past heritage of abandonment so much there was an internal war exploding in my being. I spent months in that war. At times I did not think I would win. It was my soul against status quo. Although only my imagination, it felt as if something had a hold on me torturing my soul with nighttime beatings, berating and inhumane chaining leaving me wanting to give in. I was deprived of food and sleep but my hunger to speak my soul eventually triumphed and status quo let me go when I realized it was me holding the key. The door was always open, I simply couldn't see. I wanted acceptance so very much I held on to the chains when all I had to do was let go.

There is magic everywhere if we only let life move us with its ever changing currents. My worry of not finishing the book and the spray running out before I finished was met with a loving blessing when my good friend Sarah, who just so happens to be my beautiful single neighbor also in her forties, stopped by with an essential oil made just for me. It is another one of life's synchronicities to have purchased a house unknowingly next to a woman with the same desire to be living dreams not waiting for a man or society to catch up with our knowing—life is to be lived fully now with hearts open, giving, daring, and sharing. She had no reason to make me the oil, not even aware I was struggling to finish, or I was losing sleep over it resulting in little to no focus. Sarah did not even know I lay on my yoga mat the night before unable to sleep, crying my eyes out over how difficult it has been to complete this task, wanting to quit, wanting to treat my words as I had in the past; losing them, destroying them, or burning them for fear my words were full of sin. And that's why I knew it was a miracle when I read the hand written label on the homemade essential oil Sarah gave me that read "Wake up and Concentrate."

Our soul knows. Strip down to it and let the signs steer, the wind sail, and the earth shake that spark free. So many of us think happiness is something we will find in the future. When I look like this, possess this item, this person, this degree, this job or this level of repetitive security. The soul knows nothing of time. It lives in this moment almost like it has no life in the past or future. If we believe happiness is only possible in the future, we will never arrive because the future remains just outside our soul's life. I never again want to be the person who only recognizes a joyful moment when it ends. The commandment list is my reminder of the life my soul wants me to lead, to recognize it when I am letting my soul show and appreciate it daily. As a counselor, I knew what to do for happiness, I knew how to get others to listen to themselves. That's what I was doing, getting them to listen to their soul. If we could only learn to do this from the beginning on our own, there would be no need for counseling.

My advice was not my advice at all, but merely a reflection of what they were saying they wanted. Many times people would talk and talk telling me their idea of happiness but it was not until I would either stop them, and say "repeat that" or summarize what they themselves had said that it would resonate with them in a way something changed. You could see it in the faces, the change. It would happen in my office, the knowing would leave them in awe. The awe is where God lives. It softens our face; it stands hair on end, tears our eyes, and sends chills up our spine signaling your soul just spoke something divine.

Carrying the knowing back into everyday life often put them right back doing what they had always done, following the script of the past so the future stayed the same. I myself was doing the equivalent in my life because believing it, really believing it was the biggest battle of all. There is so much programming to unprogram. The list is now my soul contract to push me to my highest self. Qualities I did not like in others are qualities I do not like for myself and want to eliminate in my life because my soul cannot thrive. It sounds simple enough but implementing it is not. For instance, if you do not want cocaine in your life then do not allow someone in your life who uses. In the same instance, if I do not want an alcoholic, controlling, lying, cheating person in my life then I had better stop being one. In doing so myself, I can comfortably tell others that although I may love you, I do not want this in my life which means I choose my life over an issue that is yours to mend if you so desire. The commandment list is my reminder of who I am. It is me. I am.

OUR FATHER

My father was visiting me when I was finishing this book with editing. I was on edge, thinking "just a few more edits and I will finish." I continued to write in the living room where my sacred writing station was. It was where my imagination had learned to flow. My father apparently had not expressed his true feelings over me living in a house we bought together because his unexpressed agitation and my desire to live a life unscripted would soon reveal more painful lessons.

My dad loves to party. He is the life of the party and since he stopped drinking scotch, he is great fun. But I had changed and I was no longer joining him in the party as much. Instead I was working on my book and I felt he was interrupting me, wanting me to be the way I used to be. The fact we bought the house together, and I took over the living room to write, progressively agitated him because I was making him feel he did not belong in his own home.

I had been trying to stay up late and finish edits. He would party then come home and make remarks like "you are addicted to that" and "Jesus, you are still working on it." I waited until he went to bed and got up around midnight but he kept interrupting me. Early morning I hurried to get to my writing station and do what I could before he awoke but soon thereafter he walked in. I got snooty saying, "Dad you keep interrupting me and it takes a long time to get back in the flow." Keep in mind, I was not kind. He left hurt. Had we had a conversation at all it would have been a great opportunity for us to evolve but instead we acted as our script portrayed and my heart and my dreams were nearly ripped away.

It was so very odd because I was writing a synopsis for a publisher in the form of a fairytale summarizing this book. I was discussing the Monster Quo, "Status" Quo, and how he programs, controls, and covers our soul with beliefs our dreams are nothing but vain hope. I wrote all the things he convinces us we must do; school, work, marry, and make money. "He will tear you down if you veer from his script" was the sentence I was writing when my dad walked in, this time after drinking.

He began to berate me and my dream, calling my book shit and telling me I think I know it all. He did not stop there; he continued saying my entire family did not like me anymore. He said "call your mom, see for yourself. You are living off the reservation with all your Indian feathers and dreams. Your spirituality is bullshit. You are crazy and need a counselor yourself. You think you know it all but you have wasted your education and your son's college fund to allow him to follow a bullshit dream like your own."

I was fairly calm at first but he pulled me into his anger and I began to cry saying "nothing was ever good enough and I could never please you. The day I graduated from Grad school, you could only tell me I should have gone to medical school. I only disappoint you because I am not like you. Good! I never wanted to be anything like you. You pushed me to know it all, then you call me a know it all!"

By this time, I was yelling too. It felt horrible to talk back. I apologized saying "I love you. I am sorry I was pulled into your anger." It made him madder. He continued to discuss me acting like the house was all mine and then yelled I should go somewhere else to finish my bullshit book! I walked into my room taking my entire writing station with me to get my bullshit spiritual things and my shitty book he knows nothing about, out of his sight.

I was reminded what it was like to live with someone still programmed by inheritance. It was surreal and eye opening because I had all but forgotten the reason I had married his demons twice— infidelity and raging alcoholism. I put this man on a pedestal and even resented my mother for leaving him, but now I get it.

I cannot stand to say these things about my own father. But like an explosion of knowledge rather than break things apart; there it was putting the puzzle together to complete a picture I never wanted to see. My relationship with my father was the reason I carried condemning energy and the reason I married that energy. Here he was berating my dreams, my voice, my spirituality, quoting Quo trying to make me align with his beliefs the way my own mind had beaten me my entire life.

I could not decide if the proper response was to stay and find my peace amongst the painful pose and racing mind symbolic to the teachings of my yoga meditative practices. Or if I should take that little girl who always wanted to run by the hand and say "let me rescue you." She was tired of me believing the lies. The way parents talk to their children becomes their inner programmed voice and I have been working so very hard to unprogram.

But look back at all the cursing I did in this book. It is not me; it is a piece I have been trying to leave. I do not say bullshit out loud. If I am mad enough to curse, I go big and say Fuck! It is not my voice inside my head, it is his when he is drinking. Drunk or sober, I get the privilege of hearing that voice over and over. It is like a recording comes on inside my brain and I am tired of meekly letting it play.

I found some peace in writing it all down but still the night was sleepless. Despite my vow not to cry; I cried all night long. Well, I did stop to do "something different and rescue myself." I meditated through my tears until about 3AM and then I booked a one way ticket to Thailand. I packed a bag thinking how I had been waiting on a sign to travel so when someone says "take your shitty book somewhere else to finish it," listen to the hidden message beneath it.

He was absolutely correct. It is shit! And just as Diane had taught me in Peru to give my shit to fertilize PachaMama, I decided to see it as a sign and finish the shit I started. I did not leave to make my dad feel guilty; I left for love; for the love of me and my dream. There is a lot of leaving in my life, yes. And I have in the past left to escape but this time I was not leaving to escape my soul. I was leaving to keep her near me and continue on my dream.

I love the dad I know beneath it all. I can see him. I know who he really is, but he does not when he is drunk. For a moment I forgot who I was too. It took every ounce of me not to instantly forgive him. I knew he would be so very sorry in the morning. They always are. I knew it would break my heart even more to see the amazing love I always wanted come through my door to apologize and comfort me. It would feel like I matter and my entire life of trying to get someone to see me; be proud of me and love me properly was finally becoming reality. He would soften, cry and be back to his amazing kind hearted self. Everyone is human, and everyone makes mistakes but I believe it is time we stop sweeping our pain under our shame.

I desperately wanted to stay as I always had absorbing the love that would temporarily come off him until the next binge to begin the sermon chanting his negative mantra of life commands. This man who denies religion is so full of rigid beliefs and judgments Controligion is his devout faith whether he believes it or not. He clings to ideas so programmed by society's way, his faith outweighs his belief in me.

I hated to leave my loving Dixie dog and NicaKitty who had both listened to my pain and snuggled with my broken heart all night. But I could not stay and enable that behavior even though he was very sorry and crying the next morning as I loaded up to leave. I got in the cab and fought tears all the way only to break down when the taxi driver turned on the radio playing "No Woman, No Cry." The words trying to soothe me shook the salty strength from my eyes.

I wrote my father a long apology taking responsibility for my energy and letting him know my love for him remains. I understand his remarks stem from fear and the fact I gave up a stable income to follow a dream. Yes, I became a "know it all" full of overconfidence in speaking facts, unable to speak my own voice; I spouted science just to speak at all. I invited the experience still residing in a body wanting to remain the sufferer. But it became all very clear the remarks from my high school boyfriend's mom that "I had daddy issues" were in fact true.

It is the reason I have body issues. I watched him degrade my mother's weight, my sister's, and every woman who did not fit his picture perfect image. It is the reason I invite men into my life who have substance abuse problems, dishonesty, and cheating. As much as I hate to admit; his dysfunction is what I seek. I wanted men to be that man in my life no matter how unhealthy. In making it okay for him, I made it okay for them.

I looked back at the original unedited manuscript and I said bullshit more than a dozen times. These words do not come out of my mouth, yet as I struggled to find my voice they flowed like water breaking a damn. In my healing I have found those words are not even mine, yet it is the voice that resonated in my head with a list of doubts and don'ts. It is not me but my conditioned fear. It is the part of me I slowly shed as the new fresh skin of my soul revealed.

I desperately tried to see the other side of the coin, to see my father's opinions of me are somehow a blessing teaching me I am different. I want to celebrate that. We can learn a lot from people who believe like us. We can learn a lot more from people who don't. His opinion is programming. I do not want to be liked by the program; I do not want to be liked by Controligion. I thank god o' mighty I am not like that anymore. If you do not like me or my shitty book it is because I am not like you and that is okay. I want to be different. It is also okay for you to stay the same. He does not have to believe in my dream. Of course it would feel terrific to have his support, to have him understand and see me. It would make me believe in me; make me doubt myself a little less. But I need to learn to doubt myself less on my own.

Dad drinking is like a warrior pose—comfortable at first but then it begins to burn the longer it's held. I practice relaxing what I can and focus on parts where I find great comfort and love. I like to be around him in small doses and there is nothing wrong with that. I think it is normal part of evolving past our heritage. It makes me very sad to think of his upbringing. He will not even discuss his father who was a horrid alcoholic. There is a little boy in him wanting to be loved so badly and I want to be the one to do that. My dad is doing all he can to be better than his alcoholic father who hurt his chance of dreaming. I am certain when he says hurtful things it is not even his voice but the man who spoke that way to him.

Dad has evolved. I believe it took a lot of leaving to get him to change. He quit degrading my mother and sister so much after my mom left him. He quit drinking straight scotch whiskey during his second marriage. He began running marathons and quit smoking. We all know he loves us dearly. He is doing all he can to put down the bag of shit his father made him carry.

Trying to tame that part in me is denying part of my existence. I am learning to accept it. I love that he is the life of the party and I love that part of me. I just need to balance it, sometimes begin again. If I spend my entire life finding balance, it is okay because I am learning to love and accept all of who I am.

It makes total sense now that my dad would love all the frogs. Just like my father; sweet, brilliant, soft hearted but then completely disappearing for days on end beneath their work. And when work no longer consumed them they could hide under their dysfunction; binging, degrading and pointing out other women's beauty exceeding my own hurting and then leaving me, yet always returning to comfort me in the pain created—maddening love feeling like home.

I will not keep trying to love any of you who cannot love yourself. You may all be trying your best to be that man for me but I am sorry, I cannot allow disrespect for you nor me. Please stop seeking me, smothering me with unhealthy issues because you may love me, but love yourself first, find your balance, heal your hurts and drink responsibly. The very word "responsibility" means you can be trusted to maintain "response ability". Which to me means keeping your ability to respond lovingly. I will work hard to do the same. I am helping myself. Help yourself.

This skeleton was the most difficult for me to face, more than my own shame. I say it now because I believe most people never confront issues with their parents until they are gone. I would want my son to tell me. I would do my best to remedy my issues to evolve his life past mine. I do it for those who had childhoods much worse than mine. So maybe you see it is okay to feel ill feelings for your upbringing and you deserve to heal those feelings. You deserve to be happy.

There is a huge contrast between sober dad and drunk dad—hard to believe he could be anything but loving. It is easy to forgive him because it is not him but rather something invading his brain making him robotically blurt lines from a horrid dark play. Then the invader leaves and he is back online with only minute memories of what occurred. That invader is his past, his childhood, his father's words that were his father's and so on. Just like our mind that makes some 60,000 negative thoughts with most the same as yesterday, he carries a heritage that won't let him stray. He tries. I love him through his tries. He pushes for improvement. He pushes hard maybe too hard because in his pushing, he pushes everyone around him. The problem is to push me to achieve, to compete for success and glory means I am not okay as I am today. I just want to be okay now and loved the way I have and always will love him—for the beautiful soul he is.

Finding no support from those we want it from most can make us feel alone, but twist that perspective to see the power in it. I am enough on my own. I like to think my father has some soul contract he is obviously not aware of, to teach me the toughest lesson. He loves me so very much he came into this world willing to hurt me to heal me. I did not believe in myself. It was necessary I learn my vision is strong enough to supersede my potent need for approval of others; even the one man I so desperately crave praise, our father.

HOLY MOTHER

In going through this process of healing by looking my past in the eye, I have gained an enormous respect for the females in my life. My blessed mother has loved unconditionally the men in her life despite all the pain I witnessed her endure. It must have been horribly difficult to leave my father at a time divorce was rare, but I am now absolutely positive she did the best thing in the world for us, for herself and for him. I believe it is time we stand up strong and not allow unhealthy behaviors in our lives anymore. Maybe then more men will wake up and make a change. We have to hold them accountable and walk away. Leaving does not mean I do not love you, it means I may not be the one to evolve you.

She still loves my father to this day and although they have been apart for over thirty five years she allows him in her home with love and open arms. She always has. She even let him bring his girlfriends to stay in our home after they divorced so he could spend time with us. She understands his battle. She can see who he is beneath his heritage. I love her tremendously more than ever for giving me that gift to love the heart beneath the storm. Both of my parents are remarried and they all spend time together at family gatherings. They put aside any ill feelings they may have felt so my sister and I could still have a whole family. I respect them immensely for never making us choose.

Controligion and the fairytales that followed taught me to doubt women and the fruits they bestowed; poisoned apples, witches, curses, doomed to pain, yet my deepest pains I can name have been due to men not women. Not one man was close in reality to the dream the stories portrayed yet we are supposed to worship them? On the contrary, I am finding it is the women in my life who are living a life worthy of worship. I am even discovering sacred divinity in our sexuality. I used to be so angry at the gossip of other women because I could not let my body be human for fear of their judgment.

Now there is a movement of women uniting to reclaim our sexuality in all its divinity. We refuse to call each other names that our jealous egos once proclaimed. We understand freedom means free to experience life, love and all the acts that go with it. We are fully connecting with another in search of our higher power, cheering each other on rather than condemning, lifting each other up rather than damning.

Expressing ourselves authentically is one of the most heroic things we can do as women. In the past our feelings were labeled as crazy, hysteria, medical dysfunction, unscientific and loose. Now as we rise the world will realize our feelings are the power connecting us to our higher being. It is our duty to stop suppressing and start surpassing. If that means we love despite pain then that is what we do. But always loving ourselves first which may mean leaving. My very own mom and even Mother Earth have stood strong loving despite getting hurt. To love get hurt, love get hurt, love get hurt and still continue to love is not gullible in my book. It is tremendous love! Godly love. We are warriors of love. We are whole on our own. We are holy.

The following poem is for my mom who put her pain aside to love unconditionally. I love you beautiful momma.

WARRIOR PROSE
Someone has to be willing to go all the way feminine
Unguarded, heart exposed, delving deep seeing all it means to be woman
It is not weak as many believed

But an unimaginable form of strength
To open up wide letting massive love flow
Despite fear of an outcome unknown
We have tried this alone all along
Because our strength was diminished with judgmental wrongs
Now we awaken and break through the chains
Banishing judgment that kept our hearts strained
Standing together we can now dry our tears
Our army of love has been building for years
With calm in our hearts and the silence of peace
We open up now to let our love scream
We have much to learn of our role in this reign
But we walk on our teacher; who's been treated the same
This once worshiped beauty is awaiting the day
Man awakens to see the error of his way
She's been raped of her innocent fruits left ravaged in pain
She's been labeled as evil and burned at the stake
She's been injected with chemicals to control her offspring
She's been chopped up and stomped on with no concern for her dreams
She's stood silently strong as waste trashed her veins
Comforting others to mask her own pain
Rigid rules coated in plastic that won't go away
Ruminate her oceans like thoughts in our brain
But just as any loving mother will do
She is willing to place it aside; all the pain she's been through
Because she knows something bigger than I and or you
Man will hurt tremendously when they see what they've done
But it's that moment of suffering where we will evolve
They will need us even more for our comforting strength
The softness we've longed for will fall at our feet
And in that instant all the pain we've endured
Will equate to the love we now know we deserve

~Juls ♥

337

G-SUS

Yep, I have added a book of G-sus. But not in reference to God's son (as you may conventionally know God); it is my son. I have always considered him my savior. His birth changed my view of life and he continues to inspire me more than any human I've known. I have a habit of shortening names of the people I adore so for the sake of easing any discomfort you may have of me calling my son by a homophone of Jesus, let's just call him G.

There's an entire book residing in my head on raising children. I grappled with if I should include this because I have come to the realization it is not up to me to tell or even influence people on what to do but I decided to include a short version to be authentic me. It is the one thing I did in my life that went against society, religion and the norm. It is the one thing I am the most proud of. I listened to my soul on how to handle almost every situation. I did not know I was doing the right thing because there was no one before me that had raised a child the way I did, at least not to my knowledge.

In return for doing something only my soul nudged me to do, I got a son who has always shocked me with his ability to understand living. He has the most remarkable soul but more importantly he has the power to hear his soul. I believe we all would be this remarkable if we had the ability to tune in to our divinity. He understands what it is like to want to be something that goes against the grain of a hard core society. I believe it is because I did my best to not smother him with my beliefs, or Controligion's view of discipline by fear. It was upon his birth I began to realize the answers were in me and I stopped agreeing with any doctrine causing people to do things in their hearts they knew was wrong. The bible is one such fascism advocating judgment and punishment with pain and fear.

I did not beat the devil out of him as so many of you have been fooled into believing is within your rights as a parent. I get sick when I see a parent hit a child. It is barbaric. It is abuse. Children die of abuse because the parents report "it began as a spanking." There are over forty countries that have outlawed it by everyone including parents. It is ridiculous and unnecessary. The system in the United States supports abuse. This is why Child Protective Services has such a difficult time distinguishing spanking from abuse and is often forced to send the child back home where days later the child is found dead! You call yourself adults while you lose control over your own emotions, beating a small defenseless child. Beating! Call it what it is. Spanking, slapping in the face, pushing; It is beating. It is abuse. In a country it is outlawed, your child has a bruise, you go to jail. End of subject.

Backing weakness up with words of the Bible, words written by primitive men, translated a thousand times over is sickening. That verse you cling to in defense to mask the guilt you feel, your crutch for continuing to act like an uncivilized heathen does not even appear in some Bibles and is often worded different depending on the Bible referenced. "Spare the rod, spoil the child." Well for your information the "rod" in biblical times was the shaft the shepherds used to gently nudge sheep back into line. Gently nudge, not beat them with it. As far as that goes, the word rod is used interchangeably with the word sword, which often means the word of God, The Bible. Hello! What if it means spare the Bible, spoil the child? Or what if the word spare is a command to spare the rod and spoil the child, to not use force but instead spoil the child. Not literally spoil as society defines it. We all need to earn to learn. Spoil as I know it is to go bad as a verb, but as a noun it can be defined as a treasure acquired. Like maybe love?

Wouldn't that be the greatest treasure of all? Maybe we are supposed to spoil them showering them with love and fulfilling their every need. I said every need, not want to those who have already formulated a defense. Maybe we are supposed to allow them to go inward and seek the answers for themselves while providing loving boundaries and tons of communication.

I know it is scary to question the Bible. But as G says, "The Bible is the oldest game of telephone." Maybe it is time to question it. One of the reasons I went this far is to knock me out of my stupor and maybe, just maybe get you to question it too. Spare a child some pain. If you think you are beating the sin or the devil out of them, think again. No! Hell no. You are beating God out of them. Adam and Eve were sinners and there for we are born with original sin? Come the fuck on. Do you really believe that? Stop beating babies. You are setting them up and breaking them down to be drones. Good job parents. Good job! The only touch a child should ever receive is comforting love. Your behavior wins every single time. They are mirroring you. They are becoming you. I did not want my son to become me, but rather be who he came into this world to be, a soul who just left God's wing.

It was not easy. I originally said I would save spanking for the big things. Because I myself had been programmed and was not sure I was doing the right thing. So if he was going to harm himself, run into the street etc., I might. Our brain automatically triggers the response we grew up with. It takes all your guts to not hit when you are mad. I believe it is more complicated to parent without spanking because it takes patience, it takes creativity and it takes time. I remember wanting to hit him at times when I did not understand his reaction but my heart prevailed and the only touch I bestowed was comforting love. It took me years to have the balls to speak up about this subject. I even hid the fact from many when we would go inside to visit about what he had done wrong and he returned crying, parents often remarked, "Wow, you must have hit him good." His tears and the amount of time we were inside made people think I had just done the same programmed monkey response they do. But no, he cried because he now understood and it took time because communication takes time. That is all. It takes your time.

Not using force was the greatest gift I could have ever given myself because in teaching him to communicate, I taught myself. We learned to talk to each other even when we were mad with one another. We talked a lot and now that he is an adult it has more than paid off. The few times we have butted heads, I am amazed when the response I normally got from a man was to walk away; he stays. He has often come after me, when I wanted to leave the controversy. "No" he says sit down and let's talk and we do and we hear the other and we figure it out together, not always his way or my way but we find a way in the middle we both feel good about. If only all disputes in life could be handled this way, we would never go to war; not in our homes, not in our countries, not in our own minds.

In one last effort to spare a child, children who die from abuse, the parents' defense is "it began as a spanking." So if you are hitting, you are engaging in and supporting the beginning of horrific abuse and often death. You think you are so smart, you know when to stop or how hard to hit? You have enough control? Then use it to be strong enough not to hit for those children whose parents are not as strong as you. If we knew we could parent effectively without hitting then why wouldn't we? Just do one thing for me, look at your child's hands. Look at those tiny hands the next time you are angry and see

341

how small, how small and precious they are. Then look at yours. Look at your big brutal hands. Take a breath, watch your hands soften to comforting love and put your arms around that baby. Say "I love you. Let's talk."

I am not going to provide you with statistics or research. I did that in Grad school and wrote my thesis over this very subject. This book is not about referencing it is about speaking from a voice coming from a place statistics do not live. The Bible did not give you stats, did not reference and you believe it. If you need research look in the scientific journals. I dare you. Or simply sit in silence and have an honest conversation with your soul. Your soul knows. Then go apologize to your kids and start parenting with love, taking time out of your hell hectic schedule to listen to them for once. Walk away and gather your peace. Be brave to return to them with love. Ask them why it was wrong, where they learned it? How they can prevent it from happening again. Become a parent who teaches not harms. See them and you will see; you are looking in the mirror.

So I raised a son without hitting him ever and to this day we have the best connection of any parent child relationship I have ever seen. Because we talked, we talked a lot. Not hitting forces you to do something else like learn to communicate. From the beginning, I knew he was here from love, for love. It was the greatest love I have ever felt seeing him for the first time. In that moment I recall thinking that at twenty two years old I would only get to love him from this point forward. But he, if I did it right, if I could be good for him, would love me his entire life. Think about that. We love our kids from the moment they are born, yet they love us their eternity. It is a huge responsibility to be the love of someone's life; the love of someone fresh from Heaven.

The day he was born I knew he was closer to God than my sinning soul had ever been. I used that to my advantage every chance I got. I would whisper to him daily to "remember, always remember who you are, where you came from." When he began to babble I would sweetly ask him. "Who are you? Where did you come from?" And he would giggle like he knew the punch line to a joke no one had yet told. I spent every day making that child laugh because it made me laugh. It felt so good. His laughter was the song angels sing. I would put him in his swing before he could even walk and play music so we could dance. We would dance and we would laugh. It was joyous. I cherished every day with this Godly soul and had the amazing experience of hearing this just off God's wing child tell me amazing secrets.

Like the day we were walking to the park and he decided he finally wanted to tell me where he came from. A year earlier he had told me he knew I would be his mom when I was ready. This time he explained further; he remembered more but it was hard to tell me because there is nothing like it here to show me. He was in a bubble. He was floating he said and it was good. "It felt good." He turned to me nodding his head, smiling to reassure me how good it was as he touched his heart. He said "there was not any time. No time Mom, just floating fun now. No hurry. I knew you would be my mom and I wanted you to be." Then he said "do you know what your soul is?" This five year old was asking me what my soul was. I said "tell me." Again he patted his heart and then rubbed it in a larger circle saying "It is all the good inside of you, all the good, always there, always right. All the good, where love grows, that's your soul." I said nothing more trying to absorb it, I just smiled as we walked side by side almost dancing with each foot step, knowing he was correct and I was correct in not beating that voice out of him, that well of good inside him—that God. It takes devotion to believe God is in us all and allow that moral responsibility to grow on its own. We each have a moral compass in there but it takes faith to let it lead.

No hitting and no religion. I wanted to allow his own spirit to steer him with an open unprogrammed mind. Even though I still did not understand how I had systematically become the victim of control, I knew I wanted him free, leaving no room for prejudice or judgment and no guilt to weigh down his wings. I wanted him to live off his wisdom from his soul, his passion not my own. I was determined to not be one of those parents who drowned dreams by molding kids into their vision of a desire their miserable life had failed to achieve, often wanting what they think is best, but that is what is best for them as parents. To keep their sanity and worries low, they don't want you on a path they have not walked because they cannot see the end.

I did not want him to be me just as I never wanted to be my parents. Love them, yes, always trying to please them, yes, but I never wanted to be them. When I disappointed them it was one of two things, either I was being the part of them they did not want to see or I was breaking away trying to be me. I am lucky; most times I knew the difference and rather than steer him from a path I feared, I supported him knowing this is how we become a different species. Maybe one that can be free in each his own divinity.

Let them know love. Teach them about nature and let them get dirty playing in it. There was a time when our children did this but even they are suffering as we label their behavior unruly. Behavior that is bucking the system screaming my body was not meant to sit behind a desk, behind fake lights or eating fake food. We cut out their play time and put them in what we deem as play for countless activities and sports often run by heartless adults. With parents screaming more orders from the stands like that little child has your life in their hands. Our social system does not allow play for learning in a way we cannot measure. No, we must test them, instilling in them early on they are wrong, born wrong and therefore must follow a big ass book of rules that advocates beating them. We shut down their creative souls early on by drugging them, whipping them, brainwashing them with lies, forcing them into a box to look and act like everyone else. Like you.

With G being closest to heaven, I was his student, often putting down my script to play in mud. I always marveled how he was happy alone the way I was as a child. We all were happy without romantic relationships for that wondrous childhood part of life. G has carried into adulthood that same happiness. He will throw himself a party for no random reason. I laughed hysterically at him dancing and singing when I walked in on him one time. I ask what the occasion was because with the mood and the music it appeared he was preparing for others to join him in a party. He danced a jig proclaiming "it is a party mom." I ask, "Who else is coming? You are the only one partying right now?" He just smiled, continued dancing, saying "one having fun is all it takes, just one having fun."

We both have been chasing dreams only our souls believe possible. I wrote him this verse while sitting in the stands at one of his practices watching his dream come in and out of view. Because that is how dreams work. You get a glimpse of your soul and have complete faith but people and life place barriers to test your belief in your dream.

The most uncomfortable place to live on earth feels like freedom inside a trap. It is enormous consuming your world, yet ironically cannot be found on a map. It has no borders to contain its hollow deep, so it seeps into every moment that you breathe. It has no coordinates, it's not near any other place, in fact it does not even occupy space. It is nowhere and it is everywhere, like a shadow cast both day and night. Not visible, so frustrating, how can it be, its' intensity alters all you perceive. When you are there uncertainty grows as you begin to swing aimlessly from above to below. Its' temperatures storm vast extremes. It is cloudy and sunny, hot and cold an ever-changing constant of certain unknown. You cannot plan your days, your nights, living in limbo becomes your life. The future remains unstable dreams as you anxiously attempt to calculate change. There is no living in between; no middle ground, no middle way, just wake and go unsure each day. Not many people go there, it is scary as Hell, teetering on the edge of life that could fail. It is draining, it causes pain, its life's greatest teacher yet it has no name. Lessons of patience and faith in one's self are waiting on the other side of this unstable jail. You will battle many forces, pushing to extremes, while obstacles dare you to turn back from your dreams. Sleepless nights, worrisome days still giving your all in hopes it will pay. This is the life chasing stars yet unseen; this is the life of a boy with a dream. ~ ♥Mom

Children are magic, still close enough to heaven to hear God. They take things literally responding from the heart having not yet been programmed to be a mental robot. It is why I think it so important we encourage children to speak. They have so much wisdom to help us get back to our soul who loved openly before life experience pained us into drones.

I am convinced if we would stop trying to mold our children to fit our imperfect world and instead let them teach, peace will prevail. Please stop trying to beat evil out, you are not beating it out, you are beating it in. Listen to them. Really listen, hearing their wisdom. Let them teach. It is our children who will change the world. I believe with all my heart if every child could have this kind of patient love there would be peace on earth.

If you grew up in an unhealthy home, you will inevitably see doing for yourself as selfish. Because limited love was given, you will limit the love you give yourself and feel uneasy doing so. We have to stop seeing self-care as selfish. But if that is what you want to call it for God's sake (since God is in you) be selfish! Be utterly selfish. Our children will only reach the level of happiness we ourselves achieve.

On the other godly hand, If we are loved, truly loved then we will grow to love ourselves, our ideas, our voice. The greatest gift we can give our kids is nothing to give at all, but allowing them to hear their own soul and because I did, I only had to allow him to grow gently guiding him with love.

I want to thank my five hundred year old son for his gentle whispers of wisdom. I know he was in my life before. I am so lucky to recognize this and to cherish our time. I only wish to be as wise as him when I evolve. I do not want to put any unnecessary pressure on anyone and just because I say such wonderful things about him does not mean he is exempt from mistakes. I do not view mistakes as bad. They are learning and if I am going to be a wonderful parent; I better wish all the best learning in the world upon him. That very well might mean he makes what many people will judge as horrendous mistakes, but not me, I will love understandingly knowing he is seeking just like me. It is in the seeking that we hear our soul speaking. There is no goal to attain just the simple act of following a dream. It is not whether you arrive at the goal but if you dare drive in the directions of your dreams. If you want to live a dream life then follow your dreams. It is in the following not the achieving. My greatest wish is he understands he need do nothing at all. His very presence is my present and if he spends the rest of his life throwing rocks far into the sky just to see how high they fly or skipping rocks on water to see how far they soar then that is a life full of achievement galore.

I do not know how long we will get to be together. I do not have all the answers; in fact, I have more questions; bigger, perplexing questions but I do not feel the incessant need to answer them because as G says "We will not know the answer, until we know the answer." I cherish every single breath I take in his presence. So my dear G, if there ever comes a day I am not physically with you, I want you to know where to find me.

Close your eyes and breathe. Listen to your sweet soul. Hear what it says and when you decide to take that chance, that fiery chance that lights up your being. I will be the next voice you hear cheering you on saying "Yes G, go. Get living!"

EDUCATION

I did not understand all the answers are within. This is where the formal education I received gets a big fat grade of F. I would love to tell the government, whom I still owe on those student loans, I would like a refund. We are trained to be cynical not intuitive. Instructed to think others' thoughts and speak others' words then graded on our ability to do so. We are all doing as told fearing punishment by number or letter scores ridiculing our soul. I learned to be everything to everyone but myself. No education in the world can teach what life has to teach us. You have to experience it and you have to screw up. Sometimes you have to screw up big time, several times, because lessons do not come wrapped in shiny pleasant paper but in a gut wrenching box of fuck ups.

No book, theory, fact or classroom was going to untangle my heritage. I knew a great deal about nothing. Knowing is why we remain such fools clinging to beliefs we are in the know, while we ridiculously repeat patterns sowing seeds of change that never grow. I had vast knowledge while not understanding a thing. My Summa Cum Laude 4.0 rank did nothing for my soul but confuse me even more. My father pushed and pushed for me to obtain educational status, boasting I would be nothing without it. Other men did the same but when I got it they all called me "a know it all" or even a "bitch" when I tried to defend my stance with my so-called educated facts.

My entire family, according to my father and my second ex-husband, did not even like to be around me anymore because I always came across as "so smart." Then try to date and open your mouth one time with an interesting topic and risk getting the response I always got "I am not good enough for you." Nothing was ever good enough for anybody because I never felt good enough for me. I had no faith in my own spirit to guide me. So I sought superficial labels to give me a name. Over and over again I ended up leaning on something or someone to identify me, label me, because I had no clue who was underneath the programming. I had it all backwards trying to evolve outside not realizing we grow from the inside out. Every person who crosses our path mirrors something inside us that needs attention. There is great education to be found in places other than the formal system. Pay close attention to what someone says about another person. Pay closer attention to what you say about them. It is always our own potential to bear the same flaw that rubs us raw. People literally get under our skin to force us under our skin.

CONTROLIGION

By now I am assuming you understand to not knock on my door with your message of redemption. If you are a member of such a wonderful sect then why do you feel the need to force it on others? If it is that superior, relax in your knowing and let the masses seek you and your message. Focus on your happiness. Seek yourself, seek your truth, and maybe consider going outside the concentrated camp. There is beautiful wisdom out there. I know it is difficult. Religion was created to control society and we are social creatures wanting love and acceptance. Why would we ever want to challenge something that would place us on the outside when all we ever want is to be in? I understand. It feels safer underneath the blanket of status quo's cozy fabricated confines. Controligion caused me to fear my future, be depressed at my past and anxious in my present. I wanted out. I wanted the truth even if it is only my truth. I wanted out of the lies—their lies, my lies—out so far I could rewrite my programming. To fill my script with other religions, other cultures to shake up the shit I was thrown and maybe somehow emerge with my own ideas, my own guidance, my own holy guide. I wanted my own 'aha' moments. Not follow those before me preaching the connection they had with God. I wanted to connect with God. We are capable of that. We have a savior here now within our own soul. This now can be our Heaven.

So many of us invite the experience of being the victim because our society honors victims. Controligion worships the one who suffers most to push the idea of suffering on us all. I do not believe we were meant to suffer. I do not believe Jesus, if he even existed, would want to be remembered as the victim. He would not want to be seen and worshipped hanging lifelessly from a bloody cross. He would not want us to be scared and fear death so much we fear living. He would want us to know our soul. Love is the same in that space for us all.

Religion cheats us out of having our own 'aha' by keeping us busy focused on someone else's recollection of miracles. Miracles follow intuitive soul. Misery follows instructive society. That is exactly what Controligion wants, eyes shut in faith dreaming someone else's dream in the past to deter focus on the now, as we chant amen to robotically agree. Open your eyes. Heaven is here. Miracles are happening now.

I believe we all have the ability to hear a message from our Holy Spirit. We just have to learn to tap into it. In some cases, I hope I was able to do that with this book. There are parts I read that feel so good in my soul I just know we are not alone. I am not the sole author of this book, something divine shared wisdom with me at times. Just as the authors of the Bible occasionally had great insight with warm words of soft, accepting love, you and I have that same ability. But we have to learn to sift through it in our words and even in the words of the Bible because society, government and egotistic wants can confuse our humanness to include ungodly biases and desires. Nobody wants to be alone, not even in their beliefs.

The judgment of society and religion is why I hid my whole. No one wants to believe they are going to Hell. It was sad for me to sit with clients who had spent years in deep depression thinking they were doomed. They too had hidden their truth and the relief they got from telling someone who cast no judgment, felt like the best church in the world to me, to them. As I see it, religion is no different than addiction because it keeps us from feeling the now—continuously pulling us to scriptures of the past, casting judgment on our fellow cast.

No one is born a sinner. We are born love. Controlling authority does not want you to know this. It takes away the power they have created over the masses through fear; fear Hell, fear God, fear your voice, fear your choice, fear your feelings, fear yourself, fear closing your eyes and be afraid to open them. You wind up with a fear of death and ironically a fear of life. Now fear death, maybe I can understand, but to fear life? What is the point? I refuse to live a life fearing. It is not necessary to fear to make proper choices. We do not need to instill fear in our kids by beating them. You are not beating the devil out, you are beating it in. There is no Hell unless you focus on fear and succumb to the curse. Living in fear burns—it is living in Hell on earth.

All these beliefs revolving around religious attempts to control us with fear of an eternal Hell, ironically steers us to choose Hell on earth; staying in unhappy marriages, with jobs we hate to support the lifestyle we create to falsely appear joyful and holy on the way to church in our shiny luxury vehicle. We wake up with no clue why we are unhappy when everything looks so nice outside. We bury the grimace to get through the day, forcing a smile on the mask we parade. That nagging inner voice is begging to be heard. It is our passion, our happiness but we have to let go of rigid beliefs, let go of the script to break the spell. It will be scary as Hell living life with no set protocol but it is the way life is meant to feel. This is a being alive.

I live amongst people now who have broken away. We no longer want to be told how to think. We want to tap into our own Holy Spirit writing our own Bibles for living. We want to live like we did as children free of time, free of schedules doing things that make our heart sing and our bodies feel alive. So alive it can overwhelm at times bringing tears to our eyes. We want to travel, write, read and sing.

Play instruments, learn languages, engage in nature, get dirty, hold hands, ride bikes, skip, jump rope, run, not just in straight lines but over obstacles, through rivers, over mountains, climb, swim and play. And we want to do it all judgment free with little possessions to weigh us down.

Schooled in a train of thought where altered states of consciousness were abnormal and should be treated as illness, I was told most homeless were mentally ill. People with nothing are unstable. But maybe those with more than necessary are the ones swimming in insanity. Trying drastically to keep up, doing the same pattern day in and day out to look nice following the rules of masses. In religion it is thought to be sin to veer from the awareness of the rules. Anything different should be punished, burned at the stake, cast out by exorcism, ridiculed or drugged. I have since learned there is energy in the universe that can alter consciousness to bring awareness beyond the norm placing us outside status quo. That awareness changes everything you know so rather than fearing rejection from the masses you feel pride to be different. To live meagerly makes me wonder if homelessness is not in fact godly because now my view of wants feels like madness. I see people still in the box and I see robots—driving to work at a prescribed time in expensive vehicles with faces of gloom while their human vehicle rides along like a strapped in puppet.

Whether it be relationships, jobs, suffering, love, tradition, religion, or history books, it is crucial we have enough faith to let go when things have reached their end. We have to demand society stop the hold and control of everything. Keeping traditions is boring us, chaining us to unhealthy relationships our entire life is smothering us, keeping foods lasting on shelves is killing us, coating things in plastic for simplicity and profit is bankrupting Mother Earth, preserving the past is slaughtering our future. Close the door, turn the page, and shut the book. Let go and be free for the next moment with an open heart for the miracle about to bestow.

I have built my church on a rock but it is not a building, it is my temple, my body and I go inside every day while sitting outside on God's lap as she gently reassures me with her breeze from the sea. She is alive and with me every day. I simply have to be present with her as she rocks me on her axis and blankets me with her clouds. Just like any great mom, she feeds me, nourishes me, comforts me, allows me to rest in her arms and if I listen she will guide me every step of the way teaching me lessons to reach my highest self.

MARRIAGE

Controligion is the reason I fell victim to the monstrous demands of status quo. It is why I felt incomplete without a man and fought each day to feel happiness alone. My running away from status quo to a land Quo had not yet conquered was the beginning to his end and the hold he had on me. Paradise got status quo out of my life, Peru got him out of my mind. I now believe my incessant need for marriage or any form of sought security; financial, religious or even eternity was fear. Fear learned from these same sources. I no longer see the traditional view of marriage as happy or even healthy for me. It has been my deepest programming and the most difficult belief to overcome. Maybe marriage fulfills some souls lifting them up to evolve but maybe others need space to breathe, to learn internal strength.

There was a lot of leaving in my life, yes, but I am learning to see it as the greatest lesson and not so much a bad thing if we are leaving to protect our spirit and our dreams. Divorce may have been the greatest thing to happen to me and possibly the greatest thing to happen to humanity; pushing us on through this awakening. The divorce option gives freedom to say I will not stay allowing you to be complacent in your unhealthy ways. To know I have a choice if you disrespect me, reminds me to treat all relationships lovingly because if I am not helping your soul evolve then you have the freedom to leave me too.

I find connection in ways other than romantic. But I believe there is no set protocol. Some people need another, some for life, some for a small time and some people need no one. Each path is just as sacred. You are on a sacred path. I no longer want to become stagnant in anything not even love. I want to change and move and flow and let you in and let you go. To have an open heart means to let someone enter but it also means to let them leave.

Leaving is okay when the relationship no longer serves the soul. I was forever complaining rather than changing. Now when I catch myself complaining, I know it is time to move, rather than stay and be the victim. If I find myself making threats, like one more time and I will leave. I stop. I do not let myself threaten I am done. I have a conversation with myself: "are you really done because if you are then leave." If you are just threatening to get the other to change then you are manipulating.

Maybe true unconditional love means we no longer need to be bound to another, owning them like property but love them in their element as they are, take that moment and cherish hard knowing soon we have to let them go. Learn a lesson, teach a lesson and move on. To think this helps me treasure the small amount of time we may have to dance joyously knowing neither of us needs to be bound for eternal happy. That to me is a spiritual connection beyond the marriages I have seen where couples stay together because Controligion says we must suffer to be happy.

What if marriage was created by religion to control another soul? To possess another, to possess anything for that matter is not good. Hmm, in religious terms anything possessed needs an exorcism. Maybe my moving was just that, to escape the idea of being possessed by marriage. It was my exorcism. I myself never flourished within those unions. My outward appearance may have fit society's idea of happy when I was a wife, but my soul suffered. In fact I shrank. My voice shrank; my spirit never soared as it is now. I have had so many more happy moments, 'aha' moments, creative moments while being alone over three years now than all my years of marriage. It is again part of the fallacy they preach, brainwashing us to believe there is honor in suffering sacrifice. True love may not be "until death do us part" holding on for dear life. Perhaps it is letting go to let each other choose each day what benefits their own soul.

That is not to say commitment is wrong; I am stepping way out of the box to shift my own consciousness. But trying to get another to commit, to remain constant is control. I had to run away from society to a place where relationships are unwanted because I had to be single. I had to. I needed to. I wanted traditional commitment so badly; had I stayed I would be walking down the aisle again boasting this time, no really, this time it is real.

Society wanted me small, kept and chained. I was so programmed I thought I wanted it too. I had to force myself to be alone because I had not yet learned how to be with someone else and still be my own. I would have never finished this book because work and wifely duties would have gotten in the way. I would have continued creating dependence making more and more money to increase my spending to increase my debt to increase my work load. There would have been doubts swarming all about and just as I lost my words or burned my words, abused and neglected my words in the past I would have done it again. I would have never learned to hear my voice. Media, religion, culture, people, material things, desires, wants, traditions, would have clogged my soul with every plunge I made to unclog it. I would have continued to adorn the camouflage smile and the shiny diamond for all to see how happy marriage had made me.

I know we have evolved past a species that needs to reproduce and I often think of my gay and bisexual friends as superior beings for that very reason. To love regardless of gender, loving whom you love—how evolved is that? Some argue gays cannot reproduce so it goes against the word of God. No, it goes against the word of some very old men; very, very old dead men in a history book that may or may not be real. Again we have evolved past the days when we need to reproduce to survive the species. I mean what if they have evolved more making us "straight" heterosexuals the inferior beings? Our soul has no race, religion or gender confining it in borders.

I was taught the Holy Spirit was outside of me, with the trinity being father (male), son (male) and Holy Spirit (male). It is not out. It is neither male nor female. A spirit is a spirit without any humanness whatsoever. Male or female is a human chromosome thing. Maybe we are meant to be androgynous and not marry but to be free to encounter other spirits learn and evolve. Rather than the length of the relationship matter, maybe it is the depth. It is the bi-sexual beings who fall in love with soul. Maybe they are the most advanced of us all. Maybe we are evolving to beings able to love whomever we love. Pure soul, no race, no gender, but simply who that person is from the core. That is freedom. That is love. To think there are countries where death is the penalty for loving a soul is blasphemy. To live and love freely takes great strength but to love and risk living is in my book godly.

I want to say again this is all just my voice I lost and have now found so please understand there is no judging or ridicule to your religion and or marriage. Just because it did not work for me does not mean it does not work. If your religion gives you peace, wonderful. And if marriage makes you happy then do not listen to the half fail statistics because half work. Half work! Do what feels good for you.

Looking back at my marriages and the brief stint of relationships, not one frog lasted more than a few weeks, (okay well Matt was two months but he said "we're not dating") I can say my lonely days are far less than when I was married. Listen to that, I am nowhere near as lonely as I was married or dating. Stick that in your boot Matthew, Mark and Luke.

If in the end people find happiness then I believe divorce is worth it. It is all about evolving. We may simply be evolving past all things keeping us tied in need. We are meant to change not be chained. Sometimes the weaker one needs the relationship to end in order to find their strength, while the stronger being needs space to soar alone to seek their dreams.

WORK

In earning a living by modern standards, I was wasting away life. Being indoors was keeping me literally from seeing the light. Somehow I was meticulously separated from nature that was so much a part of my childhood. If I was not outside playing in it, I was escaping the inside by writing about it. I was never meant to be an inside cat. I got so far separated from Mother Earth, it is no wonder I fell for every man made chemical, electrical and medical gadget. Society has lost the connection with nature making anything natural an oddity, so odd we try to poke and prod it to prove it. In the end we cheapen it. Finding Paradise put me back in touch with the natural world. With each encounter with Mother Nature, I began to question my so-called knowledge.

I connected with the earth and my spirit more and more. It changed my western thought so fast I felt remarkable confusion. I saw there was more mystic healing power in nature than I was aware of. Things cannot always be measured. I started to feel all my years of schooling, all the money I spent with the student loans I still possessed, no that possessed me, were a trap. I began to think everything I knew just might be wrong. Imagine that. What if you wake up, I mean really wake up to discover everything you know is wrong! The thing about the spell is you do not realize you are in it until you step out of it. This so called "new Psychology" is just a copy of ancient wisdom. Charging people money and hooking them up to give them what? Oh yes, focused relaxation. That's what I was schooled to call it. The whole idea is teaching self-regulation where each person is his/her own master. These new waves in Psychology are nothing more than a reproduction. This is meditation, this is Buddhism, this is Hinduism and countless other ancient philosophies I was now making money on while measuring scientifically. It felt like extortion to some extent.

I began to believe I was taking advantage of people praying on ignorance by throwing brain words out there. Indeed, energy changes but it can also be done the old fashioned way through healings of the ancient; chanting, yoga, meditation, music, dancing, healthy eating,

Mother Earth's medicines and her healing earth energy. Biofeedback works. Western Society wants to see proof, but I now believe you do not need fancy equipment to gain focused relaxation. It was like I was trying to mechanically alter a practice that has been free and easily accessed on one's own for thousands of years.

Molding people to some scientific perspective of normal, began to seem like just another means of conform. To teach normal is to judge. It is to say you are not okay as you are. We are ruining uniqueness by normalizing what could be awesomeness if we could only alter perspective. I was working under conventional wisdom trying to measure and represent it in stats, graphs and numbers. Like sacred ancient wisdom could not be real unless we could qualify and quantify it in some fancy chart or scientific statistic. It seemed I was banking on the visual aspect of it to produce income for a once free spiritual path. Trying to fit mystic wisdom into some code society can understand and communicate started to feel manipulating. On one hand I was glad to offer an alternative to prescription drugs because at some point medicine needs to stop labeling and prescribing. You are smothering the nagging voice. That nag is the teacher. It does not have to be defined as painful. It only feels unpleasant to push us into change. We must find faith in our strength to fully feel our feelings even the painful pieces. It is those painful pieces that complete the puzzle.

HEAVEN

There really is no time in heaven as my son G taught me. I truly believe I am living as close to a version of heaven here on earth as my humanness can get. I have witnessed my programmed mental reality let go of societal measures as I merged into this spiritual realm with hours slowing, so we group the day into either morning, noon or night. I rarely know the month, and it takes work to recall the day of the week. I used to fight the freedom with sticky notes and to do lists to keep my ritualistic mind online. It used to drive me crazy to witness my mentality try to remain calculated. Once you let go, I mean really let go, it is quite humorous to go about your Sunday routine and begin to prepare mentally for Monday..... And then, as you refill your morning tea at half past noon, tilt your reading glasses to drool over your Man Candy Calendar (thank you Sarah) that merely exists for mid-life lady pleasure, not for a timely measure, the eye can't help but drift from June's monthly catch to the day of the week. You will screech with delight to see, it is Saturday! It is just Saturday people! Hello Heaven. Winning.

I wrote that in my journal one morning when I began to shift from society's calculated measure to this new way of life. I do believe I am experiencing what so many feared would be the end, the end of time because as we awaken we only live in the now. If you have ever watched the video discussing what you would do if money were no object, this is where I live. I live among artisans, artists, dancers, composers, musicians, writers, singers, adventurists, farmers, dreamers, unconventional thinkers, heart feelers who follow passions and live like children playing loving laughing and best of all, I am one of them. Some days I am filthy with nature from head to toe. I love it! We all know sterile environments hinder children's growth. Getting dirty actually benefits the immune system. More importantly it benefits the soul.

I now know the season we are in by the creature in my house. Scorpions indicate dry season. Then the influx of crabs proclaims the rains are coming and once the rain starts the huge bullfrogs frequent my home. The permanent resident geckos that for the longest time I thought were birds, having not seen, but only herd the chirp live in my ceiling. The bats that literally hang around sometimes inside my house, the monkeys and the odd still unidentified creature that is in no way scared of me climbing down the tree a few feet away from where my hammock hangs. They all like to stare at me like I have rudely entered their habitat. The once upon a time girl who was chauffeured by friends is now driving a stick shift, down rough dirt roads and narrow by ways backing that baby up like a boss. There is also the adventure of riding my bike with one hand to carry as much of my laundry and or recycling into town. There is no room in the bike basket for carrying things because my little dog has made that her space. She loves that pink bike too.

At times I have ridden my bike the mile and a half into town six times in one day when trying to get errands done. My hair resides in a permanent ponytail and the daily makeup routine has been traded in for a slather of homemade coconut oil sunscreen. Dirty feet and sweat are no longer even thoughts of care. Air conditioning is a luxury but not really wanted once you accept sweat is okay, not dirty at all and actually healing to expel toxins. I even have a friend here who jokes "all good things require sweat[7]."

Crossing a river with crocodiles could be considered a downfall to living here but most of us mentally turn it into an adventure playing games in our mind as we tell ourselves "what are the chances" and just swim faster. Then there's the fear of the boa that ate my friend's cat. I consoled her saying "so sorry, the cats here are small" and she warned me her cat was bigger than my dog. The positives far outweigh any difficulty; indeed these difficulties simply make me feel

[7] My friend Mitch gets credit for this cute description of sweat.

more gracious to have a naturalistic life. I have no television to drag my energy down with media negativity or bash my body image with females looking unrealistically. I have no watch; time is of no concern, in truth on most days, I don't even know what day it is. And best of all I have no scale that used to be the daily measure of my worth. I could not tell you what I weigh nor can I believe I used to do that to myself every day.

Living in Paradise and spending time in Peru have made me appreciate Mother Earth like I did as a child. Eager to be out in her presence every morning, playing with the varying toys her daylight brought; green grass, trees, rain, puddles, mud, and nighttime lightning bugs. The stars and the moon are healing I swear and the sunrise and sunsets are a soul's best repair.

I appreciate the sun so very much and the moon even more especially on the dark patch of path on my way home where no street lights live. I treasure experience over exquisites, natures stones, shells, wood over jewels, dirty, walked on feet with worn skin of my own over shoes wrapped in death. Going over waterfalls and jumping off cliffs is part of life not just something done on vacation for fun. To live in a place where I am seen for my spirit is so freeing. Had I walked in the grocery store as I do now back home, no makeup, swimsuit, dirty bare feet, I would have felt judged or afraid for someone to really see me. Here I get hugs and kisses because I am truly seen. I am honored by my friends for who I am at the soul level; my frivolous behaviors are not judged but merely seen as part of my growth.

This is my heaven and these people are angels, admiring and at times adoring my raw flawed humanness by eating desert with me for dinner, ignoring rules, smoking pot, breaking into spontaneous song and laughter, dancing and loving. I am hugged and loved like it is our first and last encounter every time we meet. All of this and more is where I find sources of happiness besides romance. I am in love, with my friends, with my family, with nature, with my breath, with myself and the experiences I am now allowing. As I started listening to my voice and following that hidden compass magic began to happen. There was more chaos around me than I have humanely known yet inside, I was strangely peaceful. The long battle, sleepless nights over business, my heart ache over my business partner all pale now in comparison to what I have. I have found myself and really found myself in an incredible destination in love with myself and Mother Nature. I had the most amazing experience with nature that taught me a lesson in love.

It was one of those moments I recognized myself again; that little girl who so loved nature as I held a starfish in my hand. I found him on the bottom of the sea while snorkeling. He was brown with brilliant indigo stripes radiating off his center and down his rays. The guide with me asked if I wanted to take it home. I thought maybe it was dead and thus why he asked. I put my face back in the water to watch it in my hand as I contemplated if it were alive. At that moment he wrapped his rays around my hand and held my hand! I swear me and the starfish were holding hands. I did not want to let go and he did not want to let go of me. I kissed him gently as I put him back on the bottom of the sea. I went to bed with love on my mind. I could not stop thinking how good it felt to love a starfish. A starfish! But in that moment a feeling inside me shifted and it was love. That is the kid I used to be. That is who my soul is and I am so glad I found her again. I am beginning to see how love reciprocates because I truly feel the world is in love with me.

I wrote this piece shortly thereafter in honor of my fairytale home.

I dream of a place where mountains make clouds and as odd as it seems the ocean makes land. The plants grow ginormous with little work of a man, while the extremes of the weather keep you humble and tan. The alarm clock each morn is a soft sun filled hand brushing your cheek with a whisper of sand. Monkeys scream songs very few comprehend, while horses dance freely as their spirit intends.

The locals are fairytale wondrous souls greeting strangers with smiles that melt hearts once turned cold. Time slows to a trickle of a joyous beat and worry is unheard of in this land of retreat. Dogs meditate unleashed by obedient rules and the children are cherished to be childish fools. Laughter is the measure of how your day went, while friendships are earned by the smiles you lent.

Your worth is not made by the amount that you own, but instead by the holas you earn pedaling along. Your senses are challenged by mystical abnorms. Like the sound of the sunshine amidst rainbows that smell, while musicians play music with notes you can see. Laughter tastes so good in this town by the sea.

This is my Heaven, peace in my soul, my heart, my Paradise, my fairytale home. ~ *Juls* ♥

MEDITATION

The issue I had with prayer is I was taught to talk to God in my head, which always ended in me begging and pleading. There was already enough talk going on in my mind; the majority being an internal voice of don'ts. It was not until I began meditating that I learned to stop it. I was a good counselor because I could listen so fully to another I forgot myself completely becoming one with their experience. In meditation, I learned to give that gift to myself. I learned to stop talking, listen and I became flooded with positive do's.

I learned to listen to my heart, to the gut feeling, to Mother Earth; her nature, trees, sun, moon, stars, the wind, the sea and all her waters running free. This is meditation. Listen for a message. What we are begging and asking for in prayer is often not even what we need. It is usually a programmed belief for a desire we think we require. At first meditation feels annoying until you learn to see your worrisome thoughts as separate from your soul. Soon it transforms into serenity and feels so peaceful.

As a child I had a divine curiosity, meditating long before I knew that was what I was doing. If you think about it, we meditate all day long. We focus on thoughts; from waking in the morning thinking how much we dislike this or that and allowing that thought to ruminate often giving thought more power than it is worth. Meditation helps to let the thoughts go by softly without attaching meaning. Instead of negative thoughts bringing you down, your mind will begin to pump positive thoughts in synchrony with your soul. I like to think it is opening the door for my spiritual side to merge with my physical reality, bringing it forth a little more each time. It is the space my dreams gain the necessary fuel to come alive.

When I meditate, I feel confident in my being, in my past and in my future as inspiring ideas emerge. You will know you are there when it feels good. It begins to feel so good you want to do it again and again. It is a space of faithfulness inside helping me ignore the doubtful outside. But it begins as a very small space. In a thirty minute meditation I maybe got only five minutes of bliss coming and going in waves. I learned to be patient and gather the spaces and now they come in longer more blissful waves integrating my soul. Soon there is no difference between who you are inside and who you are outside. My soul wants me to stay with her, trust her because she is bringing me in alignment with more bliss than I know. She wants to assist me. Meditation helps her assist me to my greatest capacity.

As far as earthly medicines that help us tap into our soul: Ayahuasca, San Pedro, marijuana and even natural tobacco; I have learned can all be spiritual. When used in ritual for spirituality and connecting to nature, healing and insights can occur. I do not condone anything that does not come from Mother Earth or has been chemically altered by man's hand. It frustrates me so many of us claim to be healthy; rejecting man-made chemicals in food, pesticides, toxins in water, and prescription drugs, but then hide in a bathroom to snort poison that goes straight to the brain! I don't believe we can claim to be awakened and light up our brain with an artificial sweetener acting on the reward centers mimicking love! It damages chances of experiencing the real thing. Fake love, fake anything is not enlightening. And selfishly, I want to love you. I can't compete with powdery love. No one can.

Although some people use pot to meditate, I do not use any substance because I try to reach the state of bliss without it. I do believe pot is okay but because it alters consciousness and I am trying to experience altered states and visions on my own, I prefer not using so I can be aware the state was reached solely by me. I have done it, felt the bliss and it is very similar to a pot high but you can recall your insights when you are not high. Plus pot numbs dreams and I need the dreams. It is part of the enlightenment process. That is not to say I never smoke pot anymore. OMG no, I love it. I eat it! But just like everything else, it's about balance.

As for shamanic healing by medicine, if you are going to do it, do it properly with a healing group and be prepared for immense changes. It works, but you must be willing to change with the new insight rather than go back to living your robotic life. I do not see myself doing the medicines again anytime in the near future. I am happy and have settled into my life as a human just trying to get by. I still welcome enlightenment but I have slowed like the growth of a tree letting life push me to grow when nature says so. Seeking anything now means I am not pleased with myself. I have seen my soul. I have seen me. I am pleased.

I knew academically through my training in cognitive therapy about changing thoughts but it was meditation that truly taught me how mindless thought is. It taught me to let go of my incessant need for approval from you. When you learn your own thoughts do not matter, you also learn the irrelevance of thoughts of others.

Enlightenment is not a one-stop shop. Just as in getting glimpses of God in meditation, enlightenment comes in pieces. It is not about sweeping pain and shame under the rug presenting false positivity. It is about facing it head on trying to brave the pain to see what is underneath having faith in your strength it will not knock you to your knees. And if it does, then faith in humanity to lift you back up. It is about accepting all that is, letting go of control, allowing whatever flows your way to flow. It is about breathing in the spaces between the waves of pain letting go of self-judgment and loving yourself for all you've become. It is about seeing yourself in others compassionately caring knowing one mind gifts you the lesson of seeing how you might be in their circumstances. Then coming back to you compassionately caring for all you have been through. It is about accepting others in their beliefs and allowing them to walk on their own two feet. It is a never ending journey full of ups and downs. It is faith through the downs staying present with the pain knowing an up is coming that will blow your mind away.

Meditation is what it took for me to unlock my inner strength and stay in touch with my dream. There are many kinds. I tried guided meditation, sound meditation, mantra meditation, walking and dance/moving meditation. In the beginning I liked listening to a guide, it helped keep my mind focused. I took a class and began using mala beads and a repetitive mantra to keep my mind busy. Now I light a candle in my sacred space, breathe some cleansing breaths and simply listen. I do this almost every morning. In the evenings, I walk to one of the beaches for sunset and do a combination of eyes closed meditation followed by open eye meditation so I can watch the sun's healing rays turn from day to night.

Meditation brings a brief space of peace that comes and goes. It is glimpses of God. And why I can say I know where God lives. In the beginning, I would sit as long as I could, gathering as many of those spaces, piecing them together until I felt I had a message. Before long you will seek that space of knowing and it grows. It grows so much it will flow into your everyday life. Knowing and flowing. That is how I live now. When I live according to my soul's commandments, I get confirmation in the form of what some call synchronicities. These small coincidental miracles confirm I am living in synch with my soul. In meditation, I listen and I learn to be happy now even amongst chaos, to feel peace despite pain and to feel love in everything whether it comes back to me or not. I learn who I am. It is not what looks good to others, to society or Controligion but what feels good to my soul. The soul is where wisdom lives. Walk inside. I dare you. Somewhere between the pain of the past and the fear of the future, there is bliss. God waits for you there.

PRINCES OF PEACE

I wrote this book for women because being one of them, I struggled to break the spell more so than men. But I have since realized this is not true. I was pissed at society for masking my soul but more pissed for hardening the hearts of the men I tried to love. I believe now, although I blamed the world briefly, I have taken accountability for my actions. Still I feel I loved completely men who could not see me. I know this is not just my issue because I am surrounded by women where I live and in all my travels who are fed up with men unable to love. I believe it is up to us to stop allowing them to be dishonest, emotionally weak, addicted escape artists. We are doing them a disservice sweeping their behavior under the rug. Stand up, stand together and let's love each other until they wake up and worship us the way we have them for years.

I am sick of watching you treat women disrespectfully, lying, cheating, abusing yourself and others, while we take the hits on our heart over and over. If you disrespect me or you, I vow to love you by leaving you. I will not stand by anymore waiting for you to change. I will not try to love it out of you. I will walk away and I will not return. Maybe my leaving will wake you up and open your heart for another woman to love but with me you had your shot. I only need one chance to love you properly and from now on that's all you get. If you did not realize what you had to begin with that is your fault to fix, not mine.

If we think our women have been suppressed and cheated out of knowing their soul from the confusion over society's judgments, wanting us to be virgins, yet portraying us as meager bodies to be gawked at, look at our men. Men who were all once little peaceful boys losing hope as their dreams were snuffed by Quo and

Controligion. I cannot imagine what it is like to be a man in this society. If I thought the spell cast on me was bad, filled with societal pressures, what must it be like to know you are responsible for the safety, happiness and financial success of an entire family, an entire nation? Men are programmed to feel worthless if they cannot be protective, be tough and financially provide for a wife pleading for him to be the opposite of toughness inside. We cannot expect men who were beaten and told not to cry to turn off and be our soft place to fall.

Little boys are hit more than little girls because daddy's feel they are roughing them up. Next time your son does something, think about how you would have responded had it been your daughter. Can you practice equality in your home? They are raised to excel with all this energy to make their parents proud in sports then contain it all behind a desk for eight hours. It is no wonder they are over diagnosed with attention disorders, their bodies are screaming for someone to pay attention to their suppressed needs. We don't let boys feel emotion. We shove them hard into rigid boxes and then expect them to open up softly with empathy? How can we raise a peaceful nation if we are not allowing peace in our homes? Learn to respond to your boys with peace and see the world change.

The government tries to make men feel unpatriotic if they refuse to go to war. The energy of that is simply overwhelming. My encounter with my deceased grandfather in Peru helped me to see your sorrow as he and I both cried over the waste of war. We both pleaded to make it stop. I feel for you so. I understand women are now soldiers as well, but for many, many more years the responsibility fell in the hands of men. Everyone is just the doing best they can, given the energy they must carry. If it is tough for me expecting to be rescued then how difficult must it be living with the expectation to be a hero? All the pressure to be strong beneath the idiotic belief boys need to be toughened up is actually dominating your powerful truth. It is another way for commanding people to prepare you to go fight their wars.

Boys have been exposed to so much turmoil and then convinced to suppress their emotions or face the wrath of yet more torture. It is no wonder their amygdala for emotion is smaller. They never got to use it. The brain is like a muscle; don't use it, you lose it. Suppress it and it suppresses. Our society beats you physically to toughen you up. Then systematically beats you down mentally deceiving you into choosing behaviors favorable to a government's goal. It is psychological warfare! Your beliefs become the systems. You become so dependent on it and so entrenched you will fight to protect it. You have been abused and made to feel like you have to fight, you have to be hard, and you have to kill. It is learned helplessness. Beat to be stronger then left with the impression the weight of the world is in your hands to promote peace with war. If you fight against anything, fight the system by finding peace inside your soul. Live a life your little boy heart can be proud of.

We cannot expect you to be everything—brave, tough, emotional, financially supportive then come home to rescue a woman, sustain an entire family, a society, raise kids and do housework because we can't decide who does what. As difficult as it was for me to break free from the idea of who I should be to follow a dream; a writer of a book many called a pipe dream; think how difficult it must be for a man who is supposed to support an entire system to follow a passion that may not pay a dime. Because of these insurmountable obstacles, in some form or fashion I will forever support my son. Until his dreams, whatever he dreams, come true. I only wish all boys could have the same support.

Each frog I got to know, I was merely getting to know myself. It is no wonder I woke up not liking what I saw. I was so afraid of the mirror because you were showing me my very own flaws. You are not frogs you are princes full of peaceful potential. I know it is difficult to break away from the pressure of society and hear your soul. You have been beaten down by wars, by manipulative honor and false glory for far longer. You are generations and generations of horrid memories of fear and death. It is no wonder we all struggle to know who we really are. We need to learn compassion to all for what we have each been through. Imagine the worst pain one can endure. It is only relevant to your experience. There is no greater pain than your own. Whatever your greatest sorrow is; is the greatest sorrow. Pain in this life is no different than pain in past lives. What if you knew your past life, your children's past lives? What if you knew your soul was neglected, abused, the victim of war and torture? What if you knew your son's past life was far worse? And now here on their birth you hold in your hands a chance to heal. Heal it. Teach them to hear their soul and let them dream peaceful dreams. Let them be a prince for peace.

LOVE

It was quite a stretch for me to write about love when I knew nothing about it. I always felt I got rations; little bits, pieces here and there. It was never satisfying, like drinking salty water that rather than quench intensified the thirst.

I waited and waited to finish this book so I could tell you a love story. Time and time again as each relationship fizzled, I said "this is not how this story will end." I kept holding out for what I thought was the happy ending, thinking love was just around the corner. Actually, the kissing frog portion of this book spans almost three years; not the one year as the title implies. As soon as I returned from Peru and stopped kissing the whole damn pond of frogs, love emerged. I quit trying to predict what was around the corner before I went around the corner, letting go of my membership to the Fiercely Independent North American Women's Club and love filled my soul. It was revealed in Peru when my grandfather demanded I look at him and see, as I had demanded for others to see me. But that was simply the fertilizer I needed to grow and just as nature matures slowly over time, it was not until I focused on my needs, making this book a priority, giving my soul nourishment that I truly started feeling the love he said I was.

All this time I was seeking loving qualities in others, I was finding me. I made the list of what I wanted and little by little became that. Each person added or deleted items and molded me to see where to find my love. We are all just mirrors into each other's souls. Look out, and then look hard within. There was something deep within me carrying a story of struggle. When I braved it up enough to face the story my perception changed and suddenly the way the past resonated within changed also.

I am the one in control here, always have been. It was not that I was a victim sitting back drawing negativity, I chose this like I chose my beliefs. Some people get furious when they hear negative people in their life are a reflection of them. I understand. I was one of those people. But it is not necessarily that we attract an abuser because we abuse others but we in some way abuse ourselves. I cheated myself, I used addictive behaviors to neglect my soul's calling and I verbally abused myself mentally. The attraction was to behaviors mirroring false beliefs I held about me. I was not in touch with my soul and neither were any of the men I felt attracted to.

An immense shift occurred when I saw the real me. The people I thought I was in love with, lost my attraction. I still love them on a compassionate level which I am discovering is maybe the greatest love. But as far as me feeling I can't live without them; not much unlike our addictions, that feeling is gone. I believe it is because I have healed enough to see behaviors I used to recognize as me, no longer identify me. I don't confuse love with pity anymore. That was the way I felt about me. I am not here to save anybody but myself. I found my strength I know resides in us all. I have faith each of us can and will save ourselves. We can be a victim or a creator. One takes negative memories to use as a crutch, remain the same and blame. The latter takes negative memories accepting responsibility for choosing the situation to learn, evolve and change.

Learning to love, respect me and my soul's dream turned my life into fantasy. The commandment list is what healthy love looks like to me. I no longer want a man to have my same qualities but bring his own interesting loving abilities. I had to sift through a lot of unhealthy habits to reach my soul. I found my dharma; my life calling to follow and the energy I get from it is overwhelming. I just had to learn I was not getting love out but in. I am the one experiencing my own love. Whether we connect with nature, another, or take the time to sit and connect with our self, the connection is divine opening our heart to the love we already are inside.

Learning to accept loneliness was something I had to accomplish daily. It was as if all I learned got wiped away under the amnesia of my programmed society brain and coupledom seeped in wanting me to feel less than on my own. Now I understand loneliness is the opposite of love and a necessary part of life's process. To feel lonely is to have an open heart. Open for me to fill on my own evolving by pushing me to move toward my soul's calling. Loneliness is motivation to evolve. I let myself sit in it as long as necessary, but then I got up and let my soul breathe by completing tasks on my list that lifted me. The only thing I needed to do was stay flexible and ready for change rather than static in the same state.

Loneliness lifts but we have to be ready to move out from under it. It is rare for me to feel lonely now. I can't recall the last time I did. But when I do, I let loneliness remind me I am open and ready for another to journey with me. Sometimes I have to force myself to go out and meet people because I now know connection is just as important as introspection. There is a time to interact and a time to be alone and integrate. I work hard to keep myself happy to attract the same. But I am still learning. I go months without romance in my life and on occasion a lesson walks in my door. When it ends, I try to see the pain as enlightenment. Despite my past belief that to love someone full on meant the pain would be greater in the end; I have found love without limits does not leave you empty but closer to your soul. And being closer to her makes it easier to hear her. She reminds me you cannot love too much and she replaces the sadness of letting go with an abundance of self-love. I have great respect for my spirit I bravely set free with his being.

In love is something so much grander than we have defined. It is not in the lasting but in the changing. It is a grand mass encompassing all the beginnings but more importantly it is letting go in the endings. I struggle still to want to save people, but that is a pattern of my past—always falling for people who need rescued because I needed it. I no longer need rescuing. I need him to meet me where I am. I have learned going to extremes to help others, only leaves them feeling more obligated to me. It is a form of control for me to do so; an attempt to buy false love. I deserve better and whoever he is deserves better. To struggle on his own and find his strength.

It is one thing to need me, quite another to want me. I want someone to want me. This is not to say I will quit giving. I am a giver but the key for me was in learning when to stop. There is a point in all giving when it turns rancid into hindering. You will know because you will feel it shift. It is a feeling. Giving that is helping will feel good to you. Giving that is hindering will feel bad to you. It is then time to realize your giving is no longer good for them either. You are making them feel their strength lies within you rather than allowing them to know their strength too. That is when to stop and let the person go; to find their own help inside believing in the God in them to be their guide.

There are so many lessons left to learn. I have faith, I am being guided and the lessons are being placed in the order they need to be. I am standing strong like a lone tree watching life's ups and downs focusing on my inner peace. I know life will take me where I need and place the people there to teach me. In choosing love realistically, I was trying to hold on to mental practicality. Choosing love rather than falling was my way of predicting the future, marrying men I thought would be there forever. Choosing love with the mind is what I needed then to realize structured security and practically is the safety net for the fearful. I feared being alone, clinging to coupledom for strength unaware how much strength I had on my own.

I could have never handled falling in love with my soul mate in the past. I would have drowned trying to hold on when it ended. I almost did that anyway with the bits of love I got. I now know how to stay grounded, how to find peace when the heart aches and how to find love in nonromantic ways. I have to prove to life my heart will stay open when pain tries to close it. I will walk on stronger and I will be ready to connect with my soul's fire. I will cherish it; cherish the hell out of it because as fast as it came, it will go. It will only come when I am already happy. Joyful energy will attract it. Be ready and be full; fill your own gaps so it will not knock the breath out of you when it leaves. Sometimes the feeling fills you up; but sometimes you have to fill up with the feeling. Even living in paradise there are good and bad days; both are of utmost importance. The good days lift you easily: enjoy and celebrate your ease. The bad days give you opportunity to exercise your power lifting yourself up; enjoy and celebrate your strength.

There is a connection so deep just waiting for me when I am ready and willing to fall. It is scary. It takes sheer guts. It is going to take more trust. Not in a man but in myself. That is what trust is. It is about trusting we will be okay no matter what storm life brings; being comfortable in the posture, relaxing what you can, finding peace in the soul when the mind is racing and loving, loving, loving the fall and all. Everything I have been through is preparing me for that. This I believe, heart racing sitting in the raft making a split decision whether to go over that waterfall or not, jump off the cliff, or simply let him stay; one in the same; One in the same.

Still, I have come to terms with the reality this life may not bring another romantically to share this journey with me. I do this not just for me, but for everyone who spends their life seeking and wishing. When we are wishing, we are missing. I used to cry when I thought of living the rest of this life alone. Tears would fill my eyes while my heart would yearn. But now I feel empowerment in that acceptance. Power in knowing it is up to me to be happy ever after. I will not wait for him. After all, this awakening has just begun, it is going to take a man at the same point on the path I am. If I am going to fall allowing my spirit to completely melt into his manly grace, it is necessary he be awake.

At my age finding a man single and on the path to enlightenment will be rare. I am not saying I am in any way better than anyone. Far from it, I have just worked hard to open my soul, to climb the mountain we are all climbing. Attempting to pick another up to my space on the mountain would require I go down. I hope I love myself enough now to not do that. Love myself enough to peacefully stay at my pace, climbing higher. Maybe he will catch me as rare as that may be, or maybe, just maybe he will come down for me. Yes, I am worth that! Uncommon as it may be it is not impossible. Knowing this makes me so grateful because I will cherish our time even more because it may not last forever.

Accepting it may not be this life has helped me focus on me. It is like crossing the Red Sea where you must forge on in faith without worry of what might be left behind. I will not wait on the other side while the opportunity passes letting the sea engulf me. No, I will still love with my all. I will not put up walls and I will not be guarded in love. I want to be untamed, dreadfully thoughtless throwing all my spirit, following my heart into the deep, going far past my ego just to see how far depth goes. No fear, I have faith. I have faith in me.

The strings of habit weave us together so intricately there is no way to neatly unknit. We must unravel completely losing all semblance of stagnant routine in order to begin a new dream. Drenched in programmed beliefs, I did not know myself. Now that I know, I am not chasing anything. It was another form of control, trying to be everywhere, for everyone just in case he held the key to my soul. Everything in my being wants control, except my soul, my soul wants to flow. I no longer need such control as I have found I am the keeper of my soul. I was forever looking for my prince. Forever hoping he would find me. I only hope if my Prince of Peace is out there; instead of looking for me he is looking for himself, his inner peace.

He is not at a bar, drunk out of his mind flirting with every woman who catches his eye. When I realized this I knew why I was going out so often. It was to find him. Erasing that possibility, I discovered most of the time I don't even want to be out. I want to be loving me in my solitude— taking nature walks, writing, yoga, dancing, and cooking. If I am out, I want to be with close friends visiting, camping, hiking, river rafting, and whatever other adventure we concoct spur of the moment.

No, the man for me is not drunk at a bar; he is at the top of Kilimanjaro or rafting a swift river, working for peace, meditating by the sea or on a walkabout seeking inner strength. He would never in a million years tell me he is not good enough because he knows he is good enough. He's doing all the things my soul seeks and our paths will cross when I do the same thing. My Prince of Peace there is no need to find me, I found me. Find yourself. I will be busy loving me.

Self-love is not selfish. Imagine you have a battery in your heart that needs to be charged every day. What charges it are things that make your soul feel good. You know it is running low when you feel bad or sad. I was always looking for someone or something else to charge my battery. The problem is, charging someone else's battery depletes your own. I was asking men with low batteries to charge me up. It is up to us to charge our own. We are responsible for our own energy. I was so programmed to be happy for others, I did not even know what made me happy. The list helped me figure that out. It is why I can say without a doubt I really love myself now because I am all those things on the list. What I wanted on that list was me but I had to learn to wake each day and feed my soul not wait for someone else to feed me. All the old adages of "you complete me" or "you make me the happiest person in the world" are now my mantras to myself. Can you wake each day and do whatever it takes to make you the happiest person in the world? Because that is what self-love is all about.

The town I live is not a place for dating. It is a place for late night hook ups. I have learned it is not what I want. It is not bad as I used to believe it to be. The funny thing is when I thought it was bad, I was participating in it. Now I see it simply a path not good or bad, just different. I know it is not my path because my soul is no longer content with the emptiness of casual sex. It never was. It just took me living in that a bit to understand why I felt deprived. My soul yearns for an authentic connection it too can participate; not be pushed aside like my panties by a man that can't even take the time to undress me properly. Although that can be very sexy, it is synonymous with the fact he will never spend the time to unclothe my heart. The energy emitted by a man that wants nothing to do with my soul does not turn me on. Still I will not let myself judge myself because I am now approaching life from a less logical standpoint; going with my feelings in that very instant not with some rational plan I concocted that would either leave me wandering what if or with the guilt of doing it anyway, breaking the rule I myself made.

My intention is fully for my soul mate but until then I will love and let go when it no longer feels I evolve. Discovering he is not the one is just as important as discovering he is. So I go throughout the nots until his hand finds mine. I know he will understand all I have been through because he will have been through it too. I will not shame myself in the morning as I used to but gently walk back to my path and continue on my way. Nor will I make some outlandish commitment to stay celibate for over a year. Been there, done that and I am here to say nobody is giving out spirituality awards. I cherish my soul so much and its vehicle now I feel overwhelming motivation to care for all her parts because I understand how she runs, what she needs and how to love her on my own. There is a tremendous difference between pleasing the body and pleasing the soul. I am focused on the latter and a spiritual union that supersedes human desire. Thoughts aside, I am vacationing as a human so as the saying goes, when in Rome.

Can we imagine what a world for our girls would be like if we would stop judging and be open with love for them and what they and their bodies feel? If we would stop judging each other with horrid names when we each know deep in our heart we are the same just wanting to love and be loved. Can you imagine how comforting to talk about your deepest pain and know your girlfriends will not criticize but instead lift you up? It would look like my world now where I feel so loved by my friends, I do not need to seek taboo sex with a man to maybe or maybe not get his touch and a scripted promise of love. It would look like women standing up and feeling proud to protect our bodies, I mean when you are a fortyish woman and you have to be accompanied by one of your best girlfriends (thank you Micah) to buy a box of condoms, something is freaking wrong. It would look like a place to be free to talk openly and support each other entirely. It would look like women not labeling each other or our experiences as either good or bad. Just experiences because we understand all things, even things society or religion label as wrong are simply pushing us to evolve.

If something you thought was a mistake changes you for the better, then how can it be wrong? I will no longer make rules for myself like I will not have sex until I meet the one or try to abstain to be worthy of holiness. I will not wait for society to catch up with me by trying to act demure and virginal. Besides, the original meaning of virgin was unmarried. Not unmarried in a bad way as society has brainwashed us to believe, but virginally goddess like, a free woman not possessed by anything, not even a man. Our little girls need to hear this. They need to know their bodies, their feelings and their choices that accompany those feelings are okay. We are natural beings. It is part of our nature, Mother Nature. It is beautiful and when you know your soul, connect to your soul and want to share your soul, sex is sacred.

One day I believe we will once again honor women and our sexuality in all its divinity. It is about being mindful in every moment not mindless. If we have learned to love our souls, exercise and listen to our soul then we will protect our being, we simply will. There is no need to instill fear or make something lovely taboo. My only rule is to stay in the moment and see the beauty of what is occurring right now. Feeling what I feel and if it is love then it is love and all the acts that go with it.

It has been almost a year since my last trip to Peru and I have not been lonely although I am alone. I do not feel the need to go out and find him or to give every frog in the pond a chance to be him. I am content. Other than the one time I cried a painful cry over finishing this book and the recent incident with my father, I have not cried out of despair. I do, however, cry more than in the past, but it is tears of joy almost daily when this overwhelming appreciation hits me. It really feels like I am in Heaven. There is this amazing connection to people and to nature with everything seeming so vivid. The emptiness I described feeling after the first trip in Peru shifted. It no longer feels unpleasant. All the past has been cleared and although it took some getting used to because it did feel empty, now it feels good. Maybe this is what normal feels like. Maybe we are supposed to have space to be fully present, to fully take in each moment and then let it go leaving space for the next. I was defining it as emptiness. That definition in itself had a negative connotation, but now there is room to be filled with joy. It feels like freedom. I am learning to let go constantly so it clears the way for the next moment to let the universe have its way with me. Whether it is happy or sad, that clear space allows for authentic feeling of the now. It is free space ready to be filled moment to moment.

I think more than anything I feel free because I have let go of fear. There is no more fear of judgment, aloneness, travel, adventure, love, life or even death. Fear consumed a lot of room and left little room for joy. Letting fear go created so much vastness I understand where

God lives and although I have felt it and said it many times only now have I found the words to verbalize it. She lives in the spaces. The space between all connections like the instant a magnet gets close enough to begin the pull. There is a brief moment you feel the energy connect. That energy is love. That energy is God. To love anything on this earth is a divine connection; to connect us to our divine self. You can feel her in your meditation in the space between your thoughts. You can find her in the space between the feelings, the touch, the kiss, the hugs and entire relationships. It is the relationship between everything. For someone to say you do not want a relationship is to say you do not want to know your own divine self.

By learning to rest in the space between, I am learning how to be less attached, more loving and finding her more often. She lives in that 'aha' moment of space between unwise thoughts and wisdom found. She is in the space between laughs, between hearts and between minds. She lives in the spaces between breaths, between life and death. You feel her when someone passes away and when someone is born; in the instant it begins and the instant it ends, like before and after a beautiful storm. My favorite place to find her is in connections to Mother Earth; in the space between me and nature she whispers her wise words. I do my best to catch her when she shows me brilliance in her skies, in the space between the sunrise where dark becomes light and the space between the sunset when the day becomes the night.

It is my goal to spend as much time in these spaces and in doing so I see there is no time. That this moment only exists when we show up fully with all our senses twisted; feeling the sounds, tasting the scents, while hearing the sights with faith in no future, faith in no past, only this moment that will instantly pass. To stay fully present is to constantly pull from your thoughts to your soul where acceptance cannot judge—from your head to your heart beating wisdom of love. To be in love with nature, with another or yourself is to be so tuned all your senses are mindful grasping the spaces between the moments. Learning to be alive in these spaces is allowing your divine being moments to experience life. Love is our being. To be loving is to let your soul be living.

Dear Frogs,

I wanted to love you all but you blocked my love saying you are not good enough, somehow putting me on a pedestal you could not reach. We were drawn together because I too did not feel good enough. Listen up. Just as I believe you are a reflection of me, I am a reflection of you. You can achieve, you have more power than you can conceive. You can be good enough, but first you must be good enough for you. Be good enough!

I loved you all, at least to the level of love I myself had known. In that moment it was the greatest love I had been shown. To love you is to see you are me given all you've been through and I am you wearing the combination of variables I was exposed to. I loved and I cared and I hurt when it ended because that is what I do. I fall hard and fast and I always hope it lasts.

You do not have to be anything on my list of qualities I seek for me but come with your own set of abilities so I can learn about you while learning about me. I do not want you to vow your life to me or claim till death do us part. I only ask you share the choices you make and give me the freedom to decide if I want to stay.

Commit to your own authenticity. You be fully you—brave with honesty, sharing with love so I can decide if you help me evolve. I do not need a second chance and neither do you. It is a cop out to say you are not good enough. It is a way to escape your own potential to keep from having to evolve. One day you will find yourself in love with the soul underneath the programming and see you were always good enough.

To be in true love is to see the soul whether it be another or your own. All the good. It is why we seek to be seen. It is a state of bliss more powerful than the greatest love we've known. It is where we came from, it is where we will go. To be in love is the closest thing on earth to heaven we can know. I can look at you and fall in love because I see you; I see the good of your soul. Should my love not reciprocate I have learned to let go. I trust that the world has better plans for me I cannot yet see. There is a love seeking me so vivaciously all I need to do is breathe.

I leave you with a word of warning! I have been told I cannot separate sex from love. This is true. For some time I tried. But no more will I strive to be something I am not. I am love. I know the good that dwells within you and I love it all. I do not know how to kiss you and not, nor how to touch you and not feel touched. And I do not know how to make love to you and not love you.

So on this day I vow to stop trying to not. I vow to love in all I do whether it be friending you, helping you, touching you, cooking for you or making love to you. Guess what? It is a relationship. I fall in love in everything I do. It is too much effort to try not to. It is a lie to not be myself. If you do not want to be loved then you better not walk this path with me, not even for a brief moment because this is the path to love, step on it and fall the fall or do not get on at all. ~ Juls ♥

THE END

Please do not fear the end. The end is really a beginning. To those who are suffering now, it does not matter the cause. Pain hurts. Heartache has no safety valve, cutting straight to the core with physical symptoms that feel unbearable. Whatever your deepest pain, I have felt it exactly the same, not for the same reason but pain doesn't mind reason. Please hang on knowing it comes in waves. This is why you may have a good day, a good moment then the next feel wiped flat out unable to breathe. Know the wave subsides and every wave you triumph strengthens you for the next. Eventually the waves lose intensity and you gain some peace in between. At first you get hit over and over as your mind adjusts then maybe just once a day, once a week, a month, until one day you awake and realize it has all but subsided and you see your strength. You will see your strength.

I believe to fully experience happiness, we have to accept sadness; experiencing it just as fully. We are conditioned to believe hard times make us flawed but I believe to allow this down time just as much attention, if not more—feeling it without numbing it, friending it without abhorring it, walking through it rather than around, is what perfects us spiritually. Feeling it will not weaken you, on the contrary, it strengthens you. If I could be there with you, I would want you to know I love you at your worst. Swollen eyes, haggard from no sleep, crumpled on the floor begging for peace; I love you. You can stay there as long as you need. You will not wither. You will find your strength and the pain will ease. It is in these moments we learn to see. Love yourself through it. Walk through pain, face it, lay down in it and rest. Get up and walk again, repeat until you reach the end.

All of this may mean nothing now, but I hope it gives you some peace. Have faith in yourself. You are strong enough. One day you will look back and see how the work of art unfolded but for now be gentle with your canvas. You can't see the picture while you are still in it.

You have plenty of time. Learning to be mindful helps relieve anxiety of hurry, feeling the clock is ticking. I continue to grow slowly and accept to do so now without forcing it. I am riding the wave as a human happy in the life I lead; letting enlightenment flow when it flows not frantically seeking it now that I am content where I sit. As it turns out my loss in conventional faith strengthened my own faith in me and unknowingly in you too. I can say beyond doubt no matter who you are, your past, your beliefs, you are on the path you need be. I have faith in the God in us all. I have faith it all turns out okay. I am not above saying I am still just as lost even standing on the other side of a crazy mid-life crisis. But crisis in a positive way, maybe an awakening—a mid-life awakening. Still, I am no far better than anybody.

Oh, I spent some time in spiritual land trying to gain more awakening, swearing off men, sex, drinking, vowing secretly to be on my own to obey some unspoken code of chastity, pushing negative emotions away to adhere the new age movement of positivity to be better than any human known. I am here to say it is hard. It is lonely. I don't want to be the know it all, do gooder, got it all together anymore. I don't want to float on a higher consciousness cloud of all knowing looking down upon you as my feet dangle inches from the unstable ground; full of fun, adventures, of lows, ups and downs. I want to be here now; on this shaky ground, standing firm in my flaws. I want to be the life of the party. I want to flirt. I want to dance and laugh, fall in an out of love, feel the bliss and the pain, laugh and cry and hurt. Trying new things and people; falling down hard time and time again scraping my knees, getting up and doing it all again. I want to fly home and see my family who are so comfortable in their ways, I can relax knowing what the day and night looks like just as confident as I feel the sun and moon will rise. Then I want to return to this ever changing country full of unknowns to shake me out of my rigid routine shell.

It is not that I have to be some grand guru or repeatedly have breakthroughs but waking each day with faith it is okay to be me now in this human being. To make choices I might regret just to get the answer. To answer my own questions! I have to experience it to answer it. So if I even have an inkling I might like it, guess what? I'm going to try it. Because I have faith in me and my ability to pick myself up, heal my heart, catch my breath and walk on ready for the next event. There is no becoming just being. Being a cat or being a human, being a writer, being in love, being happy; just be it. It is not floating on some enlightened cloud. It means combining the two into one unity; finding spiritual things in being human and human things spiritual. Everything is necessary. Let people be. Allow them on their path. I don't want to change you, I want to support you. Trust in humanity. Nothing is coincidence anymore. Trust your path. Reasons will reveal.

My path has not been easy. I am not rich. I did not move to a foreign country to chase dreams with tons of money. I moved with limited means to get by long enough to give the dying spirit inside half a chance to experience this life. I have debt; more than I like to admit, but I have faith in something I almost let society extinguish. I have faith in me and the little girl inside who once had a dream. I see glimpses of her more now than ever. She comes to me in whispers, begging with a child's eagerness for me to try new things, play, sing, dance alone and for God's sake keep writing. She does not care if any of it ever makes me rich or famous. She simply wants to be herself and accepted, not by others as we have been programmed to believe, but by the woman who surrounds her spirit and holds the key to set her free.

I have found spreading love freely—the kind you genuinely give with no expectation of return—is the key. This is so much more difficult to do than one might think because we have been programmed to believe there are limits to love. That is why my connection with Mother Earth is so important. She is the classroom teaching us true love does not diminish when given; it grows. Go outside and love a tree, the breeze, an animal, an insect, the sun, the moon or simply a drop of dew on a leaf and you will see. Messages of love emerge in the flight of life, the colors of the sky, the buzz of a bee or the sound of the sea. Being mindful and sensitive to nature's signals makes it impossible to feel sad. My heart opens to compassion for all life and I feel love. I feel satisfied. She always pushes me to write. I feel down when I don't. I call it "dharma neglect". Whether I am immersed in Mother Earth or in my writing, I feel in touch with my intuition, my soul: the moral compass that needs no religious education to become more divine. It is divine.

Every frog was doing their best. My parents were doing the best they knew how going above and beyond their own childhoods. Everyone is just evolving at different rates. We are all energy looking for connections to evolve us. The lesson is in the connection. I see souls now like mercury drops that come together seamlessly to form a greater spirit. The more experiences the bigger your drop of love. Maybe in the end we mesh together to from one big energy field of love in some cosmic phenomenon of bliss.

My exes taught me to let go of the fairytale outside of my soul. Ruth taught me to stand for something right or wrong, stand and stand strong. All the frogs taught me about the love I sought and reflected back what I needed to work on to reach it. John taught me I am just as holy as the rest and to stop looking up to others because worshiping another's knowing will not create the miracle for me. Peter taught me to love and let go. I said I left my job because I was creating dependence rather than abundance but it was everything in that society programming me to be dependent—religion creating dependence for eternity, government for safety, men for security, the mirror for beauty and work for prosperity.

It took a long time to realize I was not breaking the rules but the rules were breaking me. I always wanted to follow but with so many things to explore; my good intentions got in the way of enjoyment. Now, I just want to let myself do what I am going to do. No more setting limits or rules. I am free to make the choice in the moment based on that moments feeling. I have come to cherish my gullibility. Living like a fool has taught me to stop judging the rightness of anything. I jump off the waterfall when I feel it, though it might take some friendly encouragement[8]. It is the innocence of a child trusting life based on nothing but my inner feelings.

There is no frog turning into a prince. Unless the frog was me and maybe it was not in seeking the kiss but in following my bliss, I turned into the princess. I broke the spell. I live in the fairytale. And the fairytale continues to grow because in the end, I do not fear heights and I am no longer afraid of the lows. I am not scared to jump, to fly, to drive, to try new things, to go alone, to live alone, to fall in love, to trust, energy moves on and I will move on. I no longer seek acceptance because I already feel whole inside and I accept myself. More than that, I feel no fear of rejection from anybody's reaction. My passion to be true to my soul exceeds the human prayer for approval. It is my universe, my script and I am the writer of the script. I am the casting director choosing who will be in my play and who gets cut. Matthew, Mark, Luke and John, you have been cut. Learn a lesson, teach a lesson, and move on. I rescued myself and this princess lives happily now.

Tonight I did a dance, a sexy dance with my naked self, laughing in front of my tiny mirror reflecting minute glimpses of what I would call hot. Seeing a forty plus confident woman proud of her spirit, her body and the adventurous life she created makes me love an outside version of me but I am crazy about the internal goddess I have grown so fond of. She is sensual and passionate about life. She is a wondrous, dancing, free spirit soul having faced challenges that suck every ounce of air, yet maintaining enough calm to remember to breathe new life into cells on the verge of collapse. The reflection is the same soul that emerged on my birth absorbing love freely never knowing reasons not to. Allowing love in and out as easy as I breathe.

I will stand courageous, putting my heart out there to love everything and everyone who crosses my path. Knowing I full well

---

[8] Thank you Benji for your waterfall jumping and matrix beer catching skills.

may get hurt but doing it anyway. That is bravery my friend; to love for the sake of loving. There is nothing wrong with seeing God in everyone. No, it is not gullible, more like gallant. There is light in me and there is light in you. God saw the light. It was all good; as that little boy once told me, "it is all the good inside of you". Thank you G-sus. There is no end. There are only beginnings. There is no scary Hell and there is no apocalypse. We go on, and on and on.

Imagine yourself totally exposed; hair unkempt, unshaven, not an ounce of makeup, dirty feet, naked walking this earth with all life looking on. Every human, every living ounce of nature in the entire universe is looking deeply at you. That kid who made you cry, the friend who stabbed you in the back, the man who broke your heart and family who judged you without trying to understand you, all looking at you. Now imagine family that has passed, ancestors, and every living thing that has gone before you. They too are looking completely at you. Everything you have ever felt uncomfortable with is showing; all your scars, all your flaws and things you never let another see. Stand there authentically and tell them your story. Tell them all the pain; the things you did that left you feeling guilt and shame, the horrible things they did to you, the heartache and every ounce of suffering. Tell them all in such great detail that each being feels your pain so completely, your choices so deeply, feeling your feelings, thinking your thoughts as if they were living this life as you.

Their hearts break wide open with love for you. They now understand you so sincerely compassion gushes out of them to comfort you. And you feel deep empathy from the ones that pained you. They all see you now and think you are the most beautiful being they have ever encountered. You are flawless in their eyes. They tell you they understand your struggle and love you now more than ever. And because you feel their pain for living life as you; you know it to be true. Close your eyes for a moment and focus on your heart feeling how this would feel.

It feels like acceptance. It feels like unconditional love. It feels like bliss. Everything you have ever done has been accepted and forgiven with no penance, only love. All of the pain you struggled with has lifted knowing they all get you. And in that instant you feel and get them too. That universal group who just loved you through and through, that group is God and because you were the one imagining it, feeling it, you can rest assured, you are part of the group.

To be seen, understood and loved is to be loved by God. That is how I believe it to be; not a judgment but an acceptance day. To feel you are still loved despite things you condemn, is redemption here on earth. This is what your divine love feels like. Can you love you that much?

Facing the nightmare that people would see what I'd done has freed me. I realized it was not so much a fear of going to Hell, but fear of rejection by you. I face it head on letting you be the judge of me now while I'm alive so I'm out of the hell in my mind. If we could only all live authentically judgment free there would be no need for doctrine, clergy and therapists or psychiatrists drugging our individuality. It is one of the reasons I decided to put it all out there. It is my way of proving how loving acceptance can be.

I could have chosen to hide it all and retain your praise but it was still there rustling in my gut with or without your love. To hate me for my truth means you loved me for my lies. This is who I am in this world. It is my need to stand in my truth. I now find strength in my past knowing I took the best possible care of myself I could. With the tools I had been given and the misinformation presented, I did all I knew to do. I would not change anything; I feel no more shame as I recognize the experiences as more than coincidence and necessary part of my path.

Enlightenment comes in small doses; glimpses of bliss and God. To be mindful is to fill the mind full with present sensations paying attention to every changing half second of incoming information with a grateful heart for all that enters our senses. We are one mind meeting ourselves again and again learning to love it all, experiencing all variables. You are me in your unique experience and I am you in mine. We are learning to love ourselves in every fashion. It is all about learning compassion.

Over the last few months I continued morning meditations to complete the process of the Munay-Ki Rites I received in Peru. In one meditation, I saw myself as each person; the liar, the cheat, the drunk, the insecure, the odd poet, the manipulator, the prisoner, the lost and the unsure. I saw the spiritual seeker full of honest strength, the writer, the musician, the artist, dancer, singer, adventurer and lover of all things. I saw myself but this time I did not judge. Just as I will not let self judge another, I will no longer let self judge self.

Even as all the things I have tried to change came into view, I found surrender in being; the one deep in thought alone with nature often appearing odd to others, brilliant at helping but at a loss when it comes to me and receiving. Trying to hold it all together during a mid-life crisis as I gave my life away to find my soul. I saw my closet full of skeletons that now walk shamelessly on less lanky bones tapping out words for all to see. I saw me dying to love, literally dying but nervous with kisses, awkward with sex, afraid to look the hot guy in the eye and the lover of touch so weakened in its grace I gave more than I craved just to feel embrace.

I realized it is all who I came into this world to be. It is me. Trying to change it is no different than taking a mate and trying to change them. Why can I not love it all? Accept it all? What if this is all I will ever be? What if I will never be published and I just wrote this book for me? Can I go out of this world in love with myself unconditionally? Yes, because I am embracing who I am today, not living in my past story or someone else's. Nor am I waiting to live in a future that may never arrive. I will not let my past dictate how the story ends because I have changed to be something different than I was yesterday, different from tomorrow loving myself so completely through the changes from this moment forward.

We cannot contain love; not inside a religious building or book, a chaining ceremony of marriage, a spoken promise that could easily break or our heart that can do the same. We cannot get it. We can only be it. It is who we are. All we need to do is remember who we are. And in doing so I get to be the brave hero in my own fairytale, breaking the spell to find love once again in myself and in every ounce of life.

I went to the stretch of beach today I used to go at night to cry. I sat down at the edge of the sea amazed at the beauty before me and again salt water filled my eyes. Tears trickled from my cheeks becoming one with the sea in awe of the love of nature surrounding me. I do not need society, religion, a bible or a man for redemption. I do not need to be saved, simply savored because I have love gushing out of me. Nor do I need anyone to see me. I see me. It is not being rescued by the feeling another person gives us. It is us. I am the image in my mind I have been in love with my entire life. Look at me, I am you. What is my last name?

I do not want anyone to think like me. It is exhausting. I have learned it is okay to be alone, even in my thoughts. If whatever you believe takes you closer to love, embrace it. I had to lose myself completely in Mother Earth. She is my bible now and I want to seek every passage to learn more about the God I see in her nature, her people; all their religions and all their beliefs. I am not done. It is only the beginning. I will travel this land seeking more connection with her. For it is in those connections I see glimpses of myself. It is a quiet strength, a powerful peace and the most beautiful soft place to fall. When I see Mother Earth, I see you, I see me. We are God.

Whatever path you take please know you and only you know what is best for you. Therapists, doctors and clergy are human. They may have great ideas but they may also push things that don't work for you. It is like reading a self-help book where only parts of it help you. This is okay. Take the parts that work and choose another book.

With all we have been through it is a miracle we still love. Being on this human journey is hard, but only when we let our mind drive. Pull over, rest a bit then hand over the keys to your heart. Give up your space in the driver's seat. Relax in your breath. We are always pushing, seeking, achieving to adorn ourselves for what? Labels, recognition, acceptance, status... Maybe today you can just be enough. Trust your soul to be your guide and ride, baby ride. Watch for the little miracles that will appear. When we follow our soul all life transpires to keep us inspired.

My wish for all humanity is for each to feel love deeply regardless of relationship status. It is possible. It is the miracle of love. Let your soul rise to comfort you for all you've been through. Hear her soft whispers and trust she will guide you. When we let our soul free the universe speaks in synchronicities. It is in this space you'll find faith in your dreams despite the outside treachery. May we all evolve past fear of a judgment day and break the spell of quoting Quo. He is not worthy to be your judge. No one is. Not even you. There is a little girl inside who is so proud of the woman you've become. Listen to her because in the end, she's the one! Be free to follow your own soul's commandments where your amor lives happily this very instant.
NEXT LEVEL

THE BEGINNING

Acknowledgements

I would like to thank my friends and family for allowing me the space to search my soul and honor her calling. There were countless people who came into my life as I began to follow my vision inspiring and helping me along the way. The town I live is full of angels who never once doubted my dream. I know they will love me even if they don't agree with my beliefs. My beta readers not only helped finalize my manuscript, they motivated me to keep believing in me. Thank you tremendously Sara Denneny, Patricia Mayborne and Mitch Maitland, your help pushed me when I myself was out of energy. There is one more living soul that kept me going when I was close to giving up; her name is PachaMama, our great, loving Mother Earth.

She inspired the final poem. It is her petition for an end to Controligion.

Controligion Petition

43 years; 41 I lived by your design and 2 immersed in mine
You taught me rules, punishment and blame, fear of God and shame
You taught me to seek education, work hard for my future, suffer to someday live free
You taught me to support a system masking corruption parading war's a way to peace
You taught me women are evil, cursing our future with temptation of poisoned fruits
You taught me to have faith in religion that froze my soul leaving me virtually mute
You taught me to hide my body, restrain sexuality and perfect myself for a prince
Who'd then expect me to fill his needs with my body of shame in his presence
You taught me worship of men and sweeping behavior beneath the doormat I'd become
Forget and forgive this is just what men do, besides you can't be whole on your own
And you taught fear of everything outside your factions that went against all you preach
So that someday my soul might peacefully rest in a heaven I'd be lucky to reach
Now two years later I've escaped your chains; moving to a faraway land
I've learned on my own without your ways that happiness is held in my hand
I've learned that your fears you bestow upon others are the tool you use to control
I've learned to hear my voice your penance of guilt used to shame and weaken my soul
I've crossed many borders you attempted to build restraining all that's chaotic
But what you try to fence out is a mirror of you masked beneath what you call patriotic
I can see clearly now as I stand from afar all of your hypocritical missions
Clothed in fake peace pearls strung on heavy coats weighted from love with conditions
I've learned that women are to be worshipped we have much to share
While men fight to put down armor fear forced them to wear
But I have great faith, not in your god but in one you have yet to meet
Although she lives in your land, you walk on her back, she's practically under your feet
She's in the spaces before sunset where day becomes night
And colors bursting at sunrise when dark becomes light
She's taught me to love despite pain when it goes
And an open heart means to take you in, the door must not then close
I've learned all this from Mother Earth who speaks to me so easy
Teaching me to go with change like her rivers flowing freely
She's shown me heaven is not to be sought by passing all of your tests
That God lives now in me and you, not reached when we confess
She cannot breathe in guilt or shame, she simply begs for peace
Trade in judgment for love, we are one just pleading to be seen
Your so called care that instills fear is indeed horrific dualism
We can't evolve, it's not love, it is sugar coated terrorism ~ *Juls*♥

Made in the USA
Charleston, SC
23 February 2015